Crazy Basketball

CRAZY
Basketball

A Life In and Out of Bounds

CHARLEY ROSEN
Foreword by Phil Jackson

University of Nebraska Press • Lincoln & London

Library of Congress Cataloging-in-Publication Data
Rosen, Charles.
Crazy basketball: a life in and out of bounds / Charley
Rosen; foreword by Phil Jackson.
p. cm.
ISBN 978-0-8032-1793-5 (cloth: alk. paper)
1. Basketball—United States. 2. Continental Basketball Association. 3. National Basketball Association.
4. Rosen, Charles. I. Title.
GV885.7.R648 2011
796.323'640973—dc22
2010026921

Set in Sabon.

Contents

Foreword

PHIL JACKSON

There is a lot of craziness in *Crazy Basketball*. I guess knowing Charley Rosen I'm not surprised at the erratic element of coaching and living on the edge of basketball for fifty-five years that he would give us this edition of his love-hate relationship with the sport that he has defined so sardonically as his life's work. I've been a part of this world of his almost since the beginning, having started Charley out on his professional coaching career. He was a coach in junior high and then in college before I met him, but the best of his "crazy" has been defined inside this work.

"Basketball isn't just a metaphor for life—it's more important than that!" is engraved on a plaque in my office that was a gift from a fan. I credit that statement directly to Charley. We put in thousands of miles journeying to and fro in basketball business, mostly me in the driver's seat and Charley navigating or "conversating." In traffic waiting to turn left, a truck coming through the intersection was a "moving pick," and on it goes with life experiences served in basketball terms. We had one laugh after another over the years working together, writing a couple of books, coaching in the CBA, and doing basketball camps at Omega Institute. After the Bulls won their first championship in 1991, Charley predicted that I would win five championships in Chicago. When my stint in Chicago ended I moved back to

Woodstock in 1998 and we started to write a book together, each of us taking an alternating chapter about our relationship to basketball. The next spring I took the job as coach of the Lakers and the book became *More Than a Game*. We have collaborated on many efforts over the years, although my living on the W(B)est Coast these past ten years has distanced our relationship.

We started out working together in Albany, New York, for the Patroons of the Continental Basketball Association. It was a good union for us as Charley kept me looking at the details of the game: what player matchups worked, how we could improve our personnel, and where we could get a good Chinese dinner or a home-cooked meal. We worked together for three years and they were good times. It was the foundation of my career, and Charley had an important role in it. This book relates the story of one of our road games on a four-hundred-mile trip driving into the night from Tampa to Pensacola, Florida—true story and there are many more of the same from those crazy daze.

The act of moving from an assistant coach/trainer to a head coach in that league changed Charley's life forever. He had to leave behind his settled life as a writer and get into the nomad life of coaching basketball in a league that would never let one feel stable. Charley did much better as a coach than he is willing to admit, surviving those harrowing days in that league. The challenges of coaching players at the edge of the NBA and the fame in the "bigs" made that life even more unstable. Everything seemed to be an impediment that kept players from being under the lights of the NBA, be it playing time or number of shots taken or the rebounds gathered as stats. The numbers made all the difference to those players. We used to say that most of the players in that league were talented enough physically. They might have to play a position larger than they would in the NBA, but usually they lacked a dimension in their game to make it. Rosen adroitly points out these features as the myriad of players flash before us with their strengths and weaknesses. There is some pain in watching these players strive and fail in accomplishing their goal.

There is an old story about Zen enlightenment. One day the Master announced that a young monk had reached an advanced state of enlightenment. The news caused some stir. Some of the monks went to see the young monk. "We heard you are enlightened. Is that true?" they asked.

"It is," he replied.

"And how do you feel?"

"As ordinary as ever," said the monk.

Somehow one gets this feeling reading *Crazy Basketball* and how the CBA affected Charley's life. Charley has become enlightened about basketball, but he's still as ordinary as ever. However, as he leaves coaching and resumes his writing career, his love for the game becomes real when he writes or talks about it. The feelings of playing come through the pages: the "knowing" of that physical pleasure of setting a pick, or planting a well-placed elbow, or hitting a timely jumper; and the frustration of dealing with the impediments that make the game tainted are gone. The monk has been born again.

Introduction

For many decades, I have been guided on and off the court by my own personal mantra: *Life is a metaphor for basketball.*

For me, this brief statement signifies the understanding that basketball reveals virtually every aspect of the human condition:

- From passion to indolence
- From discipline to chaos
- From saintly unselfishness to the worst kind of self-absorption
- From joy to despair
- From a loving sense of community to virulent hatred of both teammates and opponents
- From grace under pressure to abject cowardice
- From decisive shots made and missed, to decisive shots not taken
- From the birth of a new consciousness to literal, physical death

In other words, it reflects everything except sex and taxes—which do happen in basketball but only off-court.

And it all happens within clearly delineated boundaries and universally understood rules—so unlike the vague and ever-changing conditions that govern our "civilian" lives.

Therefore my immediate goal in the following pages is to abandon all metaphors and get down to the reality of The Game. This, then, is strictly a basketball autobiography, in which other aspects of my life—such as marriages (3), divorces (2), graduate degrees (1), children (2), grandchildren (4), and stepchildren (2)—will be ignored unless they are directly relevant to my fervid pursuit of the bouncing ball.

For the record, however, here's a list of my civilian employment:

- Summer camp counselor
- Parking lot attendant
- Survey interviewer for the New York City Department of Health
- Nautilus instructor
- Junior high school English teacher
- College English teacher
- Freelance journalist for dozens of magazines, from *Rolling Stone* to *Men's Journal,* from *Sport* to *The New York Times Sunday Book Review*

My initial contact with a backboard and a rim took place when I was nine years old and had been sent away to a summer camp for troubled youths in Pittsfield, New Hampshire. Most of my problems grew out of my anger at being so big and so clumsy and, therefore, readily exposed to ridicule. In addition, I felt both anger and guilt because my father wasn't a "real" father.

That first backboard was nailed to one of the telephone poles that lined a dirt road bisecting the campgrounds. In the absence of any kind of balls, I would often amuse myself by trying to throw stones through and at the hoop: pebbles and baseball-sized missiles from long range, as well as large rocks that I had to shot-put toward the rim in approximations of lay-ups.

Nobody seemed to notice, or perhaps it was believed that my rock shooting had some beneficial effect in dissipating my anger.

By the end of the summer, my shooting percentage was about 20 percent, the backboard was reduced to splinters, the rim was scarred and bent, and the pole was seriously gouged.

Maybe that excuses the occasional brick I subsequently launched over the course of the next fifty-five years.

Crazy Basketball

1

Portrait of the Hooper as a Young Man

During the late 1940s, the only sports played on Fulton Avenue in the West Bronx were baseball, punchball, stickball, two-hand touch football, off-the-bench, -stoop, -curb, or -wall, and kick-the-can, as well as tie-a-little-kid-to-a-tree-and-leave-him-there. Because the nearest basketball court was way over on the other side of Crotona Park, the neighborhood version featured a small pink rubber ball (a Spaldeen), and the lower metal square of a vertical fire escape ladder, which served as the goal. Dribbling was difficult, toughness was all, and everybody could dunk.

All through my childhood, my father was acutely ill—his tubercular left lung had been surgically removed back in 1937 in a primitive attempt to prevent the disease from spreading. He couldn't take ten steps without having to halt and catch his breath in small, gasping doses, and he spent most of his time in bed within easy reach of a gray torpedo of oxygen, forever repeating his anguished lament, "God, what have I done to deserve this?"

Naturally, I felt an overpowering sorrow for his affliction. But I was so very young, and also plagued by a confusing jumble of fear, pity, anger, and shame, so I took every opportunity to get away from the apartment, and I played every sport with a fierce energy that often outpaced my meager skills.

I first started to take basketball seriously when I was thirteen. In the Bronx, the ethnic makeup of neighborhoods changed dramatically every mile or so, and during one of my long, brooding, solitary walks, I became intrigued and then lured by the sound of a bouncing ball.

That's how I came upon a "steady run" in the wintertime locker room of a public swimming pool in a "Negro" neighborhood not far from Fulton Avenue. It was a full-court game played between portable baskets on a cold stone floor. I wandered in out of sheer curiosity, and I was instantly welcomed. "Lace 'em up, big fella. You got next with me."

The game was presided over by Bill, rumored to have been a Harlem Globetrotter in his distant youth. It was a ferocious and honorable game in which the shooter was the only person who'd ever dare admit to being fouled, and all the other players rebounded as if they were wolves and the ball was a lamb chop.

I loved the company of those joyful warriors who played with such aggression and passion. Smelling of booze on Sunday mornings. Laughing away everybody's mistakes. "Keep on shooting, Mister Charley," Bill would urge me. "You throw enough shit against the wall, some of it's bound to stick." But at the time I couldn't master the fine art of shooting a . basketball—it seemed to squirt out of my hands like a huge watermelon seed. "Young Mister Charley," Bill would exclaim with a laugh, "even if you was standing on the beach, I don't believe you could piss in the ocean." Yet Bill continued to encourage me ("big as you are and bigger as you gonna be . . .") to persevere.

Which I did.

So, a belated thanks to Bill and the joyful company of weekend hoopers who taught me that it's equally as important to play well as it is to learn from one's mistakes.

Thanks for the run, guys.

My first formal game was in a ninth-grade tournament at Junior High School No. 44, where my class (of intellectually gifted students) was trounced by class 9-14, a low-IQ team of unruly young men who'd been left back several times and who shaved every day. My main memories of playing in the cold, windy schoolyard were of wearing my long pants with my shirttails flapping, of getting razzed for being so clumsy as to stumble over a foul line, and later getting beaten by my father for tearing my pants.

Even so, I was recruited to play with my classmates in a local community center league. And whenever we dared to defeat the Jabones, another team of tough guys and troublemakers, we had to fast-break all the way home.

After long, lonesome sessions in the playground I ultimately developed an awkward, but adequate, corkscrew jumper to complement a hook shot. At the tender age of fifteen I was a senior at Theodore Roosevelt High School, and having grown to six foot six and 210 pounds, I tried out for, and made, the varsity team as a third-string center.

The coach was a math teacher named Howard McManus, who was smart enough to let our All-City guard, Jackie Thompson, run the team. Coach McManus's only advice for the rest of us was this: "Bend your knees, boys. Bend your knees."

It was early in the season and we had just finished routing Grace Dodge Vocational High School in an afternoon home game. I already understood that winning was better than losing, but I was absolutely ecstatic because I had come off the bench to score my first varsity points. Five of them—on a put-back lay-up, an elbow jumper, and a free throw.

FIVE POINTS!

I was so happy that, instead of taking the Third Avenue Elevated train for the four stops from Fordham Road to the 174th Street station, I decided to undertake the two-mile journey by foot. Merrily I skipped through Little Italy and across Tremont Avenue. FIVE POINTS! I aimed to cut about fifteen minutes off my travel time by taking a shortcut through the wide construction site that obliterated 177th through 175th streets in preparation for the Cross-Bronx Expressway.

It was dark and the dug-up landscape was beyond the reach of the bordering streetlights, but my neighborhood buddies and I had easily scampered across the same route during the daylight hours on weekends on our way to the movie theaters on Tremont. And besides, I was floating in my own delirious reverie.

FIVE POINTS!

I literally came back to earth when I tumbled into a freshly dug ditch. Fortunately, the ditch was only four feet deep, and I escaped with only a deep cut just over my left eyebrow. With blood gushing over my face, I managed to transverse the construction site with no further injury, whereupon I ran the ensuing ten blocks to the emergency room at Bronx Hospital.

Turned out that I needed five stitches to close the wound. In my dazed adolescent mind, the five stitches somehow equated with the five points. And I would gladly have suffered twenty stitches to score TWENTY POINTS!

Alas, those were the only stitches and the only points I amassed for the rest of the season.

Meanwhile my father's condition deteriorated. Every three months or so he'd experience a crisis and be rushed off to the hospital. "This is it," my mother would sob. "This time . . ."

The varsity coach at Hunter (now Lehman) College, a tuition-free institution in the Bronx, was a childhood chum of my uncle Richard, and somehow, despite my inferior high school grades, I was encouraged to matriculate there.

The freshman coach was Tony Russo, who stressed guts and grit and ridiculed me whenever I played "soft." At the time, the pro game was mostly played below the rim and, for big men especially, the emphasis was on belligerence and bone-on-bone confrontations. At every level that's the way coaches coached and the way players wanted to play. A big man's utter ruthlessness was expected to trump a smaller player's skills.

By now I was bigger (six foot eight) and stronger (230 pounds) than any of my opponents, and I overcompensated for my basic shyness and confusion by being mindlessly aggressive. Coach Russo employed some kind of high-post offense that I was spectacularly unsuited for. I averaged 8 points per game with the frosh and went scoreless the night before my father died.

My father was forty-six going on a hundred when he finally succumbed to an attack of something quick and painful. I accompanied my mother in the ambulance ride, and just before we reached the hospital, Daddy roused himself. I remember that his blue eyes were tightly clenched and staring at a space just above my head. The last words he ever said to me were, "Hi, kid."

He died that evening, and, just three months short of my sixteenth birthday, I was tortured by conflicting emotions. I loved him as best I could, but like all adolescents, I needed a loving father's guidance and example so that I'd know how to be a man. I never stopped being afraid of his constant pain and his disfigured body, and I desperately needed to be free of his tragic life.

Everybody said that his death was a blessing, a merciful end to his suffering. Yes, his suffering, my mother's, and mine, too.

Suddenly I felt free to be a child, and several months later I became the tallest player in the brief history of Hunter College basketball.

2

Undergraduate Hits, Misses, and Turnovers

Hunter's varsity coach, Mike Fleischer, had been a classmate and close friend of the infamous CCNY hoopers (who'd won both the NCAA and the NIT championships back in 1950 before being exposed as point shavers and dumpers). One of Coach's best pals was Ed Roman, a hulking six-foot-six board-banger with a surprisingly deft shooting touch. Except for his corrupted dossier, Roman certainly possessed the smarts, the size, and the talent to have been an outstanding NBA player. From time to time Roman would show up at the Hunter gym and tutor me in the theories and practices of pivot play. Footwork. Balance. Boxing out. The works.

It was just a week before the varsity's preseason practice was set to convene when, during a three-on-three scrimmage, I tried to bully my way around Roman's wide body (as per his instructions) and attack the offensive boards. A quick bang to freeze him, then a half spin, and I thought I was there, when all at once the lights went out.

Out of nowhere, his elbow had blasted the middle of my face into a red, pulpy mess.

Coach Fleischer drove me to Fordham Hospital, where a

doctor inserted two metal rods into my collapsed nasal passages and, with one blood-soaked and agonizing yank, realigned the broken bone into at least a semblance of its original position. According to Coach, the blood, the swelling, and the subsequent black eyes were all badges of honor. I was now a bona fide "big man," theoretically unafraid to stick my face into the rebounding scrums in the shadow of the basket. Coach further consoled me by saying that a busted nose was easily preferable to a sprained ankle, because the latter would prevent me from playing. "Don't worry," he added. "Before you're through, you'll break a lot of other guys' noses!"

Since I couldn't help looking to Coach as my surrogate father, I trusted that everything he said was in my best interest.

Fleischer had played baseball at CCNY and had been a teammate of Floyd Layne's. Of course, Layne was better known as a basketball player, albeit one who was convicted of conspiring with gamblers to shave points and dump games.

Actually, Layne was one of many. Several others at CCNY, NYU, Manhattan College, LIU, Kentucky, Toledo, and Bradley committed the same crimes and suffered the same fates—expulsion from school, public excoriation, and in some cases prison terms. Several of these disgraced players lived in New York and played weekends in the Eastern League for fifty to one hundred dollars a game.

It chanced that Hunter's practice season prefaced the start of the Eastern League's season by a week or so. And since EL teams rarely had the means to conduct preseason practice sessions, the local EL players were looking for runs. The connection between Coach and Layne resulted in Floyd bringing a team full of his EL compatriots up to the Bronx to scrimmage the Hunter varsity. Chief among Floyd's playmates was Sherman White from LIU, who was without doubt the best player—college or pro—in the world. A smooth six foot seven, White was the forerunner of such fliers, leapers, and creators as Dr. J and Michael Jordan. Too bad White had been still another victim of the betting scandals.

How good was White? When NBA teams came to New York to play the Knicks, a great many players journeyed to his hometown of Orange, New Jersey, to pay their respects by scrimmaging with White at a local gym.

All told, Floyd's team included about five or six onetime fixers.

I was eighteen at the time, and playing basketball was the joy of my young life. In my barely postadolescent imagination, basketball was heaven on earth, and therefore all basketball players had to be saintly. And if I played with more exuberance than skill, I was still the best player on the Hunter Hawks.

In any event, Layne's team of veteran players destroyed us. Their skills were incredible, plus they knew how a slight push on the hip or a well-placed elbow could gain immense advantages. If I turned my head for an instant, Ed Roman cut backdoor and wound up with a lay-up. Every one of my minor missteps and hesitations was costly. It was all I could do just to get a shot off.

But more than anything else I was stunned by the total lack of joy with which they played. For sure, basketball was a serious business—but not even the slickest of plays or the most miraculous of shots could make them smile. In fact, there was something almost sad and wistful about the way they conducted themselves.

Of course I knew about their shady pasts, yet I was completely puzzled. How could anybody as talented as these guys play basketball and not have fun? It seemed inconceivable.

Eventually, I played some pickup ball with Layne and Roman and got more of an insight into their respective mindsets. But their underlying grief seemed to make playing the game more of a chore than a celebration.

And that's why, many years later, I was moved to thoroughly investigate the events (and the causes thereof) that led to so many broken lives. The result was a history, *Scandals of '51*. But when that proved to be unsatisfying (to me, but thankfully not to the critics), I wrote a novel, *Barney Polan's Game*, in another attempt to explore every aspect of the unfortunate situation. A third book, *The Wizard of Odds*, resulted when Julie Molinas recruited me to write his older brother Jack's biography. Jack was by turns a fixer and dumper at Columbia and in the NBA (as were several others in the league), a procurer of undergraduate fixers in league with the Mafia, a double- and triple-crosser of the wrong people, a bookie in Attica, a player in the porno business, and finally a murder victim.

Along the way, I also learned that dozens of other college and professional players had also been in league with gamblers but had escaped detection for religious and political reasons.

At some level of my continuing naiveté, I still feel that (too much) money and basketball is a dangerous but necessary parley that, despite the many blessings that accrue to so many folks, also greatly diminishes the joy that should be at the heart of the game.

Once the season was under way, we played mostly a passive 1-3-1 zone defense and a static offense that stationed me in the low post. Our game plan called for me to shoot first and never ask questions; assists were deemed so unimportant that they weren't even recorded. As friendly as the players were off the court, once the lights were switched on, we were jealous of one another's shots and point totals, and we were far from being a team.

Coach Fleischer was a bright man who, among other things, prided himself on being more adventurous than his peers. But for his players, Coach's adventures often turned out to be either worthless or painful.

Take the time he saw the Russian National team play some college or other at Madison Square Garden. This was back in the early 1960s when any appearance on American soil by the Russkies was a rarity. In any event, Coach was enthralled by the Russians' pregame routine: after undergoing some earnest stretching exercises, the Russians spent the remainder of their allotted warm-up time in an all-out five-on-five halfcourt scrimmage.

Instead of going through artificial lay-up lines and random shooting practice, here was a true preparation for the game at hand. An exact duplication of the very same movements, skills, and teamwork that a basketball game required. What a wonderful and revolutionary idea!

Of course, before our next game, Coach instructed us to follow the same procedure. In truth, despite Coach's demands to the contrary, in our postadolescent haze we were basically a lazy, selfish team—with me and a high-jumping forward named Lyndon Prince perpetually competing for shots, points, and rebounds.

We were slightly embarrassed by the new orders. However, with the results being strictly unofficial and unrecorded, during our cramped little scrimmage we played with passion, the ball always found the open man, extra passes were always made, and our play was incredibly unselfish.

Eureka! Coach had found the answer!

But once the real game began, we were all relieved to revert to our usual me-first game plans.

Revolutions are always temporary and always wind up eating their young.

Jon Shoutta was one of only two seniors on that team—the other was Saul Goldfarb. Jon was a broad-shouldered power forward with plenty of muscle and plenty of game. Although his superior intelligence was proven by his graduation from Brooklyn Tech, one of the most academically elite high schools in the country, Jon often suffered lapses of concentration on the court—zigging when he should have zagged, and vice versa.

Late in a game versus Bridgeport, Jon went into one of his brain-dead spells and committed a pair of costly turnovers. Coach Fleischer was quick to call a time-out.

"Jon," he pleaded, "you've got to think out there."

And Jon delivered this classic riposte: "I did think, Coach. I just thought of the wrong thing."

None of his ex-teammates have been able to keep track of Jon's doings after he graduated. But we did learn at fifth- or sixth-hand that he had enlisted in the U.S. Air Force and had become a big shot who had his finger within reach of The Button. Since there haven't been any nuclear holocausts in the intervening years, it's apparent that Jon has been thinking of the right things.

There were two games during that 1959–60 season that seemed much more significant than any others. The second game of the season was against Rider College, a win for us, but marked by my catching another elbow with my face— this one painfully shattering a tooth. During the subsequent time-out, Coach said, "Not to worry, Charley. You're not bleeding and you won't miss a minute. Just suck it up and be tough."

Yeah! I was tough enough!

The second unforgettable game was at Brooklyn College, where we were in the process of being soundly trounced late in the game when Coach officially surrendered by emptying the bench. The Brooklyn College coach quickly followed suit, and everybody settled back to watch the scrubs try to make garbage time last forever. The only trouble was that one of the Brooklyn College subs (Number 46) was out of control, throwing indiscriminate elbows, undercutting the legs of airborne jump shooters, and even throwing a punch in a close-quarters rebounding melee. The referees, eager for the lopsided game to end, ignored Coach's protests, sucked on their whistles, and let the clock run down. Coach Fleischer was furious as he stood up and shouted to his opposite number on the home team's bench, "Hey! Why don't you get that jackass out of there before he hurts somebody?"

The other coach's rude reply was, "Screw you, Fleischer! You coach your team and I'll coach mine."

With that, Coach walked over to where I was sitting comfortably on the pines and said this: "Go back into the game, Charley, and take that jerk out."

"What do you mean?"

"Elbows to the face are like Christmas presents," he said. "They're better to give than to receive."

Moments later I found myself side by side with Number 46 along the foul lane while one of my teammates prepared to shoot a free throw. As the shot was released, Number 46 leaned into me and assumed the proper "box out" position, thereby hindering me from rebounding a possible miss. Standard operating procedure would have been to muscle him closer to the basket, but instead I cocked my right arm and aimed my elbow at the middle of his face. WHAM! I connected so solidly that several of his teeth were broken, and a small fountain of blood splashed into the lane. In their haste to keep the clock in motion, neither ref noticed anything amiss. While the Brooklyn College coach screamed bloody murder, Coach just shrugged.

In the locker room I received Coach's congratulations. "Good job, Charley. The guy got exactly what he deserved."

I was flushed with the elation of my first kill. So that's how it felt! The power. The sense of reckoning. Now I was a man. Mess with me or my teammates at your own peril.

But the flavor didn't last long enough. Even on the long subway ride back to the Bronx, I began to question the bloodthirsty imperatives of this strange but wonderful game. I was confused, disappointed, and increasingly ashamed of myself. But there didn't seem to be any alternative. I was too slow to ride the crest of a fast break, too white to fly, and too unskilled to either razzle or dazzle. The only lesson that I could glean from the circumstances was that I was doomed to be a banger.

I wound up averaging a whopping 17 points and 12 rebounds as the Hunter Hawks finished with a record of 9-10.

Shortly after the season ended, I had a chance to test my on-court manhood against the biggest, strongest player in the history of the game—Wilt Chamberlain.

Back in the early 1960s, the NBA season concluded in early to mid-April. And since the best parties were in New York City, many of the players who were based on the East Coast flocked there to begin celebrating the long off-season.

In any case, if Floyd Layne spent his weekends playing in the Eastern League, to augment his income he conducted afternoon and evening recreational programs at several junior and senior high schools near his home in the Bronx.

All of these factors made Floyd's springtime "runs" the most illustrious, and most competitive, in the metropolitan area. One memorable Tuesday evening, I received a phone call from Coach Fleischer commanding me to be at such-and-such a place at 10:00 p.m. The Dipper was in town and needed some exercise.

The scene of the royal appearance was in a junior high school in a racial ghetto in the South Bronx. Come game time, Chamberlain was nowhere in sight, but the bleachers had been rolled out and about five hundred kids were on hand, screaming for somebody—anybody—to dunk the ball. Mine was the only pale face in sight.

The only other players I knew were Floyd; a tough little

guard named Junior Martin; and a hot-shooting forward, Ralph Bacot, whose nom de hoop was "Durango."

While waiting for the feature attraction, Floyd arranged equitable sides and we were off—fifteen baskets wins. In theory, the offense called the fouls, but unless blood was showing nobody dared to do so.

In my own Mikanesque fashion, I managed to drop a few hook shots and was on the verge of feeling confident when the fans voiced a collective "Oooooo!" And suddenly there he was—the seven-foot-one, 280-pound colossus who had shredded all of the existing NBA scoring and rebounding records as a rookie and then bested himself in his sophomore season.

Even the players in midgame stopped to savor his dramatic entrance: Wilt was wearing a silk shirt, a gold medallion on a thick gold chain, nondescript black pants, and, on his bare feet, tasseled black loafers. Walking behind him in single file were four beautiful women: one carried a pair of huge sneakers, another had a towel draped around her shoulders, a third toted sweat socks, and the fourth had a small bottle of cologne.

The young bleacherites were respectful, and a space was cleared on the lowest bench for Wilt and his entourage. He shod his loafers, pulled on his sweat socks, laced up his sneakers, and carefully shed his chain and his shirt. The pants stayed on.

Then he warmed up for a few minutes—his trademark fallaway jumpers from the left box, some fluid hooks, and even a couple of one-handers from the top of the key. Acceding to popular demand, he also executed several rather dainty dunks.

Floyd proceeded to rearrange the sides—Durango, Junior, and I were among the Shirts, while Layne joined Wilt on the Skins.

"Shirts' ball," Floyd pronounced, and we were under way.

Matched against Chamberlain, I didn't presume to move into my favorite spot in the pivot, choosing to aimlessly wander around the perimeter instead. Durango hit a long jumper from the baseline, and we were up 1–0.

If I could be relatively anonymous on offense, guarding Wilt was to accompany him in the spotlight. What to do? Fronting him would be futile. But so would playing behind him or three-quartering him.

As he settled into the left box, Wilt actually acknowledged my presence. "Hey, boy. You can foul me all you want and I won't call it. Just stay away from my face."

Whoa! He smelled like a distillery! Had anybody lit a match in his vicinity, the entire building would have exploded. He had to be drunk!

Indeed, he seemed much more intent on passing than shooting—receiving the ball, waving it around in one huge hand before hitting a cutter or open shooter. (Wilt did, however, take—and make—a pair of fallaway jumpers.) Nor was he interested in moving to the offensive boards.

Coach had insisted that I was a bona fide big man, so I simply stationed myself behind Wilt and tried to shove him off his spot—but I felt as though I was trying to move the Statue of Liberty. On one sequence, I stepped back, then ran into him with a lowered shoulder as though trying to break through a locked door—but I simply bounced off his massive back.

The only time I touched the ball on offense, I passed to

Martin. And even though I was a surprisingly adept shooter from sixteen to eighteen feet, I didn't even dare think of shooting. In any event, Martin and Durango shot the Shirts into a 15–12 victory.

Wilt went to the bench to towel off, and then we were ready to go back at it.

This time, he was more intense. When he posted on the right box, dribbled into the middle, and flipped up a finger-roll, he wound up with a basket and I wound up with a face-ful of wet, odorous armpit.

A few plays later, I attempted the unthinkable: I was a step above the key when I received a pass from Martin, and Wilt was once again ensconced near the rim, at least twenty feet away. Sure, I was a step out of my range, but what the hell? So I fired up the shot . . . and it plopped through the net!

The young fans acted as though I'd just taken off my pants. "Ooooooooooo!"

Before Wilt could retaliate, one of the Skins' guards (not Floyd!) misdribbled and the ball was turned over to us.

Now, I'd played enough in Harlem and Bed-Stuy to know the protocol: do what you did until you missed. Sure enough, Martin presented me with the ball in just about the same spot, Wilt remained in the shadow of the rim, so I fired up another jumper . . .

WHAM!

Somehow, Chamberlain closed the gap between the time I cocked the shot and the ball spun off my fingertips. Was my release that slow? Was he that fast? Or what?

BOP!!

The shot was not only blocked, but it came back at me at warp-speed, bounced off the top of my head, knocked me to the floor (again!), and caromed into the bleachers!

Imagine the celebratory whoops from the stands—and also from the players.

Throughout the second game Durango and Martin never cooled off, and the Shirts won again, 15–13. Afterward the fans crowded around Wilt not to get his autograph, or shake his hand, but merely to touch him. (A few of them pointed at me and laughed.) He toweled off his face, his arms, and his torso, splashed himself with some of the cologne, changed shoes, put on his shirt, and, with his ladies in tow, made a grand exit stage right.

And what did Floyd have to say to me? "Good job," he said with a smirk. "I'll call Coach when Bill Russell gets into town."

So, over the next two seasons, I mastered the sternum smash and broke virtually every school scoring (24.2 points per game my junior year) and rebounding (16.0 per game as a senior) record as the Hawks barely managed to play .500 ball (a combined 31-28 during my tenure). I was moved by what Coach called "the competitive drive," which I interpreted as the urge to humiliate an opponent. Nail him with a well-placed elbow and bust his ass to the floor. If necessary, make him bleed. Annihilate his personality.

It was no secret that for Hunter to have a chance of winning any given game, I had to dominate both baskets. For everybody concerned—Coach, my teammates, the opposition—every game was all about me.

Even so, I still didn't believe that I was a legitimate player—and this belief was borne out by the biggest on-court choke of my life. The scene was Madison Square Garden just before my senior season.

Ten days prior to my stinking up the Garden, we had engaged in a preseason scrimmage against Iona at their gym in New Rochelle. Iona's center was a six-foot-ten strong man (whose name I've unfortunately forgotten) and, by official count, I had scorched him for eighteen consecutive jump shots. It was primarily on the strength of this that the Iona coach, the well-connected Jim McDermott, arranged for another scrimmage between us—this time at the Garden of Basketball Delights.

The idea was to showcase whatever talents I might have for the scrutiny of the Knicks decision makers. And, indeed, there were several scouts and assistant coaches in the stands as the scrimmage began.

At the time, I was twenty years old and completely intimidated by the entire situation. ME? PLAYING IN THE GARDEN? Not only couldn't I hit a jumper to save my life, but the ball seemed to weigh about ten pounds and I couldn't even make my lay-ups.

My failure at MSG totally destroyed my confidence to the point where all of my numbers decreased in my senior season. And even though the NBA draft consisted of sixteen rounds, my name never came up.

If the NBA wasn't impressed with me, neither was Professor Ann Mackey.

Hunter (now Lehman) College was an all-girls school until the end of World War II when returning veterans were admitted. During that same alteration in the student body, the chairwoman of the physical education department—Professor Mackey—was replaced by a man. I'd become a "fizz ed" major primarily because several of my teammates were going that route and the program seemed to offer several courses of minimal resistance. Even though I was a relatively innocent bystander, Professor Mackey often took out on me her still-virulent resentment at being replaced.

Late in the basketball season of my senior year, Professor Mackey had occasion to rage at me at the beginning of a Games of Low Organization class. It just so happened that the classroom was situated just beneath the basketball court, and the desk behind which she sat during the class doubled as the official scorer's table during ball games. To make matters worse, whoever was responsible for moving the table back to the classroom after the previous night's game had been neglectful. So when Professor Mackey entered the classroom and discovered that her table was not there, she pointed at me and said, "It's all your fault, Rosen! Everything has gone downhill at the college since you basketballers were let in the back door!"

Then she ordered me to fetch the table without any assistance.

It took me about a half-hour to lug that heavy table out of the gym, down the stairs, and into the classroom. Then she fussed and fumed her objections to my failure to replace the table in the exact same position from which it had been "pilfered" without her "permission."

And since I had missed most of the class, she marked me absent.

Even worse was my performance on her final exam. Her printed instructions were to answer each of the test questions by writing either "True" or "False." But since only a relatively small space was provided for the answers, and I was so eager to escape her clutches, I responded by writing either "T" or "F."

Even though I supplied all the correct responses, I had not followed her directions to the letter and failed the test and the course. (Not that I was an adept student anyway; whereas a 1.8 cumulative index was necessary for both athletic eligibility and graduation, I finished my career at Hunter with a 1.81.)

It's a good thing that Xs and Os aren't abbreviations for anything else.

It was the last game of my varsity career at Hunter College. Back then, freshmen were ineligible for varsity competition, and the number of regular-season games a college team could play was limited. So my last game was only the fifty-ninth of my entire undergraduate career.

Nowadays, guys who stay in college for four years can play at least 120 total games. But in my halcyon days the limited schedules made every game an extremely valuable and cherished experience.

Our record going into that game was 11-9, and our opponent was Brooklyn Polytech—easily the worst team on our schedule, which included such notable foes as Fairfield, Bridgeport, LIU, Rider, Hofstra, Farleigh Dickenson, Adelphi, St. Francis (Brooklyn), and C. W. Post. Since we were also playing on our home court, the game figured to be a romp.

In larger schools seniors playing their last game are usually honored in various ceremonies. Perhaps the player and his family are introduced before the game and his mother is presented with a bouquet of flowers. Or else some plaque or trophy is given. And seeing that I had been a record-breaking scorer (the first to reach 1,000 points), rebounder, and three-time team MVP during my tenure at Hunter, I expected some kind of acknowledgment.

Anything would have been greatly appreciated.

However, Coach Fleischer, ever the self-proclaimed innovator, had something else in mind. I and the other four seniors who had started just about every game—Lyndon Prince, Artie Brennan, Sam Giambalvo, and Hal Mayerson—started this game on the bench!

Coach's rationale was that each of us would get a rousing welcome from the home crowd—numbering about five hundred in our tiny gym—as we entered the game.

Meanwhile, I sat on the bench sunk in a profound depression. As a foolish twenty-one-year-old, I knew my points-per-game average from game to game. And anticipating a bonanza against the weak opposition, I had calculated that a 30-point performance would raise my scoring average to 23.0. Not quite as good as my junior year, but good enough to end my career on an upbeat note.

Coach finally inserted us into the lineup about halfway through the first half, and we all started shooting at every opportunity, which had always been my modus operandi, but was unusual for my teammates. And why would any of the seniors play even a vestige of defense since foul trouble would only send us back to the bench?

We were fortunate to win the game, 65–60. Lyndon finished with 10 points, while Hal and I had 12 each.

Twelve points! My lowest total of the season—reducing my points per game to a mere 21.5! And leaving me with a sad, heavy memory that used to occasionally haunt my dreams.

Anyway, Coach now lives in the L.A. area where he re-

cently celebrated his eightieth birthday. I've long ago forgiven him and I hope he's forgiven me.

I still speak to the rest of the guys several times a year.
And like all ex-athletes, our recollections of our team and of
our individual accomplishments have become happier and
more bountiful as we grow old together.

All told, I enjoyed several personal triumphs and endured
even more embarrassments during the totality of my undergraduate days.

For example:

- In my junior year I set the single-game rebounding record,
  grabbing twenty-eight in a game versus New Paltz.
- I'd always played well against Bridgeport, even though
  we'd never beaten them. In my junior year a six-foot-
  six, 260-pound football player was added to Bridgeport's team with the sole design of shutting me down.
  Undeterred, I lit up Bridgeport for 43 points, my best-
  scoring game at Hunter.
- Summertime games between various camps were always
  highly competitive since many of New York's finest high
  school and college players spent July and August working as counselors. In the summer of 1961 I worked at
  Camp Dalmaqua, and our biggest rivals were Camp To-
  go-la, who featured a six-foot-seven high school All-
  American. Turned out that I torched the young man
  for 50 points.
- After my junior season, the New York sportswriters
  voted me to the 1960–61 All–Metropolitan Small College team.

- At the end of my collegiate career, I held various Hunter records for points and rebounds and was the first player in any of the colleges that comprised the City University of New York to tally 1,000 points. My final total was 1,234 in fifty-nine games.

However delightful these accomplishments were, they were overshadowed by the following nightmarish on-court experiences:

- During my sophomore season, we were trounced at home by an all-black school, Maryland State. Their front line featured players who were six foot ten, six foot nine, six foot eight, and so intimidated me that I managed to score a mere 7 points, the only single-digit outing of my college career.

- After I'd been named to the Tri-State League's All-Star team after my initial varsity season, I received a phone call from a total stranger, who said that he was entering a team in a fast amateur tournament in the Brownsville section of Brooklyn. He'd pay me twenty-five dollars under the table, plus subway fare, if I'd consent to be his team's ringer. Sure.

- Too bad the home team featured two players from Boys High School—Billy Burwell, a six-foot-eight senior destined for Ohio State, and a six-foot-eight junior named Connie Hawkins, who was destined for the Hall of Fame. These two guys proceeded to block every shot I even thought of taking, and they had me continually ducking away to avoid being brained by their game-long dunkathon. And I never got my ringer's fee.

- Even worse was my experience with the USA team at the 1961 Maccabiah Games in Israel. My teammates included Larry Brown, Art Heyman, Mike Cingiser, Julie Cohen, and several more of the finest Jewish hoopers in America. But, since we played 1-3-1 zone at Hunter, and I was always stationed in the low post, I didn't know how to defend or play facing the basket. As a result I was so lost on the court that I was eventually designated as an alternate and never played in the tournament—which the USA won.
- Worst of all, I came down with a virulent case of amoebic dysentery and lost twenty-one pounds in the fifteen days we spent in Israel.

So, despite the gaudy numbers and the page full of school records, I left Hunter convinced that I was nothing more than a small-time big man.

Because of the red flag I'd received from Professor Mackey, I had to attend night classes during the fall semester in order to graduate. On the weekends, however, I continued my basketball career in the Eastern Professional Basketball League.

3

Basketball Follies in the Nearest East

The Eastern Professional Basketball League was initially chartered as the Eastern Pennsylvania Basketball League on April 23, 1946 (six weeks before the formation of the Basketball Association of America, the forerunner of the NBA). The EPBL's six original franchises included the Wilkes-Barre Barons, the Lancaster Red Roses, the Reading Keys, the Allentown Rockets, the Hazleton Mountaineers, and the Pottsville Pros.

Virtually all of the players lived in-state, and the best of them earned $7,500 for the season—which was equivalent to the salaries paid by the established (but soon to be extinct) National Basketball League and the fledgling Basketball Association of America.

The schedule wasn't balanced, with Lancaster playing thirty games, Allentown playing twenty-six, and the others either twenty-seven or twenty-eight. The leading scorers were Allentown's Whitey Van Nieda (22.7 points per game), followed by Bill Zubric from Reading (17.4 ppg) and Cas Ostrowski (16.0 ppg) from the championship Wilkes-Barre squad.

Van Nieda eventually went on to play for three years in the NBA.

The games were played mostly on Saturday and Sunday nights, and players from out of town would usually travel with seven or eight guys packed into somebody's car. The teams played mostly in high school and junior high school gyms, and seven hundred fans was a big turnout. The officials were usually local high school refs, and it was extremely rare for a team to win a game on the road. The players made about fifteen bucks per game, and if someone had a really good game he would try to squeeze another five out of the owner. Trouble was that many of their paychecks would bounce higher than a basketball, so right after the final buzzer players would storm the box office and demand to be paid in cash.

For the following campaign, the league was renamed the Eastern Professional Basketball League and became commonly known as the Eastern League. The Allentown franchise folded, and Wilkes-Barre dropped out to join another doomed pro league, the American Basketball League. But the Eastern League added the Philadelphia Lumberjacks, the Williamsport Billies, the Harrisburg Senators, and the Sunbury Mercuries. Each team played twenty-eight games usually in local high schools, with Reading copping the title.

For the next few years, the Eastern League played musical franchises with an increasing number of teams being sponsored by local businesses, such as the Berwick Carbuilders, the Lebanon Seltzers, and the Pottsville Packers. The rosters were still mainly populated with local heroes, including Philadelphians like Jack Ramsey and Jack McCloskey, who both went on to be successful coaches in the NBA.

In 1948 the BAA merged with the NBL to form the National Basketball Association, which reduced the total number of pro teams and likewise cut the available jobs. One result was that a number of elite players from New Jersey and New York were happy to earn anywhere from one hundred to three hundred dollars for a weekend's work with some Eastern League team of the moment.

Said HUBIE BROWN of what the early days were like after the merger: "*Remember, back in those early days there were only eight teams in the NBA and only ten players on each team. That adds up to only eighty players. Guys played in the Eastern League because there was no place else for them to play, and it was a hell of a league. Everybody played a cerebral kind of game with a lot of motion. It was a form of passing game before anybody gave it a name. A lot of the old guys, especially from the Northeast, called it Jew basketball. I'm telling you the truth here, that many of the guys in the Eastern League would be NBA All-Stars if they played today.*"

The league finally hit the jackpot two years after the college betting scandals erupted in 1951 when it admitted convicted point shavers who had been banned by the EPBL. The likes of Floyd Layne and Ed Roman from CCNY's infamous double championship team of 1950, Sherman White of LIU, and Ralph Beard and Alex Groza of Kentucky (both former selectees to All-NBA teams) became widely ballyhooed gate attractions. Jack Molinas, a certified All-Star who was booted from the NBA in 1954 for wagering on his team (the Fort Wayne Pistons) to win certain games, also headlined the league. Several suspected but never convicted dumpers—Bob Zawoluk from St. John's, Bill Spivey from Kentucky—were other Eastern League curios.

Additional noteworthy alumni of the Eastern League included Jim Luisi, a clever shooting guard, who became an actor with such credits as the Broadway version of *Sweet Charity* and several television series, including *The Rockford Files*; Jack Ramsay, who later became the Hall of Fame coach of the Portland Trail Blazers; John Chaney, who for many years was the universally respected coach at Temple University; Jack McClosky, the EPBL's Most Valuable Player in 1953 and 1954 and later the general manager of the Detroit Pistons; and Hubie Brown, who went on to coach for several years in the NBA.

As one anonymous Eastern League and NBA veteran described it: "One big difference between the NBA and the Eastern League was that a ton of players and referees in the NBA were in cahoots with gamblers. Entire teams like the Baltimore Bullets were dumping games. But there were no point spreads issued for Eastern League games and all of us played on the up and up."

Even so, if the players and the refs were honest men, to ensure maximum paydays virtually every playoff series went the limit.

HUBIE BROWN: *"The majority of the guys who became great officials in the NBA all learned how to referee in the Eastern League. I'm talking about guys like Earl Strom, Jake O'Donnell, and Mendy Rudolph, whose father, by the way, was president of the league. One of the early Eastern League refs was Tommy Lasorda, who later traded his whistle for a baseball and wound up managing the Los Angeles Dodgers."*

At the time of my rookie season in the Eastern League, the NBA fielded only nine teams. With 12 on each roster, that amounted to 108 NBA players—compared with 450 nowadays. That left a lot of highly skilled players out of the loop, and many of them performed in the Eastern League, guys like Wally Choice, Julius McCoy, Stacey Arceneaux, Cal Ramsey, and Paul Arizin (who refused to move from Philadelphia to San Francisco when the Warriors relocated).

Apparently I had been drafted by the Camden Bullets in the fall of 1962, and our first practice session convened on a subzero December morning in a cavernous U.S. Infantry Armory on the outskirts of the city. The problem was that the armory had no heat. It was so cold that the players' hands and feet were totally numb for the first fifteen minutes of our intrasquad scrimmage.

Arizin arrived late because his car wouldn't start. Without even stretching or warming up he jumped right into the scrimmage. My fingers and toes were just starting to tingle and I was assigned the task of trying to guard Arizin. No problem, right? At least until his extremities thawed out. Not so. In fact, Arizin proceeded to put on the best exhibition of shooting I've ever seen. With literally no feeling in his fingers, Arizin hit his first ten shots.

Before the season began I was traded to the Scranton Miners for Floyd Layne(!). The season commenced before I had a chance to practice with the Miners, and for our first scheduled game, I took a long bus ride from Penn Station to Allentown—arriving just minutes before the opening tip-off.

Wilt Chamberlain, of course, was the most powerful of them all, but the second strongest big man I ever played against was Roman Turman. This guy was an ex-Globetrotter who stood about six foot five, weighed perhaps 260, and was playing center for the homestanding Allentown Jets.

Not only was he big, but he was also good. Turmon was averaging more than 32 points and nearly 17 rebounds per game, and he had once scored 68 in Eastern League competition. Turmon's eyes lit up when I checked into the game late in the first quarter, and he immediately took me into the low post. I was leaning, pushing, shoving, and grabbing him when he caught the entry pass, but he didn't seem to notice. Then, with the ball palmed in his right hand, he used his free hand to grab my left arm just below the armpit. Showing no strain whatsoever, he proceeded to lift me to my tippy-toes and then fling me across the baseline as though I was made of straw. As I slammed into the padded wall and sank to the floor, Turmon wheeled and executed a monstrous dunk.

But the play wasn't finished yet.

The nearest referee tooted his tooter, pointed to where I was still sprawled on the floor, and called the foul on me.

That's exactly why home teams rarely lost in the Eastern League.

The Miners were coached by Elmer Ripley, a rather fragile, white-haired gentleman. Ripley was seventy-one years old and his résumé included playing under James Naismith at Kansas and with the Original Celtics, as well as coaching stints with Wagner, Georgetown, Columbia, Notre Dame, Yale, the Harlem Globetrotters, plus the Israeli and the Canadian Olympic squads. I couldn't even begin to guess why Ripley was willing to coach in the Eastern League. I only hoped it wasn't because he needed the money.

In any event, as the EL was strictly a weekend league, we never practiced, we had no plays, and Ripley did little more than make substitutions.

No surprise that the officiating was awful. Home teams got the benefit of virtually every close call since any team that lost two or three consecutive games in its own gym would be in immediate danger of folding. So, if Ripley was rather quiescent on the bench at the Catholic Youth Center in Scranton, he was quick to climb to his feet and vigorously protest any blatantly biased call when we were on the road. And it was his behavior during these road games that truly frightened the players—our fear being that he would suffer a fatal heart attack.

No matter how wrong or how costly a call might be, all of his players shared a common reaction. Instead of protesting to the offending refs, the guys involved in the play would immediately sprint over to the bench to console Ripley.

"That's okay, Coach. It was a good call. Yeah, I really did hack him. Take it easy. Okay?"

Ripley was inducted into the Hall of Fame in 1973. And every one of the 1961–62 Scranton Miners could take a minor share of the credit for Ripley's living to the ripe old age of ninety.

The Scranton Miners were playing a home-and-home weekend set with the Trenton Colonials. One of Scranton's big scorers was Dick Gaines, a real rock-'em-sock-'em marginal criminal type from Jersey City, who, according to Hubie Brown, "was better than Charles Barkley." Trenton's best player was a hot-shot guard named George Blaney, a mildmannered white guy who was an Eastern League rookie after playing one season with the New York Knicks. During the Saturday game at Trenton, Blaney had totally lit up Gaines, beating him on forays to the hoop and also hitting long-range jumpers at will. The Colonials trounced us by 20 points. After the game, players from both teams were milling around in the corridor outside the locker rooms and I chanced to be present when Gaines approached Blaney. "Nice game," said Gaines, and Blaney responded with a modest, "Thanks."

Then Gaines reached into his gym bag and pulled out a rather large handgun. "However," Gaines continued, "if you're thinking about having another nice game tomorrow night, then I'm gonna have to blow your fucking head off."

Now, I had known Blaney for a while and had played in several pickup games with him during the summer. As soon as Gaines put away the gun and made an exit stage left, Blaney rushed over in a panic. "Did you hear that, Charley? The guy's kidding, right? He's just trying to scare me, right? He must be bluffing."

"I doubt it," I said. "I mean, Gaines is my teammate and I'm afraid to step on his shadow."

The next night in Scranton, Blaney shot 1-12 from the field, Gaines had 35 points, and we won in a rout.

In the Eastern League, crime always paid.

After just a handful of games, I was diagnosed as having some seriously infected polyps in my sinuses (belated fallout from Ed Roman's atomic elbow). While I was still in the hospital recovering from the surgery, I was notified that I had been traded to Williamsport—for Floyd Layne (!).

Over the course of my six-game Eastern League career, my per game stats were about 2.0 points and 1.0 rebounds.

Big Man with a Small Whistle and a Medium-Sized Game

After finishing my night school classes and finally graduating from Hunter, I got my first coaching job—directing the fortunes of the Veraldi Junior High School basketball team in Middletown, New York. The young men were a joy to work with—Dickie Fields, Paul Sardella, Jimmy Darling, Jimmy Elia, Emilio Estevez, and Jon Peterson, to name only those whose identities my leaky memory can still summon.

At our initial team meeting held the day before practice was scheduled to commence, I laid down some rules. The one I emphasized the most was the absolute necessity of being on time to every team function.

"If you're late to practice," I said, "even one minute late, you'll run laps until your tongue drags on the floor. And no excuses of any sort will be tolerated."

Okay. They seemed to be suitably impressed.

For our opening practice everybody was on time, except for Peterson. We began our warm-ups and drills, and after about fifteen minutes, he made his appearance—all red-faced and sweating and holding a piece of paper for me to read.

"No excuses," I insisted, waving off the paper. "Start running." Which he did, and with commendable vigor.

We continued some drills, walked through the basics of our offense, and went through a controlled half-court and then full-court scrimmage. It was during the up-and-down scrimmage that something caught my eye—after at least an hour, Peterson was still doggedly running his laps.

I had completely forgotten about him!

"Okay," I said, with as much nonchalance as I could muster. "That's enough."

Needless to say, none of the kids was ever late again.

Meanwhile, I was still playing—mostly with Rotolo Electric in the Middletown City League. And it was during a championship game that I was compelled to unloose another face-seeking elbow.

Facing me for the opening tip-off was the coach of the high school varsity, Jim Brownley, who had played his basketball at Seton Hall. Just before the ref tossed the ball in the air, Brownley snarled at me and said this: "Jew bastard!"

Instead of jumping and reaching for the ball, I aimed my right elbow and sought to at least smash his nose to smithereens. But I missed.

We went on to win the game and, from then on, Brownley was unfailingly polite to me whenever ours paths crossed.

In retrospect, I should have missed the first elbow onslaught at Brooklyn College and connected against Brownley.

I was in my late twenties, living, teaching, and coaching in Middletown, when I got an offer I couldn't refuse. It seemed there was a highly competitive city league in nearby

Newburgh, New York, and the sponsor of one of the teams called to ask if I was interested in joining his squad. He'd pay me thirty-five dollars a game, and to satisfy the league's residency requirements he'd register me in a broom closet in the Newburgh Hotel, which he owned.

Sure.

Turned out that I averaged about 30 points per game and led the team to the championship game. We were comfortably ahead when I chanced to go up for a rebound and landed on somebody's foot, thereby suffering an excruciatingly painful ankle sprain. But when I limped to the bench, the sponsor was waiting for me.

"I can't go," I said. "I can't put any weight on it. Is there any ice available?"

Whereupon he started screaming at me. I was a wimp! A coward! If I didn't finish the game, he'd tell the local police that I'd blackmailed him! The cops and the judges were all buddies of his, and at the very least I'd be spending the night in the hoosegow. Then he leaned over and whispered that he'd give me another fifty dollars if we won the game.

So I tightened my sneaker laces and gimped my way through the rest of the game. I was scoreless for the duration and we wound up losing. Afterwards, the owner stiffed me for the thirty-five dollars he owed me, but I was grateful for two things: one, that I wasn't in jail, and two, that since it was my left ankle that was sprained I'd be able to drive home.

Turned out that I couldn't play for another nine months and my ankle was sore for at least two years. When I did heal, I discovered that my vertical was only half of what it used to be, that is, six inches instead of twelve.

Subsequently, I moved back to New York and, after an insufficient recuperation, I limped through frustrating runs at various YMCAs and local after-school rec centers.

My first marriage had ended, but I was more eager than ever to connect with the "right" woman. My standard site for a first date was Chinatown so I'd at least be guaranteed to have some good eats. With Susan, we seemed to have the possibility of a meaningful connection, so for our next date I planned an excursion to the Palisades Amusement Park located in New Jersey just over the George Washington Bridge. I was anxious to make a good impression, so the day before escorting her there, I made a solitary scouting trip.

Naturally, I zeroed in on the basketball toss booth—three shots for a dollar. But the game was rigged.

There was a low-hanging net that permitted only line-drive shots. The rim was slightly smaller than normal and much tighter, and the front lip was higher than the back. Also, the backboard was slanted backward, and the ball was oversized and overinflated. If the ball so much as touched the rim it would bounce awry.

It took me two bucks to make adjustments and find the range.

The first time I nailed 3 for 3, I won a four-foot-high stuffed teddy bear. In quick succession, I also won a huge stuffed penguin and a somewhat scary-looking stuffed owl— all of which I presented to whatever kiddies happened to be in the vicinity.

All right! I had it down! There was no way that Susan wouldn't be totally impressed.

The next night, I confidently steered her over to the basketball toss, said, "Watch this"—and proceeded to miss shot
after shot. After spending twenty dollars, I had won two tiny
plastic dinosaurs!

What the hell was that all about?

Apparently Susan wasn't too bothered by my poor performance because, several months later, she and I were married—and we stayed married for a long time, even though
it turned out that we really didn't like each other. A very
long time!

One reason why "basketball marriages" last longer than
they should, however, is road trips.

While our divorce proceedings were under way, I happened to flash back on that date at the amusement park.
And it suddenly occurred to me that I had failed to recognize
an obvious warning. Twenty dollars' worth of misses, frustrations, and embarrassment . . . How could I have missed
the message?

THE BALL NEVER LIES.

Shortly after hooking up with Susan, I entered into another relationship that would be far more interesting and
satisfying. That's when I met Phil Jackson.

I had made the rounds of the NBA doing various profiles
for *Sport Magazine,* and I first met PJ in the spring of 1973
at a party in his loft in Chelsea (brought there by Stan Love,
a fun-loving, powerless power-forward for the Washington
Bullets, with whom I'd connected while doing a story on one
of his teammates). I was immediately taken with Jackson's
easy manner and total sincerity, qualities that were in sharp
contrast to most of the other arrogant, self-serving NBA ballers
I'd previously encountered. He, in turn, appreciated my big-

city cynicism, my quirky sense of humor, and above all, my passion for The Game. We also had the same taste in music: bluegrass, the Grateful Dead, and Bob Dylan.

Besides, during the off-season Phil had a weekly run at the United Nations School in midtown, and since the biggest of his buddies was only six foot three the game was in dire need of at least a sizable opponent to guard PJ. So, I double-taped my still-sore ankle and became Phil's routinely abused sparring partner.

Shortly thereafter, Phil's agent negotiated a book deal with Playboy Press and PJ chose me to be the "as-told-to" writer who was required to help PJ present his autobiography. As I became privy to his history—and some of his secrets—Phil and I became fast friends, and since then we have greatly influenced each other's lives.

In the early years of our friendship, we both had vague spiritual itches that we couldn't quite scratch to our respective satisfaction. Together we attended services at Unity churches and read the Christian mystics. On my own, I briefly explored Christian Science and the teachings of Bhagwan Shree Rajneesh. Yet the only messages I was able to receive seemed either vague or unattainable.

Fast forward to the last day of the 1974–75 season when the Knicks were playing an afternoon game at home against the Buffalo Braves. To make the playoffs, the Knicks needed to win, and the Cavs (who played later that afternoon) needed to lose.

Susan and I brought our six-month-old son, Darrell, to the game, and June Jackson (Phil's then-wife) brought their three-month-old daughter, Chelsea, along too. All snuggled in their portable basket/cribs the two infants snoozed throughout the game, blissfully oblivious to the thunderous crowd noise and the raucous celebration when the Knicks finally pulled the game out.

Immediately after Phil had showered and dressed, we all scooted over to his Nineteenth Street loft and arrived in time to see the last quarter of the Cleveland game. With ten seconds on the game clock and down by 2 points, the Cavs huddled around their coach during their final time-out while Bill Fitch masterminded the most critical play of his team's season.

We could tell by Fitch's frantic scribbling on his miniature game board and by his team's utter confusion when they attempted to inbound the ball from the sideline that the play he had drawn up was an improvisation and was not in the Cavs' game book. This was a bad idea. And the result was a bad pass and nary a shot.

The Knicks were in with a record of 40-42, and the Cavs were out.

Immediately after the final buzzer, Phil's phone rang. It was Walt Frazier inviting his teammates and their guests to a celebratory party at his luxurious midtown apartment. Of course, we had to bring the kids.

The bathtub in Frazier's master bathroom was loaded with ice, beer, wine, and champagne. The large dining room table was loaded with cartons of take-out Chinese food. And, besides the Knicks themselves, several other New York sports celebrities were on hand.

Everybody was instructed to deposit their coats on either of the two beds in the bedroom nearest the front door. And, carefully arranging protected areas for Darrell and Chelsea, we laid them down when they both fell asleep again. Every fifteen minutes or so, one of the four parents peeked into the room to check on the kids' well-being—and I was astonished at what I saw when it was my turn.

Chelsea was awake and merrily chortling, while Darrell was wide-awake and laughing as though he was being tickled. In fact, two men were standing on opposite sides of the bed and tossing Darrell back and forth!

One of them was Spider Lockhart, a glue-fingered free safety for the New York Giants. The other was Nate Bowman, a backup center for the Knicks whose assist-to-turnover ratio was an exercise in negativity. And both were laughing, bobbing, and weaving in a mild alcoholic haze.

"Nate," I said with as much nonchalance as I could muster. "Don't drop him, man."

"No chance, bro," he said. Whereupon Bowman set himself to receive the incoming baby, and then slyly bounced him in the air before securing him.

I didn't know what to do or say, so I hustled back into the living room and relayed my worries to Phil.

"Don't worry, Charley," said Phil. "Nate can catch all right. Everything will be okay as long he doesn't try to dribble the boy."

Darrell survived, and the Knicks lost a three-game series to Houston.

Thirty-three years later, both Bowman and Lockhart have passed away. And Darrell is now a red-bearded, six-foot-seven, 280-pounder, and living with his wife and their three kids in Bellingham, Washington.

Meanwhile, in addition to the magazine articles, I was also writing novels and nonfiction books. From time to time, various publicity appearances were arranged by my publisher of the moment. The first televised promo that I ever did was to hawk *A Mile Above the Rim*, a ficto-historical version of life in the NBA—and my worst book ever—on *The Joe Franklin Show*. On the air in New York City more than twenty-five years, the legendary Franklin was short and stubby in the flesh, wearing an agreeable smile and a surprisingly chintzy toupee.

"Are there any questions you want me to ask?" he said.

"No. Let's just go with the flow."

One of my co-guests was Anita Cabana, a sagging musical comedienne whose specialty was imitating Carmen Miranda. "A star of stage, screen, and radio . . . The always lovely . . . The always delightful . . ."

"Oh, Cho! Hue are so cute! For the nex' six days I am play-yink at the Golden Hind uptown on Willis Avenue. I do all the old favorites."

Sitting beside me was a young man in a Jimmy Durante costume—replete with silly hat, bozo bow tie, and plastic schnozz.

"And our third guest," Franklin enthused, "is Charley Rosen who has written *A Mile Above the Rim* . . ." Expertly, Franklin held the book at the proper angle for a closeup.

"One of the all-time great sports novels by a truly great writer. I urge all my good friends out there in videoland to go out and buy *A Mile Above the Rim*. That's *A Mile Above the Rim*. We'll be right back after these important messages."

When the red eye of the camera blinked off, Franklin blew his nose and said, "Good! Good!" Then he rubbed his hands together like a fidgeting housefly. "This is going to be a truly wonderful show."

"Cho! Ju know, I am appear-ink for the New Jeer's Eve at the Pink Flamingo in, how you say, Bed-Stay?"

"Ha, ha!" said Franklin. "That's terrific! Let's use that when we come back! Great show!"

Bizzaro Durante's nose was secured around his head with an elastic cord. During the intermission, he yanked on his ersatz honker, saying, "I can't breathe under this damn thing! What a way to make a living!"

When my turn came, Franklin promptly asked me who would win the NBA championship, and cagily, I answered, "I'm just rooting for triple overtime in the seventh game of the final series."

"We'll be right back, my friends, right after this . . ."

Franklin sipped from a glass of water, but the pseudo-Durante said, "My mouth gets dry and I can't drink or I'll ruin my makeup."

It turned out that the real Durante was hospitalized with pneumonia, so his double sang "Inka Dinka Doo"—"Just for you, Jimmy."

When the camera winked again, Franklin twitched with glee: "Great! Great! Only five more minutes to fill! This is one of the truly wonderful shows! But what'll we do next?"

"Cho! In three weeks I am play-yink in Chursey City!"

"We'll go with it! I love it! What a truly wonderful show! One of my best ever!"

Sometimes being center-sized can lead to unique off-the-court adventures.

One of my teammates at Hunter, Joe Schenker, eventually became the interim president of Kingsborough Community

College in Brooklyn and used his influence to get me a job teaching English there. It turned out that the English department's secretary also ran a talent agency.

"One of my clients is a fat lady," she told me. "I have four dwarfs, three midgets, a lady with an enormous bust, and an old guy with a great big nose. The agency is called Freaks Unlimited."

Measuring six foot nine, 240 pounds, I accepted her offer to become the house giant.

My first gig was a rainy-day audition at a penthouse apartment on Lexington Avenue in the fancy 40s. I was met at the door by Cyril Starmaker, a middle-aged man in disco slacks and a blue silk shirt worn open to reveal a hairless chest. Mr. Starmaker handed me a script and told me to "wait in the foyer with the others."

According to the script, the name of the movie was *Sasha and the Undead*, and the lead was already cast—Sasha to be played by the "seductive Miss Mia Culpa."

The luxurious vestibule was appointed with several leather couches, but I was the only aspirant to sit down. Before my very face, at least a dozen midgets in natty three-piece suits swarmed briskly about the room, declaiming their lines in shrill voices:

"Oh, Sasha! I know it cannot be, but I must confess how much I love you!"

"Sasha! Look out behind you!"

"Hey, baby, what's a nice girl like you doing in an oasis like this?"

"The fools! How can they resist us? They shall die for their folly!"

"Hey, Gork, how's the weather up there?"

According to the script, Gork had no lines. By the look of the competition, I seemed to be the only qualified applicant.

None of the midgets glanced up from their scripts when the door to an inner sanctum suddenly swung open, and another tiny man strode grandly across the room toward the front door. But their collective eyeballs clicked in unified disappointment when Mr. Starmaker poked his head into the room and said, "You're next, Gork."

Inside, a spacious living room was immaculately styled in ritzy plastic furniture. Another young man with an open-chested shirt and a neckful of glittering gold chains was introduced as "George the director."

"Okay," said George. "Here's the scene, see? Lie down on the floor and wake up as though from a thousand years' sleep. You've been asleep for a thousand years. Get it?"

As directed, I laid back on the floor with my eyes closed. Then after slowly twitching one eye, I quickly popped open the other one.

"Good," said George. "Good. I love his beard."

Despite the rain, I was then asked to chase George around the terrace. "Not so fast," said George as we splashed through thin puddles. "Lumber around a little more."

"And grunt," said Mr. S.

"Unnnga!" I grunted. "Unnnga! Bunnnga!"

After that I had to make believe George was Sasha. "You haven't seen a woman in a thousand years," he said. "And here I am. Sleeping, helpless before you. Touch me. Caress my face."

"And grunt," said Mr. S.

"UNNNGA! BUNNNGA!"

My next assignment was to grab George and throw him

onto the couch. But George was heavier than he looked and to my surprise I almost dropped him.

"Throw him again," said Mr. S. "Don't be afraid to hurt him."

For my last trick, I took a running start, then pretended George's umbrella was indeed a mighty sword that sliced me from belly to spine. "Ugh!" I grunted as I plunged into a death spasm.

"Good," said George. "Let's do it again."

In all, we "played the scene" five times, and I swear that George hit me harder each time. However, when we were finished, George turned to me and said, "You're the best Gork we've seen so far."

"But don't call us," cautioned Mr. Starmaker. "We may or may not call you."

The best Gork they'd seen! I was born to Gork! Gorking my way to fame and fortune!

Months later, the agent-secretary reported that another Gork had been chosen.

"A big blond he-man," she said. "They're positive he's going to be a superstar."

"How tall is he? What's his name?"

"He's a six-foot-nine-inch bodybuilder. His name is Rock Lock."

According to further information, *Sasha and the Undead* was completed, received a PG rating, and failed to survive seven days at the Bayonne Bijou.

Perhaps one of these days Gork will live again on HBO.

It was during my travels for *Sport* that I accidentally came upon the very best game of basketball that I have ever witnessed: It was a preliminary to a Sixers-Lakers game at the

Spectrum some years ago. The players were mostly preteens, Westwood Hills versus the Meadowland School.

One team featured a guard whose long red sweatpants concealed his artificial legs. A forward had a deformed hip and bone-locked wrists. A center's entire body was blistered with thick, shiny scars, and most of the cheerleaders leaned on crutches.

The players were absolutely confused with joy as they leaped, stumbled, and shouted. The final score was 6–4.

For me, this jubilant competition, such as it was, represented nothing less than the heart and soul of the game.

Then in the spring of 1975 I moved a hundred miles upstate to Woodstock where I discovered to my delight there were dozens of top-flight hoopers.

5

On the Road with the Woodstock Joneses

The pickup games were organized by Rod Chando, who'd been a JUCO All-American in his prime and was the highly successful coach at nearby Red Hook High School. Accordingly, we played at the high school gym on Tuesday nights and early—7:00 a.m.—on Sunday mornings.

Occasionally, the best of the group would get together and play against "outside" teams. Our All-Star squad included six-foot-six Al Dufty, a onetime captain of the Princeton Tigers; six-foot-seven Dennis Odle, a double-figure scorer for Clemson; and six-foot-nine me up front. In the backcourt were Greg Dodge, an All-State selection in high school; and Chando. We were sometimes augmented by six-foot-seven Jack McCue, a rugged forward-center from St. Francis (Brooklyn). We called ourselves the Woodstock Joneses, and we had orange jerseys with the team name and our numbers printed in gold-flecked glitter.

One of our most satisfying performances came when Phil Jackson added Neal Walk to several of his UN School players, and we played a best-of-seven series to fifteen baskets. Which we won, four games to three. A few weeks later we returned the favor, losing 4–3 on their court in midtown Manhattan.

Eddie Mast had been Phil's roommate for two seasons with the Knicks, and although Eddie lived in Easton, Pennsylvania, we also became close friends. On one occasion, Eddie brought his guys up to Red Hook High School for another challenge series. Playing with Eddie was Bobby Greacen, who had been the twelfth man on the Milwaukee Bucks championship team of 1971 that featured Lew Alcindor (soon to be Kareem Abdul-Jabbar) and Oscar Robertson. Since Eddie had played his college ball at Temple University in Philadelphia, several of his old teammates filled out the rest of his team.

We prevailed in seven fiercely competitive games, but for one reason or another we were unable to arrange a conclusion to this particular home-and-home series.

I was in my late thirties and still a rock-'em-sock-'em force in the paint when I was asked to participate in a charity doubleheader somewhere in northern New Jersey. I was asked to bring another player and Al Dufty was eager to come along for the run. The first game pitted an All-Star pickup team (that included me and Al) against a squad that had won the city's recreation-league championship. In the second game, the winner would be matched against a team comprised of professional football players from the New Jersey Generals of the now defunct United States Football League. The gate receipts were earmarked for a local fund that benefited children afflicted with cerebral palsy.

The stands were filled with dozens of young CP victims, their friends, and their relatives. They were all somewhat downhearted when their local favorites were defeated by the All-Star ringers, but they clearly enjoyed the competition and were eagerly looking forward to the finale.

Against the rec-leaguers I had played with my usual almost-over-the-top frenzy and had succeeded in dominating the lane while managing to stay out of foul trouble (mostly because of the incompetence of the referees). Since the expected banging and rough-house tactics would be right up my alley, I was also anticipating the second game and the prospect of competing with the football players. Here was my chance to prove that I was just as tough as those muscle-bound oafs.

However, between games, the two referees—crew-cut bozos with slight paunches and stone-colored eyes—demanded a bonus for officiating the second game. The promoters were outraged. But they were also stumped. No refs meant no game and an early and disappointing end to the children's celebration. The promoters pleaded, but the refs were adamant.

That's when, seemingly out of nowhere, I came up with a great idea. What if we played the game without the greedy refs? If all the players were agreeable, we'd just call our own fouls.

Everybody seconded the motion. And the subsequent contest turned out to be the most enjoyable basketball game in which I have ever played.

The football players were uniformly powerful, athletic, and eager for chest-to-chest combat, but the big men (tackles, ends, centers, and guards) lacked the instinctive footwork necessary to work effectively beyond the line of scrimmage. We respected their professional status, and although we were only civilians, they respected our superiority in performing the requisite dance steps.

As the game unfolded, a wonderful camaraderie developed. Even though we all played hard, we played clean. And we talked to each other constantly, complimenting good plays on both sides and apologizing for any undue contact that fell short of being foul-worthy. There were no arguments and not a trace of ill-will.

On one drive hoopward I was bumped off-stride and missed the ensuing lay-up. When my defender (a six-foot-six, 270-pound tight end) offered to penalize himself for the illegal contact, I surprised myself by saying, "Naw, that's all right. I should've made the shot anyway."

During the brief half-time intermission, the players mingled near the scorer's table, identifying ourselves and exchanging personal information—even though we knew we'd never see each other again once the game was over.

"I'm from Bear Country," the tight end said, referring to the legendary University of Alabama football coach Bear Bryant. "And you?"

"Woodstock. The town that time forgot."

Meanwhile, the kids lined up for autographs—and we remembered where we were, why we were there, and how fortunate we were to still be able to run up and down the court. So we turned our full attention to the kids. The beautiful, tragic, cheerful children.

"Hey, buddy," we'd gently enquire, trying in vain to match the innocence of their joy and their forgetfulness. "What's your favorite team? Who's your favorite player?"

Too soon, the game resumed.

As before, the body contact was aggressive and intense, yet

within acceptable limits. The fouls were seldom called, particularly among the bigs. Each play, each move and countermove was executed with a sense of joy that transcended any consideration of shots made and missed, of botched passes and misdribbles. We were all riding the crest of the same unexpected, yet delightful experience.

"Nice shot, man."

"How'd you get that pass through all that traffic?"

"All right!"

The final buzzer came as a rude shock. Only then did we bother to look up at the scoreboard—and it didn't matter who had won and who had lost.

Instead of Us versus Them, instead of five against five, there were ten players playing one ball game.

Ah, hoops were paradise enow.

6

On and Off the Court with the Bard-Ons

From 1980 to 1982 I coached the Bard College hoopers, such as they were.

The student body was almost exclusively comprised of aspiring artists of various stripes. Musicians. Painters. Dancers. Writers. Which goes a long way to explain why the Bard Running Red Devils were such poor basketball players. And since they had trouble successfully running a three-on-none fast break, the players usually referred to themselves as the Bard-Ons.

At five foot seven, my small forward was really small. My six-foot-two center, the colorful Lance Lavender, once mooned his opposite number instead of jumping to capture the opening tip of a ball game against Skidmore. My shooting guard was once pulled from a game in progress by his drama teacher for an unexpected rehearsal of *As You Like It*—which I didn't at all.

The most talented player on the squad would always open a game by playing brilliantly for about sixty seconds. But then, as soon as he missed a shot, committed a turnover, or had a foul called against him, he would sit down on the court and refuse to move.

Also on the team was a Canadian hockey player who had never touched a basketball before, an ex-con, and a pair of once and future heroin addicts. Another player routinely showed up for games tripping on acid.

Our combined record for those two seasons was 3-35. It should be noted, however, that two of those wins were against Simon's Rock Academy—a high school for advanced students that was run by Bard. Whereas we'd lose an average game by anywhere from 40 to 60 points, we'd beat the Simon's Rockers by 30.

It was while coaching Bard that I was on the red-ass end of the worst exhibition of sportsmanship I've ever experienced.

Because of injuries, midterm exams, and general disinterest, only five players made the road trip to Berkshire Christian College. The star of the home team was a six-foot-eight powerhouse player who had played for the Harlem Wizards before seeing the light. In an earlier game with BCC, we'd lost by 40-plus points, which is approximately what this guy had scored.

Anyway, we were getting thoroughly trounced in the game at hand when, midway through the second half, one of my players fouled out. Okay. No problem. That's the breaks of the game. Let's play on.

Trouble was that even though they were already up by 40 plus, the BCC squad went into a full-court trap-and-press. Seeing as how they had a five-on-four advantage, the score mounted. And when I yelled my protest down to the other bench, I was studiously ignored.

Then it got worse. With about five minutes remaining, my point guard (Matt Pelosi, a wonderful young—now middle-aged—man, who's still the nephew of Nancy Pelosi) went down with a badly sprained ankle. Stubbornly refusing to come out of the game, Matt doggedly, and literally, hopped on one foot for the duration.

And, of course, the coach ratcheted up his full-court pressure. It got to the point where I instructed my three remaining fully ambulatory players to respond to every basket converted by the home team by simply passing the ball inbounds directly into the hands of the nearest player in a white uniform.

Meanwhile, the scarce but loud BCC fans yelled their lungs out as their heroes' lead increased.

The final differential was more than 60 points.

Afterward, the BCC coach dashed off the court without the formality of approaching me to shake my hand. Fuming with rage, all I could do was shout after him, "Good job, Coach! You jackass!"

Whereupon several of the fans huffed, puffed, and verbally upbraided me for using such foul language.

We may not have been a very good ball club, but we sure did have lots of fun. For a more detailed report on my coaching tenure at Bard, see *Players and Pretenders: The Team That Couldn't Shoot Straight* (University of Nebraska Press, 2007).

It was also while coaching the Bard-Ons that I came across Vern Piantanida, my favorite referee of all time. Here's why: In one game, when he saw a play the wrong way, I yelled at him, "That was a bad call!" He just nodded and said, "You're probably right." And later, when I asked why he routinely allowed Lance Lavender to take extra steps, Vern replied: "Bard was usually losing by 40 or 50 points anyway, and why would I want Lance screaming at me?"

A few years later, Vern reffed the final of a highly competitive semipro tournament played at Columbia-Greene Community College. It just so happened that the Woodstock Joneses were playing the Adams Aces, and the championship game went down to the wire. The most critical play of the contest came in the last minute when I set a marginally moving screen (my specialty) that not only surprised one of the Aces but sent him sprawling to the floor—freeing Al Dufty for the game-winning score.

The Aces were too stunned to protest the call, but I asked Vern afterward why he hadn't whistled me for the foul. "Because the guy who was guarding you didn't tell the guy who was guarding Dufty about the screen. It was the defense's fault because they didn't communicate."

7

The Crazy B-Ball Ass

My next stop on my personal coaching carousel was the Continental Basketball Association (nee the Eastern League). More than the name had changed since I played for the Miners.

The caliber of play had remained high with several over-the-hill NBA players or still developing youngsters having dotted rosters during the intervening seasons: George Blaney, Al Butler, M. L. Carr, Fred Crawford, Greg Fillmore, Sihugo Green, Art Heyman, Cleo Hill, Bob Love, Eddie Mast, Luther Rackley, Mike Riordan, Ray Scott, Paul Silas, Ben Warley, Bob Weiss, and Harthorne Wingo.

Indeed, the EL had been perpetually hopeful of developing some sort of working relationship with the NBA. But the EL's admittance of so many point shavers in the early 1950s made this impossible. However, by the late 1960s all of the tainted players had retired and there were some vague preliminary discussions aimed at the NBA's partially subsidizing the EL in return for an as yet unresolved player development arrangement.

But even this tenuous beginning collapsed in 1974, when the NBA Players Association took notice of the fate of John

Brisker, a double-digit scorer for Seattle, whose lack of off- and on-court discipline irked his coach, Bill Russell. Strictly as a punitive measure, Russell sent Brisker to the Eastern League, where in a handful of games he averaged more than 50 points. To the Players Association, the EL was henceforth deemed to be a detention hall for unruly players and the interleague negotiations were dead.

There were other bizarre dealings that likewise encouraged the NBA to keep its distance from the Eastern League. One notable example was the most risqué trade in the history of professional sports.

It seems that the general manager of Team A made an agreement with the GM of Team B to transfer the rights of a certain player from A to B. However, since Team B had no cash to spare and the CBA had no college draft at the time, other arrangements had to be made.

After much dickering the two teams finally agreed to the following terms: the secretary of A's general manager would get together with B's general manager to deliver a blow job at a later date.

One is left to wonder exactly how the transaction was officially recorded.

Through the years instability remained the most significant constant in the EL: during seventeen of the league's first twenty-one years, at least one team folded or relocated either during or after the season. In 1967 the American Basketball Association came into being and most of the Eastern League's best players eagerly jumped to the new organization, lured by pricey contracts that the EL's teams couldn't come close to matching. At the start of the 1974–75 season, the EL was down to four teams—Hazelton, Allentown, Scranton, and Cherry Hill.

Then in 1976 four ABA teams joined the NBA, and the remaining five ABA franchises ceased operations. Now there was a return migration of high-quality players back into the Eastern League. A year later, franchises could be purchased for eight thousand dollars and the EL had ten teams: Jersey Shore Bullets, Long Island Ducks, Quincy (Massachusetts) Chiefs, Providence Shooting Stars, Brooklyn Dodgers, Wilkes-Barre Barons, Lancaster Red Roses, Allentown Jets, plus an extracontinental franchise situated in Anchorage, Alaska.

The 1977–78 season provided a milestone for the Eastern League. That's when three of its players signed with NBA teams: Harthorne Wingo with New York, Charlie Criss with Philadelphia, and Brad Davis with the Lakers. At the end of the 1977–78 season, another minor league—the Western Basketball Association—folded and in anticipation of adding more quality players and far-ranging franchises, the owners of the holdover EL franchises convened on August 26, 1978, in Quincy, Massachusetts, to rename their league the Continental Basketball Association and prepare for their suddenly bright future.

Jim Drucker's father, Norm, had been a longtime NBA referee, but Jim was more interested in sports administration.

JIM DRUCKER: *"I got the job as the CBA's first-ever commissioner under very strange circumstances. . . . The ten owners met with the two candidates—me and Steve Kaufman, who's now a high-powered agent operating out of Malibu— in a somewhat sleazy hotel in the worst section of Quincy. The owners didn't want to spring for a rented meeting room, so we gathered in the cocktail lounge where the arguments*

soon became loud and nasty. Also, there seemed to be an un-
usual number of flashy but well-used women floating around.
During a break in the negotiations, I agreed to meet privately
with one of the owners who supported me over Kaufman,
but when we entered his room we found a man and a woman
fucking in his bed. Anyway, I was confirmed by a vote of six
to four. Thirty minutes after we all checked out of the hotel
the next morning, the joint was raided by the local police.
Turned out the hotel was really a whorehouse."

Prior to the forthcoming 1978–79 season, the hiring of
Drucker paid an immediate dividend when he negotiated a
million-dollar contract with the NBA for "referee development." Most of the money was used to finance the league
office in Drucker's hometown of Lafayette Hill, Pennsylvania, with the CBA's franchises each receiving about seventy-
five thousand dollars. Among the current crop of NBA refs
who eventually got their start in the CBA are Bob Delaney,
Ron Garetson, Steve Javie, Monty McCutchen, Leon Wood,
and Ronnie Nunn.

RON GARETSON: *"The CBA was never about the players,*
the coaches, nor the fans. The only reason why the league
existed was to provide a training ground for referees."

All of the Western Basketball Association's teams closed up
shop before they could merge with the CBA, so after another
round of musical franchises, here was the lineup for the CBA's
inaugural 1979–80 season: Anchorage, Hawaii, Lancaster, Lehigh Valley (in Nazareth, Pennsylvania), Maine (in Bangor),
Scranton, Rochester (New York), and Utica (New York).

BILL KLUCAS: *"I was the coach of the Anchorage North-*
ern Knights, and in the middle of the season we embarked

on what I'm sure was a record-setting road trip that lasted thirty-two days. We flew into Rochester, and from there on we traveled everywhere else in a van that I had to drive. Every article of clothing we brought had to be either hand-washed in a sink or not washed at all. It's not surprising that some of us got on each other's nerves. I'd estimate we had about a dozen blood-letting fistfights.

"We had several onetime NBA players on the team—Sean Colson, Ron Davis, and Stan Pietkiewicz—so we averaged about 135 points per game. We did make the playoffs and were fortunate enough to play all of the semifinal playoff games in Anchorage. We were swept in the finals by Rochester, and the average score was like 145 to 132. Everybody had the same attitude on defense—hurry up and score so we can score."

Even with a bright, shiny new name the league couldn't seem to avoid the same old daffy doings. Beginning on January 25, 1979, a contest matching the Rochester Zeniths and the CBA All-Stars wound up being the longest, and the looniest, All-Star game ever.

Back then, it was felt—and for good reason—that a battle of East and West All-Stars would draw mostly flies in any city in the league. So for several years, the All-Stars played a host team and a capacity crowd of 4,086 filled the Dome Center Arena in suburban Henrietta, New York.

(A footnote: Only three coaches have ever led their host teams to victories over All-Star rosters: Mauro Panaggio with Rochester in 1979, Phil Jackson with the Albany Patroons in 1983, and yours truly with the Rockford Lightning on New Year's Eve 1988.)

The Zeniths were leading at halftime, 57–48, when a blizzard knocked out the power in the Dome Center Arena. After a meeting of the minds, it was decided that the game would resume the very next night when an additional four quarters would be played.

After a total of six quarters, the Zeniths won by the whopping score of 182–168.

Five participants were already NBA veterans—Eddie Mast, Jim Bostic (albeit briefly), Dean Tolson, Larry Fogle (briefly), and Larry McNeill. Plus Fly Williams had played in the ABA.

Six other participants later played in the NBA—Andre McCarter, Billy Ray Bates, Ron Davis, Lewis Brown, Stan Pietkiewicz, and Glenn Hagan.

In its way this two-day All-Star game anticipated the NBA's annual weekend-long All-Star extravaganza.

Not long after the All-Star game was finally over, I accompanied my buddy Eddie Mast and his Lehigh Valley teammates up to Rochester for a game against the Zeniths. The ensuing game offered two surprises.

First, instead of hardwood, or a composite plastic substance, I saw firsthand that the court at the Dome Center Arena was actually surfaced with a feltlike material. While the ball seemed to bounce normally, there was absolutely no sound when it hit the court. The effect was eerie, turning the game into a contest between two ghostly teams.

And second, I was shocked during the pregame warm-ups when players from both squads attacked the baskets with such ferocious dunks that the rims seemed to be on the verge of breaking. Turned out, however, that the CBA was testing a newfangled apparatus for possible future use in the NBA—the collapsible rim.

The CBA also gained a considerable degree of respectability after the season when Commissioner Drucker negotiated another million-dollar deal with the NBA, this one for player development. The agreement allowed any NBA team to sign any CBA player to a ten-day contract, for which the player would earn about twenty-five hundred dollars and the CBA team fifteen hundred. A ten-day could be renewed for another ten days (with the same compensation), and thereafter the player would have to be signed for the remainder of the NBA season or returned to the CBA. (For the legions of players whose ten-day contracts were not renewed, another of the CBA's noms de hoop was "Come Back Again.")

These call-ups were the main motivations for top-notch players to sign with CBA teams (there were long and complex rules dealing with which teams had the rights to which players). Yet some CBA coaches (especially Mauro Panaggio) would routinely denigrate whichever of their players NBA scouts asked about.

As part of the new agreement, there was a loose affiliation between CBA teams and the closest NBA team. CBA teams now had the rights to any player drafted and then cut by their affiliate—providing that said player hadn't previously been the property of another CBA team.

The Albany Patroons joined the CBA in time for the 1982–83 season as the only community-owned franchise in the CBA. According to its charter, any profits accruing to the ball club would provide scholarships to worthy students. Dean Meminger was their original coach. At the time, Dean the Dream was thirty-four years old and five years removed from his last NBA season. During practices and games, Meminger would constantly ridicule his players, claiming that he was still better than any of them.

In any event, after the Patroons began the season with a dismal record of 8-15, Meminger was fired. His temporary replacement was one of the players, Sam Worthen, who led the team to a pair of losses before a more permanent coach was hired.

Enter Phil Jackson, who had recently retired as player and assistant coach of the New Jersey Nets and had retreated to his home in Montana where he was operating a local health club.

Before he left town, Meminger made a last request to be allowed to try out for the team. Phil agreed, and watched a painful scrimmage wherein the surviving players unmercifully beat on their ex-coach.

Jackson finished the season at 8-11, then moved out of his hotel room and relocated his family to Woodstock— a hundred miles south of Albany—in preparation for the next season.

Phil needed another supervisory body to assist him during training camp, and he asked me if I was interested. The best the Patroons could do was to pay me twenty-five dollars a week.

Hell, yes.

8

On the Bench with Phil Jackson

At the time I was signing on for my new position with the Patroons, the CBA featured a total of twelve teams. The Eastern Division comprised the Albany Patroons, the Puerto Rico Coquis, the Bay State Bombardiers, the Lancaster Lightning, and the Sarasota Stingers. In the West were the Wisconsin Flyers, the Detroit Spirits, the Wyoming Wildcatters, the Ohio Mixers, the Louisville Catbirds, and the Albuquerque Silvers. The league was still ruled by the burgeoning brainstorms of Commissioner Jim Drucker and was self-advertised as "PROgressive Basketball."

Visiting teams brought nine players, the home team suited ten, and nobody ever fouled out. Shortly before PJ signed with Albany, a dissatisfied benchwarmer had tried to drown his coach in a toilet bowl. Players, coaches, team executives, and other inmates routinely referred to the league as the Crazy Basketball Association.

Keeping a diary of that wacky season was an easy decision.

Inside a room filled with creaking institutional folding chairs just off the lobby of Albany's Best Western motel, twenty-five aspiring Patroons convene for the first time. Only three players return from last season: six-foot-nine, 225-pound Ralph McPherson, a wry Texan with a desperado moustache; Frankie J. Sanders, an irrepressible six-foot-six guard and the San Antonio Spurs' first draft pick in 1979, who lasted in the NBA for eighty-five ball games (the J. stands for "Jump shot"); and Derrick Rowland, a six-foot-six forward with an easy smile. Last season, Derrick received twenty-five dollars per week as the Patroons' "practice player," and his primary employer was Burger King.

Other names and faces are vaguely familiar: Jim Braddock was point guard for UNC's last national champs. Dave Magley is six feet seven inches tall and trim—but with his angular chin and his rimless scorekeeper's spectacles, he hardly resembles a player. His credentials include fifty-six precious minutes with the Cleveland Cavaliers. Maurice "Mo" McDanial played for Catawba College in Salisbury, North Carolina. Penny Elliot stammers that he's from George Washington U. and swears that his real name is "Penny." Most of the other hopefuls are names on a list: Yarharbrough Roberts, York Gross, Evans Ford.

Mike Sandman is the Pats' director of player personnel, an ex-collegian hooper himself, now grayed and paunching. "Welcome to Albany," says Mr. Sandman. "It gets very cold here in the winter. You'll need heavy boots and a heavy coat. Learn to dress in layers." Sandman goes on to caution the players about mishandling the local groupies. Then he reminds them of Albany's contractual obligations: Free beds at the motel. No salaries during training camp. Only five dollars' per diem for meals. In the back of the room, six-foot-seven Ford from Brooklyn takes notes.

The room's most commanding presence belongs to Jackson. At age thirty-eight, PJ is only three years removed from his playing career and he still shows the same long-jointed arms and rigid shoulders, the same friendly beard, his eagle-colored eyes still gleaming. After introducing me as his assistant, Phil talks about role players and "court awareness." "Workouts are at eleven and six," he concludes, "so get plenty of sleep."

The season begins in just fourteen days.

November 17–20

Albany is the capital of New York and, as such, has the largest per capita population of lawyers in the country. The city has a metro-area population of six hundred thousand, delusions of grandeur, nary a decent eatery (except for Lombardo's), and an alarming number of ambulatory alcoholics.

The Patroons' home base is the Washington Avenue Armory—with massive medieval walls and rookish towers set on a ridge overlooking the state capitol building. The U.S. Army stores live ammunition in the Armory's basement behind a well-guarded door marked Off Limits. Once the season starts, the arsenal doubles as a dressing room for the refs.

Across the hallway the Patroons' locker room is slung with low-hanging pipes, perfect support for clothes hangers and umbrellas. In lieu of carpeting, the bare concrete floor is covered with a white sheet. The only showers are reached down the hall and through the public men's room.

Upstairs, a six-lane track encircles portable grandstands that can accommodate three thousand fans. The court itself, which cost fifty thousand dollars, is handsomely inlaid with oaken strips, with the Patroons' wooden shoe logo (Dutch colonial landowners were the original patroons) emblazoned at center court. Too bad the Pentagon orders the floor cleaned with an inappropriate chemical, so the footing is always treacherous. The near basket is also one inch too low, the other an inch too high. And every time the heating system is activated, the government bills the Patroons seven hundred dollars. Accordingly, the practice air is frosty and the players must shoot with cold hands.

Yet consider that the Puerto Rico Coquis' training camp is being held in New York City with sixty players battling three times a day. Consider that other CBA teams charge training camp players two dollars to get their ankles taped. No wonder the Pats are considered one of the CBA's class operations.

The Armory is much colder in the mornings, so the players run and stretch for about twenty minutes before I take the big men and Phil works the guards and small forwards. The morning sessions are devoted to basic fundamentals as well as installing our defenses and offenses (mostly a flex). Evenings involve a comprehensive review followed by a sixty-to-seventy-five-minute scrimmage.

Magley's game face includes his unlikely glasses, but he is indeed a player—stabbing the net with tight-wristed jumpers and running wild on the break like a merry dunkster. Frankie Sanders can always create space for his J, and McPherson is rawhide tough. But all the available point guards are inadequate. Soft-spoken Andre Gaddy stands six foot eleven and may be an excellent shooter, but he's easily bewildered on defense. Seven-foot former Globetrotter Dedrick Reffigee is short-winded and blubbery.

Phil likes Troy Mikell, a six-foot-three high-jumping power guard who battles the big men in the shadow of the hoop. Right before the first cut, Mikell goes down with a torn Achilles tendon.

First cuts: Ford, Carter, Tallman, Harris, and Washington.

"Thanks for the chance," says Tallman.

"You're making a big mistake," says Ford. "I'm your best rebounder."

An hour later, Harris calls to ask if Phil has changed his mind.

November 21–23

Transactions:

John Schweitz, purchased from the Bay State Bombardiers, a six-foot-six shooting guard with three-point range who last season averaged 20.5 ppg for the defunct Maine Lumberjacks. In October 1992 and again in 1983 Schweitz was the last player cut by the Boston Celtics. In exchange for Schweitz, Albany sends six thousand dollars to Bay State, the maximum sum allowable in straight cash purchases. Then Schweitz arrives with a swollen ankle—and his entire season is agonized by injuries.

Lowes Moore, obtained from the Wyoming Wildcatters for the CBA rights to Larry Spriggs, currently on the L.A. Lakers' roster. Should Spriggs last with the Lakers through December 15, Wyoming will take its pick of six Patroons left unprotected. Moore is a reliable point guard with NBA experience.

David Williams, a six-foot-one guard, is signed as a free agent. The younger brother of Ray and Gus is NBA quick, but wild as a hurricane.

Bernard Randolph is dealt to Bay State in a typical CBA transaction. In the CBA home teams assume the motel fee for the visitors—about three hundred dollars a night. (This rule will soon be changed to make each team responsible for all of its own accommodations on the road.) The Pats' first exhibition game is at home versus Bay State—and under the terms of the trade, the Bombardiers will now drive the 250 miles from Brockton, Mississippi, to Albany immediately before the game, and then make their return trip immediately after the game.

During an evening session, Reffigee loses his desire and his lunch.

Cuts: Braddock, Reffigee.

November 24

Thanksgiving: Ten years ago, Phil and I collaborated on his autobiography, *Maverick*, and we've been fast friends ever since. After an early practice, we drive back to Woodstock (about sixty-five miles south of Albany) where both our families share a joyous feast.

November 25–28

The baskets are fixed for our first preseason game, and we beat weary Bay State 112–110. In the CBA, teams earn one point in the standings for winning a quarter and three points for winning the game. It's an interesting game structure—young players learn to maintain their concentration even in blowouts, and it produces four endgames-within-a-game in every contest. PROgressive. But since the best players *have* to be on-court at the end of each quarter, the point system also wreaks havoc with the normal rotation of substitutes. Since we won two of the four quarters and the game, our split tonight is 5 points to 2 (5,2).

Schweitz starts and Sanders comes off the bench scowling. And the lead-footed play of Gaddy has Phil worried.

Drive to Brockton and lose 111–104 in our last exhibition game. The Bombardiers are coached by Johnny Neumann, a six-foot-six bleary-eyed shooter who once scored 40.1 ppg at Ole Miss. After his junior year, Neumann jumped to the ABA, where he spent his money too quickly. Neumann then bounced from Utah to Memphis to Germany to the Lakers. (Phil calls him "Newbaby.") He's a fiery presence on the sideline, screaming at his players' mistakes, riding the refs with a hoarse yell that pierces through any size throng.

After the game, Neumann approaches me to say that he recognizes my name. "I read that book you wrote with Phil. It was called *Maniac*."

November 29

Drive back to Albany through freezing rain. Then mine is the voice of doom: "Hello, York? Could you come up to our room? Phil wants to talk to you."

Cuts: Gross, Tyson, Yar Roberts, Fred Daniels, Dave Williams.

"Why me?" asks Gross. After thirty minutes he remains unconvinced.

Williams is stunned. He thought he played so well. But Williams doesn't know that one of our "reserve players," Mark Jones, will be cut from the New Jersey Nets just as soon as Footsie Walker's hamstring heals. (Williams is so embarrassed that after returning home to Yonkers he stays in his house for the next three weeks—calling his buddies to tell them that he's still on the team.)

In a ragged evening practice Sanders plays the point for the second-stringers and only looks to shoot. Afterward he moans to Phil, "I've always started. I can't believe I'm not good enough to start here."

Emphasize what you do best, Frankie. Instant points off the bench, just like Junior Bridgeman. The change will even help get you back into the NBA. But Sanders will not be mollified.

November 30

Once the season is under way CBA players earn weekly wages of $350 to $450. Today, Frankie J. doesn't show for practice and $50 will be deducted from his first paycheck. "With the Knicks," Phil tells the team, "we used the fine money for a team party at the end of the season. It'll be up to you."

December 1

Cazzie Russell brings his Lancaster Lightning into Albany. Lancaster's roster includes "two newcomers" mandated by CBA statute, as well as five holdovers, and they are the league's most veteran team. In private, Phil always refers to his ex-teammate with the Knicks as either "The Snazz" or "Snazzola."

In Phil's locker-room talk he scouts the Lightning's players (there are no available game videos) as best he can, and then runs through the Pats' repertoire. Then after joining hands, the players bound up the stairs and we're off—forty-four ball games in 102 days.

Game time: Derrick Rowland plays the game of his life—shooting 11-12 and scoring 31 points from pivot and post. All season long, Lancaster is the only team to stall our 1-4 flex offense—but Ralph McPherson tallies 26 points and we win, 121–113 (5,2), before 2,155 delighted fans.

December 2

Noon practice, a short, hard workout. Magley's wife is expecting their first child—it's due in twelve weeks and he is of constant good cheer. His daily salute to Gaddy is, "Here's my mainest man!" Magley says this about his sojourn in Cleveland: "I could have stayed longer but they wanted me to do something immoral. Put me on the injured list even though I wasn't hurt. Maybe my career suffered at the time, but I'm sure I'll receive a blessing somewhere down the road."

December 3

Bay State invades the Armory. The Pats win the first three quarters, then dissipate a 13-point lead in the fourth Q. "Run the play!" Neumann bellows from the visitors' bench. "Run it exactly the way I drew it!"

There's bad blood between Schweitz and his former mentor (last year the Bombardiers were the Lumberjacks, and Neumann their rookie coach). "Trap him!" Neumann yells whenever Schweitz dribbles the ball. And whenever Schweitz defends, Neumann calls, "Four Down" to isolate John one-on-one. "Take him!"

When Charlie Jones rejams an errant Bay State shot, the Bombardiers lead 104–103 with four ticks left in the ball game. After a time-out, we run the "3 Play" to perfection—small forward David Little executes a nifty inbounds pass to McPherson, who spins and buries an eighteen-footer at the buzzer.

December 4–14

By CBA decree, assistant coaches are allowed on the bench only during home games and "ground travel" road games—to prevent the wealthier teams from having an advantage. So, on the first leg of the first road trip, Phil drives the team van through a six-hour snowstorm. The players are hugely disconcerted when PJ simultaneously drives and does the *New York Times* Sunday crossword puzzle. Then at Lancaster, the Pats lead by 13 at the half, only to lose 97–95 (5,2) as McPherson misses a last-second shot. Early next morning, Phil drives the van to Baltimore for a flight connection to Sarasota.

In the first game against the Stingers, Gaddy accumulates two shots and 2 rebounds in twenty-two minutes and the Pats are trounced.

The second game of this miniseries is a dogfight that turns up tied after four quarters. One of Commissioner Drucker's more contrived innovations is brand new this season: the sudden-death overtime. The first team to score 3 points wins the game. Drucker is on hand to insist that the fans love it, but the idea is absurd to players and coaches—deciding forty-eight minutes of honest competition with a publicity gimmick.

After free throws and elbows are evenly exchanged, the Stingers' six-foot-two guard, Billy Allen, suddenly zooms out of the pack and dribbles unimpeded downcourt for a lay-up. The Stingers are confused, the fans have no idea, and the refs deliberate with Drucker. But Phil always knows the score; amid the turmoil, he grabs his clipboard and angrily stalks across the court headed for the locker room.

On to Puerto Rico, where the Pats split two games and 14 available quarter-points. "Wait till you see Geff Crompton," Phil says when he returns. "He's six foot eleven and at least 375 pounds."

December 15–21

The Toronto Tornados blow into town, perhaps the most talented club in the Eastern Division, but a wild and selfish crew. The visitors' locker-room door is ajar as coach Gerald Oliver delivers his pregame message. Even as Oliver talks, one of his players wears a Walkman and nods in time to a headful of music.

And Frankie J. has his way at last. He starts the game to great applause, scoring 31 points in thirty-six minutes. Albany wins, 133–124 (6,1).

Afterward Phil meets with the local media, armed with his habitual cigarette and cup of beer. He seems calm and collected, but that's only because he's already learned to sublimate his ferocious competitive nature. When we lose, the strain on his face is even more pronounced.

We've been in first place from the start, but all season long, the Pats will have a bad case of "The CBA Blues"—winners at home, patsies on the road.

December 22–23

Larry Spriggs is retained by the Lakers and Wyoming chooses Dave Little.

Brockton High School looks like it was battered by an

army of juvenile delinquents—broken lockers, splintered windows, and fractured plumbing. The visitors dress in the wrestling team's locker room, where encouraging posters and sayings abound. The largest sign is white with red letters—"To be a superior athlete, you must crush your opponent and humiliate him when he's down." Without a word, Phil tears the offensive advice from the wall and tosses the pieces into a trash can.

Game time: Bay State wins, 133–124, as Joe Dawson gets 36. Frankie J. tallies 30 but throws the ball away at a crucial juncture. "That son of a bitch!" Frankie growls in PJ's general direction whenever he's removed from the action. "He's messing with my game!"

December 25–29

Christmas on the road. The Pats get fifteen dollars a day meal money—and Ralph has lost fifteen pounds.

Lancaster's Linton Townes has been called up to the NBA by the San Diego Clippers and we ground the Lightning in the Armory. Mark Jones joins the Pats after being cut by the New Jersey Nets and debuts with 13 points and 3 assists. When Frankie is taken out with 2:50 left, he storms to the locker room. All he knows is that the better his numbers, the better chance he has of being summoned back to The League—and he's also peeved that Townes got the call before he did. Mike Sandman wants to trade Frankie immediately, but Phil counsels patience.

December 30

The citizens of Albany are greatly taken with Phil. "Mr. Jackson, could I please have your autograph?"

"Come down to the warehouse and I'll give you some pastramis for the holidays."

"Say, Phil. What was Clyde *really* like?"

Derrick has a slight groin pull, so I'm called on to scrimmage in his place. Imagine my delight when Magley says I set the mightiest pick in the league!

December 31

A day off, but Phil and I do a Nautilus workout, then play one-on-one at the Kingston YMCA. He's younger and better. My only advantage is my strength. Our unspoken agreement is that I won't bang away at his left hip (the scene of a spinal fusion years ago) and he lets me dribble the ball with my left hand. Phil wins, 11–7, and my lifetime mark against him now stands at 0-48.

January 2–3

Phil and Frankie confer after a practice session, still contending on a friendly level. "I want you here," says Phil, "because I respect the possibilities of your game."

Frankie doesn't know quite what to make of this, but he keeps repeating that he deserves to start and play at least forty-five minutes per game.

January 4–8

The Pats play an inspired game to win at Brockton. "Schweitz can't dribble under pressure!" Neumann screams. "Trap him!"

"Hey, Newbaby!" Phil shouts. "You say whatever you want about your own guys but leave mine alone!"

Afterward Neumann apologizes to both Phil and John.

To heal the breach, Neumann confides that one of his players was caught stealing money from several teammates' hotel rooms.

January 9–14

Since our last encounter three weeks ago, Sarasota's coach, Bill Musselman, has signed five new ballplayers. Phil advocates the team game, while Musselman's philosophy is to ride his best horses to death, then get some new ones. So Mike Wilson, Kevin Loder, and Willie Smith, all NBA veterans, each play the full forty-eight minutes and total 97 points—but the Patroons win again at home, 126–116 (5,2).

Lowes Moore is a profoundly spiritual man, good-natured, lively, forever reading the Bible. Magley and McPherson likewise praise the Lord. Before every home game, Dale Walker, the team chaplain, conducts chapel for both teams. Frankie J. always goes, saying, "I need all the help I can get."

January 15

John Schweitz talks about his jump shot like it was part of his body: "It feels good today, Charley. I'm gonna stick it in Newbaby's face."

The players are increasingly irritated with one another. "Hey, judge!" Mo McDaniel says to everybody. "What's happenin', judge?" In a spirited practice, Mo and Ralph lock elbows and exchange maledictions. Every Sunday, Phil leads us in the Lord's Prayer.

January 16–23

Phil decides to shake things up. The players have gradually become too confrontational in practice sessions and too lackadaisical in games. Even worse, our sense of community is breaking down. We've tried yelling, cajoling, threatening, and making them run suicides, but nothing shakes them out of their game-time lethargy.

So here's what happens: Phil makes a few phone calls and zeroes in on Lewis Brown, a six-foot-eleven bruiser out of UNLV who had played two games with the Washington Bullets back in 1980. Lewis is eager to come in for a tryout. So he boards a red-eye flight from Los Angeles and is picked up at the airport, where he signs a contract. From there he is driven directly to the Patroons' practice facility, changes into his gear, and is immediately thrown into an intrasquad scrimmage.

The holdover players are alarmed that a new big man is in town and that somebody's job is being threatened. That's why, during the scrimmage, the players simply band together to beat the hell out of Brown. The poor guy is elbowed at every turning, knocked on his keister whenever he approaches the hoop, and even smacked in his face a time or two.

Finally, here is the passionate unity that we were looking for. Moreover, everybody (except Frankie) seems to loosen up and feel good about each other.

After the scrimmage, Brown showers, is driven directly to the airport, receives a hundred dollars, and flies home. His entire CBA experience has lasted about twenty-four hours.

January 24

Penny Elliot has a strained ankle, so Phil has to join me in a scrimmage. PJ is way out of game shape and Magley eats him alive. How does Phil respond? With an accidental/on-purpose knee to Magley's thigh that sends Mags to the injured list.

January 25–27

The NBA is responsible for the CBA's officials, and several refs work ball games in both leagues. We see a righteous ref only once or twice each week.

Another tough contest against Bay State in the Armory. "Three!" I yell at the refs. "Three! Dawson's still in there!"

"If I hear you say 'three' once more," says the ref, "no matter how long he stays in there I'm not calling it."

Albany wins and Frankie rushes over to the Bombardiers' bench. "Get me out of here," he pleads with Neumann. "Make a trade. Me for Perry Moss. Go ask Phil."

January 28–February 1

The Louisville Catbirds call; Rudy Macklin was cut by the Knicks and is therefore Albany's territorial property. Since Macklin hails from Louisville, what do we want for his rights?

But the prospect of Macklin playing for the Patroons is too engaging for us to accommodate the Catbirds.

February 2

In a separate inquiry, Louisville offers Al Smith for Frankie J. Smitty is a wiry six foot six and all-around nice guy, the CBA's finest shooting guard. Phil decides to stick with Frankie on the basis of his "possibilities." Smith is then dealt to the Bombardiers.

February 3

Only four available players at practice: Mo and Mark are sick, Mags is still out with his severely bruised thigh, Andre has jammed a finger, Lowes just received word that his grandfather had a stroke and he is off to South Carolina. Schweitz doesn't show and is fined fifty dollars. "I just got angry when I remembered about being cut by the Celtics last fall," John says later. "Shoot! Auerbach told me that I made the fucking team! If I came to practice here, I'd only have gotten into a fight with somebody."

Rudy Macklin calls to say he's not interested in Louisville and will shortly be on his way to Albany.

Bulletin: Citing health problems, John Neumann resigned today as coach and GM of the Bay State Bombardiers. The newspapers say "ulcer"—the grapevine reports that he had an argument over his game-time language with the team's owner.

February 4–8

Our final journey to Toronto. As a special favor, Phil the pathfinder lets me drive the van from Rochester to our final destination. The traffic lines are whining beneath me. The buffeting wind foreshadows a passing snowstorm near Niagara Falls. The players sleep in cramped and gangling positions (the heat is turned on full blast to make them drowsy). Even Phil nods over his crossword puzzle. And Schweitz whispers in my ear, "It's an automatic fine if you go slower than 80."

The Tornados' owner is the same Ted Stepien who was bounced from the NBA for destroying the Cleveland Cavaliers. Stepien now hopes to create sufficient interest and entice the NBA into Toronto. The Tornados' home court is called Varsity Arena and there's ice three-quarters of an inch thick beneath the floorboards. The Pats split two games and

14 points. In both contests Andre lingers too long in the lane, either misdribbling or committing the most offensive of fouls. "Dammit, Andre!" Phil scolds during a time-out. "Hang on to the ball!"

Afterward Andre says that Phil is picking on him

February 9

There's been no word from Lowes—not even his agent knows his whereabouts. In truth, it's fairly common for CBA players to simply vanish.

Game time: A disastrous ball game for the Pats. When Carl Nicks stuffs, Toronto leads 34–33 on the second-quarter scoreboard with only twenty seconds left until halftime. Phil stands up, touches his hands above his head, and shouts, "Time!" Oblivious, Mo takes the ball from the ref and looks to inbounds. "Time!" Phil shrieks. "Maurice! Time-out!" But Toronto springs a press and Mo's errant pass becomes a dunker for Bobby Cattage.

At halftime, Phil appears to be hot and bothered in the locker room. "You guys are supposed to be fucking professionals! You're supposed to be aware of the fucking game situation! I'm six foot eight and waving my fucking arms like crazy! Dammit! Get your head out of your ass!" Mo defends himself with shrugs and mumbles. "I know you all want to be in the NBA," Phil continues, "but right here is where we are! Dammit!" During his tirade, the coach even slams his clipboard to the floor.

Phil's face is still flushed as we cool off in the hallway. Although he hates to smoke, Phil ignites a quick cigarette. Then loosening his necktie, he says, "Do you think they believed me?"

Rudy Macklin arrives. A handsome, six-foot-seven forward, he always dresses with style—"Got to look good, Charley"— wearing his glamorous New York Knicks sweats to practice. Rudy can reach back and plunk a crooked left-handed jumper, the ugliest shot in the CBA, but on defense, he relies too much on hand jive. He looks three weeks out of shape and we wonder if he's come to play.

Lowes's grandfather has died in the bosom of his family. When Lowes does return, he plays poorly. But Ralph raises the team around him and the Pats capture five points from Sarasota.

All the players in the league are heartened when Ricky Green plays in the NBA's All-Star game. Green had played with Golden State from 1979 to 1981, before being cut. Next he'd played in the CBA for a while, then was picked up by the Utah Jazz. Green is now the first EL/CBA veteran to become a bona fide NBA All-Star.

February 12–15

Bombardier Charlie Jones has been signed by the Sixers— and an erstwhile assistant coach, trainer, and designated van driver named Jim Sleeper has replaced Neumann. It's a perfect chance for the Pats to win on the road, but Bay State is still too ferocious, winning by a score of 142–115 (7,0).

February 16–17

With first place at stake, the Pats overcome the red-hot Coquis, 118–113 (5,2). Rudy, Mo, Mark, and Derrick are ineffective, but Andre gets rough-and-tumble, limiting Crompton to 4-15. Then Lowes suddenly assumes command in the endgame, hitting a clutch three-ball.

The word among the visitors is that Compton goes to bed every night with a six-pack of Big Macs stashed under his bed—and wakes up periodically to gobble them down.

Bulletin: John Neumann returns as Bay State's coach. "It was a bad reaction to some ulcer medication," he explains, and nobody believes him.

February 18–22

I can understand why Ralph McPherson is overlooked by the NBA. He's fifteen pounds too light and his sneakers are a touch too heavy. But to appreciate fully Ralph's talents, watch how many important plays he makes over the course of a season—the necessary rebounds, the double-clutch free throws, or a basket at just the right time. A mature player, Ralph is the only Patroon invited to Casper, Wyoming, to participate in the CBA's All-Star game.

With low spirits, the rest of us practice in Albany. "I've heard rumors of drug use going on with you guys," Phil tells the team. "This is what Cazzie always says to his players: 'If you're caught doing drugs, you're gone.' But I don't want to talk about drugs."

February 23–25

Magley finally returns from the injured list, so Maurice McDaniel is cut. Toronto beats us at home. Meanwhile, Puerto Rico wins six points in Brockton and we fall into second place.

Neumann comes into Albany with his ball club dramatically improved, but Rudy and Frankie have their chops up and we rush to a 15-point lead by halftime. During the intermission, Neumann loudly accuses his players of being no-talent bums, then punches a blackboard to smithereens. Even so, Derrick plays yeoman defense on Al Smith and the Pats win, 121–111 (5,2).

February 29

Bulletin: Sarasota fires Musselman for giving his ex-NBA players too much money under the table. Wyoming waives Little.

March 1–3

Magley is increasingly disenchanted as his playing time dwindles, even listless and silent in practice. According to Mags, PJ is doing him wrong. "I'm an NBA player," he says. "I should be starting."

Rudy keeps everybody else lively with his high-pitched laughter and his sharp eye: "Hey, Cholly," he says to me, "I like your necktie. There must be a piece missing from your living room rug."

March 4

Lancaster, Pennsylvania, is the last of the old Eastern League towns—and last in total attendance. Only 395 fans on hand in a dank high school gym. Schoolboy hoopers and their dates. Assorted minor-league-caliber groupies. Neatly attired families with 2.5 children. Also a scattering of old men whose youth was darkened inside coal mines. Before the game an old-timer fondly remembers watching Phil on TV. "You had a beard back then, too," the old man says. "But, tell me, what was Clyde *really* like?" The same old man yowls foul curses at Phil throughout the game.

Game time: The refs are especially outrageous tonight. "Nice call!" Phil shouts. "Did you make that one up all by yourself?" Then with 10:40 left in the contest, Lancaster leads by 15 for the game and 8 for the last quarter. Time-out Albany. Phil points his face at the nearest ref, Ronnie Nunn. "It's a good ball game, Ronnie. Too bad you had to miss it." *"That's a T!"* Phil quickly escalates the argument, forcing Nunn to oust him from the premises. As he leaves the court, Phil flashes me a conspiratorial wink.

The assistant steps in. My first substitution is Magley for Macklin, and Rudy never forgives me. But Mags makes a steal, Ralph gets hot, and we're back in the chase. But Mark Jones is weary and commits two outlandish turnovers. We lose the quarter by 1, the game by 6 (6,1).

Oh. So that's how it feels.

March 5–6

Cleveland picks up Puerto Rico's Geff Crompton, but the Coquis win in Toronto and clinch first place.

March 7–8

For a reasonable fee and percentage of the gate, the Pats have purchased a home game from Bay State, a procedure that's only possible in the Crazy Basketball Association. The battle for second place lures nearly twenty-six hundred partisans to the Armory.

Game time: Albany leads 121–120 with ten seconds left when Bay State runs a play for Al Smith. But Ralph comes from nowhere to block the shot and outrace everybody down-court for a dramatic game-jammer.

The following night we clinch second place at Lancaster.

The Lightning now draws Puerto Rico in the playoffs and the trip to San Juan will cost ten thousand dollars. Lancaster is on the verge of folding, but the league office will pay the expenses.

March 9–12

We will enjoy a 2-2-1 home-court advantage as we prepare for Bay State. By now Phil has installed seven different offensive sets and nearly forty plays.

There is no playoff pool in the CBA. Road teams will receive 25 percent of the gate receipts, and the players' reward is the continuance of their weekly salaries for as long as their teams stay alive.

March 13

Phil has spent the night in Albany, but I have a magazine article to finish writing so I can't join him. Then a gigantic snowstorm strands me at home in Woodstock—too far south to receive the play-by-play on the radio. Instead, Phil's then-wife June and I take turns calling the Armory box office every fifteen minutes. The Pats trail by 8 to 10 points all game long and finally lose, 110–100. "We were flat and they outgutted us," Phil says. "All our worst fears come true."

March 14

With 1:20 elapsed in OT, the Pats lead the game by 2 points, only 1 point from victory. Suddenly Frankie steals and is on the break—pulling up now to send the J home from the foul line. But Frankie's feet slip on the treacherous surface and the ball bounces harmlessly out of bounds. After a strategic time-out, Bay State's point guard, Glenn Hagan, buries a three-point shot to claim the ball game, 100–99.

We're down two games to none.

March 15–17

A downcast ride to Brockton. Before the game Lowes gathers the team in the hallway, and for the first time we have our chapel in a strange land. "Do your best," Lowes says, "and trust in the Lord."

Andre rules the lanes, Ralph is dynamic, and we carry a 15-point lead into the fourth quarter. But the Bombardiers take off again—and we need a clutch free throw from Rudy to send the game into OT. Then Bay State wins the tip and Al Smith uncorks a high-arching three-ball. Phil reaches for his clipboard and rises from his seat as the rim opens to swallow the Patroons' season. But Smitty's shot kicks out and Ralph rebounds.

Time-out Albany. Phil calls Lowes's number.

After a few probing dribbles and the threat of a pass, Lowes casts a leftward-leaning jumper from beyond the pale. The net dances and the Pats win! All of us jumping, screaming, and celebrating as though we've won the championship.

Back at the hotel, the latest news is even more stunning. By all accounts, Neumann is often loud and abusive during ball games. With the cozy Brockton crowds, Neumann's language raised complaints from parents, children, and clergy, as well as the owner's mother. Neumann was fired and rehired several times during the regular season. For the playoffs, owner John Liggums delivered an ultimatum to his coach: one more T and he'd be fired for good. "How can I coach like that?" Neumann wants to know. "Even the refs tease me about it." And after tonight's dramatic loss, Neumann calls Liggums "a butt-hole" for the benefit of the local press. As before, Jim Sleeper will take over the team.

March 18

The officiating is worse than ever before. From the bench, Frankie puts his right hand to his throat and yells, "You choke motherfuckers!" But the refs are so discombobulated that they let the abuse slide.

Frankie goes wild in the third quarter, scoring 12 consecutive points on fallaway J's from everywhere. The Bombardiers' last-quarter rush closes the margin to 108–104. But Ralph and Andre sink their free throws and we win, 116–111, to even the series.

More jubilation in the locker room. New-Who?

March 19

A spirited, confident practice session. In the other Eastern Conference series, Puerto Rico loses two games at Lancaster, then sweeps three at home.

March 20

An Armory attendance record of 3,026. While the visitors are introduced, several well-rehearsed Patroons fans stand up, each one demonstrating that they couldn't care less about the opponents by perusing a newspaper open at arm's length. Even Bombardier Glenn Hagan can't help laughing.

Come game time and Andre produces 24 happy points and 10 rebounds. The Pats break open a tight ball game in the third quarter and win easily, 118–101.

First a silent prayer of thanksgiving in the locker room,

then a howling joy. Afterward a mad scramble to formulate traveling arrangements to Puerto Rico.

March 21

Herb Brown is the Coquis' coach, recently named by Drucker as the CBA's Coach of the Year. Herb is also Larry's older brother—smaller, thinner, but with the same relentless eyes. In 1976 Herb coached the Detroit Pistons—succeeding Ray Scott and guiding a troubled team into the playoffs. But the Pistons' internal problems were never resolved (the rumor is that the white players and the black players used separate locker rooms) and Herb was dismissed one and a half seasons later. Since then he's coached in Israel, France, Belgium, Puerto Rico. Anywhere. Searching for another chance.

Normally in an "air-travel" series, the first-place team would play the first two games on the road and the last three at home. But the Coquis' owner is aware of Albany's 20-3 regular-season record at the Armory and he worries that only one of his home games is guaranteed to happen. So he chooses to switch the schedule and the advantage shifts to Albany. Brown is already irate because Geff Crompton, the CBA's MVP, is still with Cleveland. He's frothing at the mouth when he discovers that his team's hard-earned playoff edge is rescinded.

Despite the ban on assistant coaches being on the bench in air-travel games, Phil convinces the Patroons' front office that my presence in Puerto Rico is worth risking whatever fine Commissioner Drucker might impose.

After traveling all day, none of us is tired. Phil designates Magley as the "home player," the Pats' tenth man; as such he will not suit up in San Juan. He's simply too soft to be dependable. Mags mopes around the hotel while everybody else heads for the beach.

"Check her out, Penny," Ralph advises. "The one in the red bikini."

"I'm checking, man. I'm checking as hard as I can."

Meanwhile, Phil and I run two miles along the peaceful water's edge.

March 22

The evening is moist and languid, the grandstands not quite full. There's only one Puerto Rican on the Coquis' roster— Raymond Dalmau, a hoops icon on the island—but he never plays. So the twelve hundred in attendance represent the largest gathering of the Coquis' season. There's a carnival across the street, and through the open walls of the arena we can see a Ferris wheel spinning and flashing like the wheel of fortune.

The small visitors' locker room is crowded and hot; the ball game, brutal. Every pick is punishing as Mark Smith, Larry Lawrence, and the Coquis' centers never miss a chance to "show the 'bow.'" Throughout the series, the Coquis only run three or four plays and seem overly intent on pounding us. Perhaps a tactical mistake by Brown.

When six-foot-nine, 260-pound Mark Smith blatantly smashes five-foot-eleven Lowes to the floor in front of our bench, I can't help myself—foolishly jumping to my feet and challenging Smith to pick on somebody his own size. Namely me. He clenches a massive fist but thankfully turns away.

The Patroons play a courageous game, battling back from a 9-point deficit and gaining full control early in the fourth quarter. Time-out Puerto Rico. Then a ref approaches Phil to say, "The Coquis are protesting the game because assistant coaches are not allowed on the bench." In any case, Puerto Rico is reduced to hurried shots and deliberate fouls and our margin is 117–109.

A postgame celebration from the squalid locker room back to the hotel. "This team is *ours*," Frankie yells. "These suckers belong to *us!*" All of us shrieking and yahooing, except for Phil, who merely beams as he smokes his postgame cigarette. Magley is still in his civvies, the only unhappy one among us.

March 23

Commissioner Drucker rules that the Pats' victory stands, but we are fined twelve hundred dollars. Not only am I barred from the bench, but I cannot be inside the arena for two hours before and two hours after the game, so I listen to the game on the radio.

"Usted está escuchando WPRC, *el sonido del basquetbol profesional en Puerto Rico. El Coquis está a la cabeza por siete. Lowes Moore apunto . . . ! La pelota no acierta!"*

The home team instigates several fights, there are technical fouls galore, it's snowing back in Albany, the Pats fade in the fourth quarter and lose 129–122.

March 24–26

Back in the Armory no one can handle Lowes, and Andre is a tower of power. There's another fight, another slew of technicals, and the third game moves into OT. Neither team scores for 1:41; then Lowes shoots the lights out with another off-balance three-pointer.

March 27

Game time: The Coquis start one last fight and three more T's are distributed, but they miss eighteen foul shots and their effort seems insincere. The Pats win, 114–109, to qualify for the championship series.

The official postgame party is at On Broadway, where several white stars hang from the walls, each star emblazoned with the glittering green name of a Patroon player or coach. There's free beer for all and free chow for the Patroons' families. Andre is astonished: "You mean it's all the chicken wings I can eat?"

March 28–31

The Wyoming Wildcatters refuse to exchange game tapes. "I've already scouted you," says coach Jack Schalow. Instead, Phil gets the scoop from a friendly Western Conference coach.

April 1

A long, tedious trip by van and plane—misconnecting at Denver, then riding a two-prop puddle-jumper through a snowstorm to Casper. The antelopes browsing on the fringes of town and the scrub brush remind Phil of his home in Montana.

April 2

A spirited shootaround at the Casper Events Center—a beautifully symmetrical arena seating almost nine thousand. The players lounge on the front steps waiting for the van to pick us up and return us to the hotel. Someone has a boom box and is playing an X-rated Richard Pryor tape full blast. Dozens of locals tiptoe through the sound and the fury on their way to buy tickets at the box office—none of them showing signs of outrage or even distress. Later, Phil and I find a Nautilus gym, then enjoy a surprisingly savory Mexican meal.

Game time: The special hero of the 5,218 fans is five-foot-ten Del Beshore, an ex-NBA player who is renowned for making steals from behind. On the game's opening sequence, Beshore tries to snipe Frankie's dribble and runs facefirst into an elbow. To qualify for bench duty, I have been duly registered with the league office as the Patroons' trainer (mostly on the basis of some undergrad courses I'd taken, plus a no-show training session back in Albany). Wearing a white Patroons' warm-up suit, my first official act is to say this: "Your elbow doesn't hurt you, does it, Frankie?"

Phil calls me the "Good Humor Man."

When Frankie intercepts a subsequent pass and speeds downcourt stuffward bound, he veers past the Wildcatters bench and flips them the bird.

Wyoming never comes to terms with the flex offense, but the game is up and down until the fourth quarter. Then Schweitz, Penny, and Mark ignite a 17–4 surge to win the game, 129–121.

Our celebration is muted since everything closes early on Sunday night in Casper, the Friendly Ghost Town.

April 3

The illusion is dead—with the NBA season coming to a close, there will be no ten-day trials for any of the Patroons. All we have is each other. Rudy conducts the pregame chapel. "The Lord is my shepherd, I shall not want."

Game time: Overconfident, we are caught by surprise in an ornery ball game. Derrick is on a roll, but Charles Bradley throws a sucker punch and both are ejected. The game gets increasingly rowdy. Then, with fourteen seconds left the Pats have the ball, trailing by two. Phil calls Rudy's number and Macklin is clobbered in the act—the loud smack on his forearm silencing the crowd, the ball springing straight up, at least ten feet higher than the rim—just as the buzzer sounds. But the refs unplug their whistles and quickly vamoose.

Later at the hotel's disco-bar, Steve Javie (the offending ref nearest the final play) says this: "I could never make that call in front of all those people. Besides, he never got fouled. Macklin should have made the shot anyway. Besides, you're better than those guys. You'll beat them two straight in Albany."

April 4

More than sixteen hours in transit. Sitting next to Johnny High on the flight from Denver to New York. "I played in Phoenix for three years," he says, "then I dislocated my shoulder in training camp. I wanted to buy a house and they said go ahead. Two weeks later I was cut." High doesn't like playing in Wyoming. "The players are too young and frivolous. They don't know what a ruthless business this is."

Three years later High would be killed in some kind of gangland drug-related shootout.

April 5

A comfortable win at the Armory, 120–111. Beshore's pet move is to dribble hard to his right, then go behind his back and spin left. A difficult maneuver for Lowes to contain, but I suggest to Phil that Mark Jones could stifle Beshore. Although

PJ is reluctant to tinker with his normal rotation, Mark gets more daylight than usual and puts Beshore on ice.

The Wildcatters' primary shooter is Boot Bond and he manages only 8 points. Also Orlando Phillips misses eleven free throws. Ralph and Lowes sustain the offense and even Magley plays well.

April 6–7

The Patroons are already lining up their celebratory parties. For special inspiration, Phil wears his 1973 NBA championship ring. But Beshore has 14 assists and the Wildcatters square the series with a surprisingly easy 128–112 win.

April 8

Playing for the championship of the CBA. The commish is on hand and the prestigious Drucker Trophy sits on the scorer's table.

Game time: The Wildcatters jump to a 16-point lead behind Boot Bond's phenomenal sharpshooting. He'll finish at 15-22 from the field, most of them long-range shots. But Andre and Ralph assert themselves. Lowes is benched and in his place Mark throws another bag over Beshore. Wyoming leads by 2 points at halftime.

Then Phil sits both Frankie and John, playing Lowes and Mark in tandem to speed up the tempo. Andre plays with a cool frenzy and only Bond's heroic efforts keep the game tight. With Mark and Andre keying a last furious rush, the Pats' final margin grows to 119–109.

The fans instantly swarm the court for a champagne bedlam. Laughing, hugging, and dancing—it's fun to be the best.

But Phil makes sure to take a moment to console the losers. And deep in their hearts the real players know that the game is already done and won, the true moment of celebration is already passed. And Magley refuses to shake Phil's hand.

The Albany crowd validates Jim Drucker's commissionership by lustily booing his name when he makes the official presentation. Then on to another madcap championship blast at On Broadway. Where Andre gorges on free chicken wings. Where a boisterous fan slips from atop the bar in mid-moon and slashes his naked ass on a beer glass.

April 9

There's a lunchtime rally in downtown Albany that draws some three thousand citizens. Each player has a turn at the microphone. Mags is witty. Lowes is grateful. And Frankie J. gloriously announces his retirement. "I've always wanted to go out with a championship."

There's another private Patroon shindig later that evening. The hot buzz is that Ralph and Andre will be invited to the Spurs' training camp. Lowes will try out with Utah. Schweitz with Houston. Mags apologizes to Phil. Derrick will start working out ten hours a day. Penny will "sleep for a week." Mark will enter graduate school. Phil will spend the summer coaching in a highly competitive pro league in Puerto Rico—he's unhappy with the flex and hopes to find a better, more fluid offense somewhere. I have a novel to finish.

The team's ownership offers us a choice: either a two-hundred-dollar bonus and a "gold" ring, or five hundred dollars. Penny votes for the latter. "No way they're gonna get us real gold rings." But the team votes for the ring and the lesser bonus. (Turns out that the rings are made of fool's gold and are worth under fifty dollars.)

Then Lowes gathers the team around him for one last huddle. "Phil wants us to decide what to do with the fine money. It comes to $270."

"That's $27 each," says Penny, and his motion is carried by unanimous vote.

And the flavor never lasts long enough for Frankie J. "It sure felt good," he says, sidling up with a drink in his hand. "I wonder how it feels to repeat . . ."

9

Good Night, Bobby Knight

Phil and his brood spent the summer in Montana, then returned to Woodstock for the school year. Several weeks before training camp for the 1984–85 season commenced, the two of us attended a clinic conducted by Bobby Knight. Sure, we knew beforehand that Knight could be overbearing and opinionated, but he was also a highly accomplished technician and we hoped to learn something about his half-court offense and perhaps his zone press.

The workshop convened one Saturday morning at a public high school in nearby Poughkeepsie, New York. The worn and scratched gymnasium floor was filed with several rows of slat-backed wooden folding chairs facing a stage that was bare except for a stray basketball and a podium. The chairs were mostly filled with fresh-eyed coachlings, some of them decked out in sports jackets and neckties, others wearing brand-name sweat suits or neatly pressed trousers and short-sleeved knit shirts that were patched above their hearts with the names and logos of their sponsoring institutions: Goshen High School, Orange County C. C., Pine Bush Boys Club. And they all stared adoringly at Knight as he mounted the stage, eased his paunch behind the podium, and adjusted the microphone.

Knight was clad in nattily creased chino pants and his trademark blood-red Indiana U. sweater. With his gray hair so neatly clipped that it resembled a gleaming war bonnet, and his stone-colored eyes staring above and beyond his worshipful audience (perhaps at the backboard and basket suspended above the far-off baseline?), the General launched into a full-blown attack.

"Sportswriters," he snorted. "They think they're experts because they watch so many ball games. But they don't know dog crap from Tootsie Rolls."

While Phil and I sat expectantly with our pens poised above our blank notebooks, the young coaches laughed to beat the band.

"Recruiting sucks," quoth Knight. "I hate it when my entire day is ruined by a seventeen-year-old."

This was followed by another round of sidesplitting, knee-pounding laughter. The General sure is a pistol, ain't he? And then Knight started talking about drugs. Heroin, cocaine, uppers, downers, crack, marijuana—they were all the same. Destroying the moral fiber of America. Turning our young people into feeble-minded, undisciplined wimps. Why, if Knight were president (this suggestive fantasy was interrupted with cries of "Hear! Hear!" "Yeah!" and even a "Right on!"), he'd make a phone call to whoever the hell was in charge of the one country, Colombia, that exported the largest amount of drugs to our otherwise blessed shores. And he'd say, "Hey, señor. This is the president of the United States of America, the greatest nation in the history of the world, and I'm giving you an absolute ultimatum, and I'm only going to say it once, so you'd better listen good. *Comprende?* You know all those poppy fields and pot fields you got set up down there? Well, if those fields ain't burned to ashes by twelve noon in exactly three days, I'm gonna send a fleet of planes to bomb your damn country from here to hell and back so it won't be good for nothing except to pave it and turn it into the world's largest parking lot!" Then he'd hang up the damn telephone and tell his flyboys to start their engines!

Yahoo! The morning session ended with a standing ovation.

Phil and I sat in stunned silence while the gym emptied. Then Phil flashed me one of his characteristic wry grins and said this: "It's been a long day, Charley, so let's make the best of it. There's a ball up on the stage, and if we clear the last few rows, we'll have enough room to play one-on-one."

So we played, shirtless and sweating, fouling each other and laughing out loud, hitting miraculous shots, missing easy ones, and never keeping score. We played until our fellow participants began to reenter the gym. Then we pulled on our shirts, grabbed our blank notebooks, and made a quick exit stage left, leaving the ball for dead on the foul line.

The defending CBA champs included several holdovers: Lowes Moore, Derrick Rowland, Frankie J. Sanders, Ralph McPherson, and Penny Elliot. I was certified as an assistant coach at home and a trainer on the road. In light of my increased duties, my salary was raised to $135 per week.

In addition, Troy Mikel had recovered from the Achilles tear he'd suffered a year ago, and he seemed like a lock to make the team . . . until he took a bad fall and tore his other Achilles tendon.

"I'll tell you this," said Mikel, "you could pay me a million dollars but I'll never ever come back to this city as long as I live."

In any event, Phil and I disagreed as to which player should be the last to make the squad. I liked Gary Springer, a bullish six-foot-eight forward from Iona who had to water his left hand twice a day just to keep it alive. But Phil overruled me, selecting six-foot-nine John Wiley from Minnesota.

"He's a lefty," said the left-handed Phil, "and I'm partial to southpaws."

Eventually, this choice would be one among several others that would cost us another shot at a championship.

Just before the season began, we picked up two highly skilled guards who had been waived by the Knicks: Clint Wheeler and Curtis Green. Besides Wiley, the only other significant newcomer was Bruce Kuczenski, who became our starting center.

We were a solid, veteran team, cruising to a 34-14 record and beating out Bill Musselman's Tampa Bay Thrillers by a total of 7.5 quarter points to finish first in the Eastern Division.

Along the way, the game-to-game CBA craziness showed no signs of abating.

Besides the actual games, most CBA teams provided additional entertainment for the hometown fans. An appearance by the famous San Diego Chicken was advertised in advance and was a surefire way to boost attendance. Accordingly, the Chicken charged a hefty fee, which he eventually increased because a subsequent CBA commissioner (*not* Jim Drucker!) demanded a kickback.

Lesser attractions were a glass-eater, a Frisbee-catching dog, and a hip-hop dance group that dressed in the home team's locker room and stole everything that wasn't locked away after their performance.

Several teams also sported mascots, but the mascot of the Bay State Bombardiers had a trick that was never surpassed.

The team had moved to Worcester, Massachusetts, and played its home games in the Memorial Auditorium. They tried appealing to their new fan base by hiring a mascot, the Bombardier, whose outfit replicated the uniform of a World War II bomber pilot replete with leather jacket, goggles, and leather hat with earflaps. The Bombardier's failsafe trick was to get a running start before diving forward, landing on his belly, and then sliding along the floor with his arms outstretched in front of him. With a good run, he could slide along for at least seventy-five feet.

During an early visit to Worcester, the Bombardier had a faulty takeoff and hit the floor facefirst. As a result, the track of his long slide was marked by a thin trail of blood.

No matter how hard the ball boys mopped and scrubbed, the stain was indelible and lasted for the rest of the season. And despite the subsequent encouragement of the local fans, the Bombardier abandoned his dive-and-slide trick forever.

Since then, the Bombardiers (and the CBA) are long gone, and the Worcester Memorial Auditorium has been torn down.

I wonder if anybody thought to save a section of those bloodstained floorboards, honoring them as a testament to courage, carelessness, and foolishness in the name of entertainment.

I also wonder what the Bombardier is doing these days.

On a longer road trip, the Patroons flew to Louisville for a game against the Catbirds.

Because of a quirk in the schedule we arrived in town two days early, and we'd normally use the extra time for a couple of practice sessions. However, just after our chartered bus let us out at the hotel, the city and its environs were hit with a massive storm that deposited at least a foot of snow. Schools were closed. Vehicular traffic was shut down. And there were no practice facilities available.

Phil and I passed some time playing Casino for pennies, watching old movies on the tube, and, just to get out of our room, going for long, trudging, snow-imperiled walks. When we finally retreated to the hotel bar, we were in for a wonderful surprise.

It seemed that the hotel had hosted a baseball card show, and several old-time stars of the sport had been present to sell their autographs. The show was over but many of the celebrities were snowed in and unable to leave town. The most notable among these fellows were Enos Slaughter and Johnny Mize, both Hall of Famers. PJ and I subsequently spent several delightful hours drinking beer and chatting with them.

Mize had joined the New York Yankees when I was eight years old and soon became one of my favorites. "The Big Cat" was six-foot-two, 235, and a powerful left-handed hitter who was especially dangerous with the short right-field wall in Yankee Stadium.

I saved up nickels and dimes from my meager allowance, and a year later I went to a local sporting goods store and proudly purchased an authentic Johnny Mize model bat. However, the bat weighed about ten pounds (or seemed to), was extremely top-heavy, had an extremely thin handle, and had only a tiny button of a knob at the bottom.

Turned out that I could barely lift the thing, much less swing it. Still, Mize was my hero and I remained stubbornly faithful to both him and the bat. Which is one significant reason why I was always a terrible batsman—and why I eventually turned to pitching.

Of course, I didn't dare tell this tale to Mize.

The day of the game the streets had been cleared—but later that same afternoon, it started snowing again. The venue was the Broadbent Arena at the Kentucky fairgrounds and could accommodate sixty-six hundred. But nobody was surprised when no more than a dozen fans were on hand when the game commenced. The Louisville front office had anticipated having a sparse crowd, and to at least create a newsworthy event, they tied helium-filled balloons to all of the ground-level seats.

The Catbirds had a nice ball club. Keith Edmonson, Dirk Minniefield, Ollie Mack, Rick Wilson, Russell Cross, Tom Piotrowski, and Rob Williams all had NBA experience. Plus Wiley Brown (Louisville), Earl Harrison (Morehead State), and Jewel Crawford (Southeast Missouri State) were top-notch players. The team was coached by the very capable Ron Ekker, who would eventually serve as player personnel director for the Dallas Mavericks.

About midway through the game, one of the balloons disintegrated with a loud POP! Immediately, several players forgot about the game and hit the floor. They came up laughing when they realized what had actually happened, but I couldn't miss the chance to razz Frankie J.

"You must owe the wrong people lots of money, Frankie. Talk about being embarrassed."

"Whatever," Frankie shrugged. "It's not as embarrassing as getting a bullet in the back of my head."

However, on other occasions that were potentially as lethal, Frankie demonstrated that there were other embarrassments that he could eagerly embrace.

Phil Jackson grew up in Montana and was therefore accustomed to dealing with winter blizzards. That's why he always drove the van whenever the weather was foul.

His driving skills were severely tested one morning after we'd played the Lightning in Lancaster, Pennsylvania. We were scheduled for a back-to-back game in Albany, which in clear weather was still a five- or six-hour ride. However, a severe snowstorm was going full blast, and in those days the only viable route from Lancaster to the New York Thruway was Interstate 209, a two-lane road with a thirty-five-mile-per-hour speed limit.

Covering the distance as quickly as possible was imperative. If we didn't arrive in Albany by game time, it was entirely possible that we'd have to forfeit. This scenario was both expensive and a severe blow to our playoff possibilities.

So PJ simply stepped on the gas and, at fifty to fifty-five miles per hour, plowed through the foot or so of snow that already obscured the road. Since it was a Sunday morning, he further amused himself by spreading the *New York Times* crossword puzzle across the steering wheel and tried to fill in the blanks as we sped along.

I was riding shotgun and was somewhat nervous, but the players behind us were absolutely petrified.

Suddenly, Phil and I became aware of a pungent odor drifting toward us from the back of the van. A quick look around discovered Frankie frantically, and blatantly, puffing away on a joint.

Say what?

Between puffs, Frankie made the following announcement: "If I got to die in the CBA, then I'm gonna die stoned."

Phil and I were roommates on the road—and one particular trip to Pensacola, Florida, found us in a rather pedestrian motel. Upon returning from a morning shootaround, we chanced to observe two refs entering the room adjacent to ours.

Okay. No big deal. Even referees deserve the opportunity to sleep indoors on beds. Well, at least some of them.

Anyway, the Patroons lost the ensuing ball game, mainly on the strength (or weakness) of a flurry of abominable calls in the stretch-run by the two blind mice. I mean, we were blatantly homered. No *if*s, *and*s, or *but*s.

Both PJ and I were still fuming after we found someplace to eat and then returned to our room. Still, we managed to quiet down and prepare for some snooze time. Unfortunately, our tenuous calm was rudely interrupted by the sound of raucous laughter coming from the refs' room next door.

Phil flipped.

He jumped out of bed and began pounding on the wall, shouting, "What are you two clowns laughing at? You're a disgrace to the game!"

The laughter instantly stopped, and even though he was still riled up, Phil took to his bed once more.

However, Phil has always been a light sleeper, and perhaps three or four times during the night, he got out of bed and resumed banging on the wall. But now his blows were accompanied by an increasing stream of cursing.

The refs checked out before we did, and the next time we saw them, the Patroons got jobbed once more.

Each of the various forms of Zen teach that peace, love, respect, and compassion should be directed to all life forms—with the notable exception of basketball referees.

For home games I had to wear a jacket and tie, but on the road I could come to the arena in my Woodstock formal attire—soiled jeans and tattered sweatshirt—and then change into my Good Humor Man's uniform in the locker room.

A few players let me tape their ankles, but the vast majority refused. Despite my ridiculous costume, I counseled players, charted plays, tracked time-outs, pointed out players who needed a blow, and also suggested possible substitutions to PJ, as well as any matchup advantages and disadvantages.

After one ball game in Evansville, I returned to the locker room only to find that my civilian clothes were missing! The players ragged me. Who would want to steal my hippie threads? Perhaps the local Board of Health had received a complaint and confiscated my stuff for being hazardous.

But what about my watch and my wallet?

Who, they argued, would want to pilfer a Woolworth special and an empty leather packet?

They certainly had a point. Nevertheless I ransacked the room, searching under, in, and atop every locker. Nothing turned up.

Then, just as we were about to depart, I noticed a telltale ragged sweatshirt sleeve barely protruding from the gym bag of one of the players! I won't disclose his name, but his nom de hoop was Mr. Rhythm.

How could he? Why did he?

Mr. R. just shrugged and offered no defense.

Phil and I decided to cut him as soon as we got back to Albany, but changed our minds when another player privately told us what had been on Mr. Rhythm's mind.

The guy was from L.A. and he simply had never seen an adult who wasn't homeless and living in the street, wearing such a raggedy outfit. He was planning on mailing my clothes back to L.A. to prove to his homeys that he wasn't lying about what was going on in the Crazy Basketball Association.

Hmmm. I guess the dress code for lapsed hippies was more upscale in L.A. than in Woodstock.

On the last day of the regular season, the Patroons were playing the Puerto Rico Coquis in San Juan, and the home team needed a win to qualify for the playoffs. But the game wasn't going well for the Coquis, and their coach, Herb Brown, was upset from the get-go.

Late in the contest, referee Ken Mauer looked at a critical charge/block situation and decided that one of the Patroons was the foulee and one of the Coquis was the fouler.

Brown could contain himself no longer. He dashed out onto the court, snatched at Mauer's whistle, then grabbed hold of the lanyard that circled the ref's neck—and, without saying a word, quickly began to twist the thing. As Mauer's face began to turn a bright red, none of the onlookers made a move to rescue him.

In fact, all of the players from both teams couldn't help laughing, with Phil and me having the same reaction. Even the fans seemed to be enjoying the spectacle. The other ref's only reaction was to call a technical foul on Brown.

Meanwhile Mauer's face had turned from red to blue, and it was apparent that Brown wouldn't stop twisting the lanyard until the ref was a goner.

At that point Brown was bear-hugged by a security guard and Mauer lived to breathe through another whistle.

For his misdeed, Brown was suspended by the CBA for the opening six games of the following season.

And that's why I've always felt nothing but admiration for Brown—for fulfilling every coach's wish.

To open the playoffs, we faced the Toronto Tornadoes in a best-of-five series. We routed them at home in Game 1, 133–109, with Frankie scoring 30 points.

Since Frankie J. would figure so prominently for the rest of the playoffs, here's a quick scouting report: At six foot six and 200 pounds, Frankie could run, jump, create, shoot the lights both on and off, and play terrific defense when he so desired—which was just about never. And if his head had been screwed on correctly, he could and should have had a long and successful career in the NBA.

He had been an All-American schoolboy in his hometown of Dayton, Ohio, and was recruited by dozens of powerhouse college programs in 1974. That included Bobby Knight, who was then at Indiana, and who, according to Frankie, offered him a hundred dollars per week plus a phantom job. In any event, Frankie wound up at Southern University, because "they offered me the best deal."

In 1978 Frankie was drafted in the first round (twentieth overall) by San Antonio, but lasted only twenty-two games with the Spurs. In almost twelve minutes per game, he shot 39.5 percent and averaged 6.0 points per game. "That's where," Frankie said, "I learned all about white drugs and white women."

Indeed, it was his love of partying that was Frankie's downfall. I can't remember how many times his wife came looking for him at a practice session because he had stayed out all night. As soon as she was sighted storming into the Armory, he would duck into the nearest bathroom and one of his teammates would tell her that he had called in sick and wasn't there.

After the Spurs cut him, he was immediately picked up by the Celtics. In twenty-four games, he shot 46.2 percent and registered 2.1 ppg. According to one member of the Celtics organization, Frankie was so "scatterbrained" in Boston that he couldn't even remember those plays that were designed for him to shoot.

Next stop was the Kansas City Kings, where in twenty-three games he shot 44.2 percent and scored 3.8 ppg. He also appeared in nine playoff games for the Kings, averaging 2.6 points in only 5.6 minutes per game.

In the CBA Frankie was a superstar with a lifetime accuracy from the field at 50.5 percent and a career points-per-game mark of 18.6. If he was totally obnoxious and self-involved during games, off the court Frankie was intelligent, good-natured, and marginally popular with his peers. Phil put up with his shenanigans because Frankie was a really nice guy and always played hard.

But it was in the second game of the Toronto series that Frankie finally disgusted both Phil and me. The game was tight all the way, but we couldn't quite catch up. In the closing minutes, Phil went with an offensive-defensive strategy at the shooting guard spot, alternating Frankie with Derrick Rowland at every appropriate dead ball. But Frankie was pissed to the max. So much so that at one point, when he returned to the bench after playing for only a single possession, he unlaced his sneakers. Then, when Phil motioned for him to get back into the action, Frankie simply ignored the summons.

We lost 124–114, and both Phil and I were steamed after the game. Since we were scheduled to leave for Toronto early the next day, we stayed overnight in a local motel. After much back-and-forth, we agreed that Frankie would be indefinitely suspended and that David Ancrum would take his place on the roster.

Anc was a six-foot-four, 215-pound strongman, a lefty who assaulted the hoop with unbridled creativity and ferocity and played rock-hard defense. He was also a seriously funny man whom his teammates absolutely adored.

Phil phoned our decision in to Jim Coyne, the chairman of the board that governed the Patroons. Then he phoned Anc with the good news and left a bad-news message on Frankie's answering machine.

Phil and I decided to drive up to Toronto together and let the players use the van. This would give them the chance to bond with Anc, and as they climbed into the van, their merriment and good cheer convinced Phil and me that suspending Frankie was the correct decision.

Unfortunately, Anc had a bad game and—despite 32 points from Lowes Moore—we trailed from the opening tip to the final buzzer, losing 117–105.

As soon as we got back to our hotel room, the phone rang. It was Coyne, asking Phil to reconsider Frankie's banishment. We were down 2–1, and if we lost Game 4 the next evening, the Patroons' season would be over. Without another playoff series, or at least a deciding Game 5 versus Toronto, the team would lose a shitload of money. Besides, all the local media was roasting Phil for suspending the Patroons' leading scorer.

I listened to the conversation on an extension and erupted into an extremely animated pantomime whose message was nevertheless loud and clear: DON'T GIVE IN!

But Phil yielded—with the proviso that Frankie would apologize to his teammates. No problem.

So Frankie was immediately flown up to Toronto in a private plane owned by one of the board members. Meanwhile, the players were alerted that there would be a mandatory team meeting in our room early the next morning.

Frankie was late, of course.

"Frankie has something to say," Phil announced.

In lieu of an apology, here's what Frankie said to his teammates: "If any of you motherfuckers expect me to apologize then you're fucking crazy. None of you motherfuckers can carry my jock, and you should feel honored to even be playing on the same team as me. So, fuck y'all."

Then he made a quick exit stage right—leaving the rest of us absolutely speechless.

The conclusion of the series was anticlimactic. Frankie scored 27 as we evened the series at 2–2 with a resounding 123–111 victory. We then cruised to a 132–123 win the deciding game back in Albany—and, wouldn't you know it, Frankie blistered the nets for 39 points.

Next up were the Eastern Conference finals against Bill Musselman's Tampa Bay Thrillers, opening with two games there and any remaining games to be played in Albany. As ever, Muss's squad was loaded with NBA veterans: Freeman Williams, Linton Townes, Steve Hayes, Ron Valentine, Perry Moss, Sidney Lowe, and Coby Dietrick.

Williams got us for 34 points as the Thrillers opened the series with a lopsided 144–129 win. But we had two off-days and therefore two practices to make adjustments—something that Phil specializes in. And Game 2 was a dogfight.

Late in Game 2 Frankie intercepted a pass and broke ahead of the field with no defender within twenty feet. However, instead of directly attacking the basket, he swerved to his right so as to pass in front of the Thrillers' bench. Then he slowed for just a beat as he approached Musselman—long enough to flip Muss the bird and to explicate in two mono-syllabic words exactly what his gesture meant. Only then did Frankie resume his journey hoopward and defiantly execute an impressive dunk. Frankie ended up with a game-high 30 points in a 113–100 win for the Patroons. There was a min-imum of celebrating as we hustled back to the hotel to rest up for a 6:00 a.m. flight to Albany the next morning.

But at around 3:00 a.m., the phone rang in Frankie's room. It was Musselman.

According to Frankie, this is what Muss said: "What you did to me was an insult of the worst kind. If you ever do any-thing like that again, you'll wind up in a hospital."

According to Musselman, this is what he said: "Congrat-ulations, Frankie. You played a wonderful game."

Before the start of Game 3 in Albany, Musselman made a dramatic entrance into the Armory—flanked by a brace of no-necked, muscular, mean-eyed, scowling, three-hun-dred-pound brutes.

When asked to identify his companions by the Albany media, Muss just shrugged and muttered something about his needing protection after being threatened. He refused to provide any particulars.

During the game Musselman's two protectors sat just behind the visitors' bench. And Frankie certainly got the message.

Not that Sanders said anything. No, not word one.

All he did was play timidly and ineffectively, scoring a season's low total of 6 points.

The Thrillers easily won the game, 90–83, but after a day off to contemplate the meaning of his days and ways, Frankie rebounded with an A-plus effort, registering 28 points in leading us to 118–113 win.

Frankie was likewise on his game (24 points) in the de-ciding contest, but the key play hinged on a mistake made by John Wiley.

All season long Wiley had been erratic. He was a decent passer (2.3 assists), scorer (8.6 points), and rebounder (6.2 per game). But both his defense and his execution of the of-fense were spotty, and he often seemed to operate on cruise control.

Anyway, the score was tied with less than a minute left in the game. As we huddled during a time-out, Phil sketched out the Thrillers' most likely play on his hand-held grease board—a cross baseline screen for Linton Townes.

"We must switch," Phil said. "Whoever's guarding the screener must switch onto Townes. John, that probably means you. We can't give Townes any open baseline jumpers. We absolutely must switch. Got it, John?"

Yes. Of course. Certainly.

But Wiley didn't switch, Townes buried the open jumper, Tampa Bay won, 93–89, and our season was kaput.

"Gary Springer would have switched," I said to Phil, and he sadly agreed.

10

The Fall, Winter, and Spring of Our Discontent

Just before our third (and last season) together, Phil and I traveled to Hempstead, Long Island, to watch the Knicks' initial practice session of their preseason. Since the Knicks were affiliates of the Patroons, we were hoping one of the training-camp players might wind up in Albany. This didn't happen. But what we observed during an intrasquad scrimmage eventually changed the history of the NBA.

Patrick Ewing had been New York's (and the NBA's) first pick in the recent draft, and he squared off against the Knicks' holdover center, Bill Cartwright—a rough-tough player whose physical play could border on brutality. And Cartwright showed the blue-chip rookie no mercy. On the opening sequence Cartwright simply pummeled Ewing with an elbow and knocked him to the floor. This process was repeated several times throughout the scrimmage. Overall, Ewing must have been dropped at least a dozen times—with his play getting less and less aggressive with every hit he absorbed.

"Hmm," said Phil.

Fast forward to June 1988, when Phil was completing his first year as an assistant coach for the Bulls. At the time—

and for several years thereafter—the Chicago–New York rivalry was especially intense, particularly in the playoffs. For the Bulls to advance in the postseason they had to get past the Knicks, and to do so they needed a big man who could at least give Ewing a hard time on defense. That's why Phil instigated a trade that sent Charles Oakley (and draft choices) to New York for Bill Cartwright (and draft choices).

For sure, the Oakman was an aggressive defender and rebounder, but he was also a poor shooter in the clutch. And while Cartwright had a chronically sore back that limited his playing time, it was soon evident that Ewing was still intimidated by his grunt-and-grind defense.

Later, when Phil replaced Doug Collins as head coach, the seven-foot-one, 280-pound Cartwright was easily able to establish and secure a position on either box, thereby enabling passes into him to initiate significant options in the triangle offense.

Indeed, without Cartwright it's doubtful that the Bulls would have achieved their initial three-peat.

Throughout the 1985–86 season in Albany, Phil and I continued our game-day routine whenever the Patroons played at home. We'd conduct our shootaround at the Armory, hustle over to the Steuben Athletic Club for our Nautilus workouts, and then play one-on-one on the club's smallish full-court. Twenty-one baskets won (but the winner had to win by two), sometimes we played straight up, and sometimes he'd spot me as many as seven baskets.

He was younger, quicker, and infinitely more skilled than I was. My "advantage" was size (about half an inch) and strength.

After Phil retired from the league (in 1980) and the spring went out of his legs, his base was more stable, his wrist much looser, and his jumper more accurate. When Phil was with the Knicks, Red Holzman would never let him dribble the ball. But Phil routinely froze me with nifty crossovers and behind-the-back maneuvers.

And me? I tried to bang him on defense, especially when he took me inside. I tried to pin his left arm and keep him from rotating his right hip. Yet I was always mindful of the acrostic scars that marked his spinal fusion, so I was careful not to Bogart his back. The best I could do was force him into shooting a turnaround jumper, which I could occasionally block.

Ballhandling was never my specialty, so Phil normally waited until I reached the three-point line before confronting me on defense. Even then he'd let me dribble leftward. In a close game, though, he'd attack me in the backcourt, and with his cobra arms and quick feet, he could steal my dribble at his pleasure.

So how did I score against one of the finest defensive players of his generation? I took long jumpers (even old-time one-handers), mostly from just beyond my range (which was about twenty feet). I shot running baseline hooks with my right hand. And I tried to overpower him in the pivot and then either utilize some kind of duck-under or reverse move to the far side of the basket.

And I did beat him once!

My shot was falling and his wasn't, plus I was a blink or two quicker than usual. We always played as fiercely as though we were brothers—pronging each other with elbows, smashing shoulder to shoulder and hip to hip. I was ahead 20–19 (with no spot!) and he had the ball, dribbling and spinning into the attack zone. We both understood that if he scored now, the game would inevitably be his. This was the play.

At the foul line extended, he pivoted to the left sideline and began his swift approach toward the basket. Realizing that he'd gained an irrecoverable half-step, I tried to swipe the ball from behind him. And, yes! He'd been a little lazy with his crossover and I managed to tip the ball away. In the process, however, I'd also bumped his hip and sent him sprawling to the floor.

"Yes!" I shouted, as I dribbled downcourt and scored the winning basket.

"Foul," said Phil, still lying on the floor.

"Bullshit. It was incidental contact."

"You knocked me down, Charley. It's a foul."

We jabbered back and forth for a while, our arguments getting more heated with every exchange. Then I said, "Assuming I did foul you, you mean you've never lost a game when a referee made a bad call?"

Disgusted, he stormed off the court and spent thirty minutes doing solitary yoga exercises in a side gym.

I'd guess that my lifetime record against Phil was something like 1-250. It wasn't until we'd showered, dressed, and agreed that both of us were jerks that we were able to joke about our respective follies.

Then we resumed our usual ritual: an early dinner at a passable Chinese restaurant and coffee laced with Bailey's Irish Cream at a cozy bar on Lark Street. With that we were primed for the upcoming game.

Unfortunately, the 1985–86 edition of the Patroons was not a very good one. Frankie J. had been released and wound up playing a few games for the Maine Lumberjacks and also for Musselman's Tampa Bay Thrillers, of all places. Ralph McPherson and Lowes Moore had retired. Our holdovers were limited to Clinton Wheeler, David Ancrum, and Derrick Rowland (who was eventually traded to Bay State for Chris McNealy, an ex-NBA player). Our most significant additions included Kenny Natt and James Banks.

We wound up at 24-24, barely qualifying for the playoffs, but, as ever, the season was not lacking in craziness.

Because of injuries and NBA call-ups, I must have played in at least fifty intrasquad scrimmages during my nine-year tenure as a head coach and assistant coach in the CBA. In all of those runs, not only did I fail to score a basket, but I never even managed to get off a shot.

Even though I had been an outstanding small college player, it was all I could do to set sturdy screens and diligently execute the offense. Civilians should never underestimate the talent of professional hoopers at any level of competition.

But I did make a pair of significant plays.

During a heated intrasquad scrimmage when I coached the Oklahoma City Cavalry, I threw a perfect lob pass to Steve Burtt whose subsequent dunk shot ended the game. Even more impressive than my pass was the six-foot-two Burtt being able to elevate sufficiently in a thick crowd of defenders and finish the play.

The only other play of which I can boast took place when I was an assistant coach with the Albany Patroons. Our star player was Clinton Wheeler, a powerful guard who went on to play eighty-seven games with Indian, Miami, and Portland (1987–89).

If Clint was an extremely talented player, he wasn't a particularly good teammate. He was all scowls, frowns, and barely suppressed anger both on and off the court.

At the time, the Patroons provided a van for the players to use—which meant that a great deal of cooperation was necessary to dole out time behind the wheel. However, it was standard operating procedure for the van to shuttle the players from their hotel to the arena for practice sessions. Indeed, it was incumbent on whoever was the designated driver to wait until the last player was showered and ready to go. The ignition key, by the way, was always stashed in the glove compartment.

But Wheeler had a habit of unilaterally commandeering the van and driving back to the hotel by himself—and leaving his teammates stranded. He did this on several occasions. The guys berated him and even threatened him, but Wheeler paid them no mind. Sometimes he even drove off by his lonesome for a Saturday night on the town.

So there we were, rehearsing our full-court press offense. Clinton was guarding the ball handler while I was lurking near the midcourt line just in case the handler needed an emergency outlet.

Seeing that Wheeler's back was turned to both of us, the player who was defending me said this: "Get him, Charley. Knock him on his butt. He deserves it."

We both knew who he was talking about.

So, as I angled up behind Wheeler and gathered myself to set a blind screen, none of his teammates informed him of a screen-left. Moreover, the player with the ball, seeing what I was up to, made sure to slightly alter his path so that my incipient screen would create maximum contact.

Which it did—knocking Wheeler sprawling.

When he climbed to his feet and saw who had done the deed, Wheeler just cursed under his breath, stalked off the court, exited the arena, jumped into the van, and drove away.

Meanwhile, I was the recipient of glad-hands from everybody else.

"I don't mind walking to the hotel," said the guy guarding me. "It was well worth it. When can we do this again?"

In the CBA (and later in the NBA), Phil was always interested in giving his assistants as much responsibility as they could handle. So it was that I was permitted to contact various coaches to inquire about trade possibilities. In so doing, one of the most fascinating characters I encountered was Sam Washington, the coach and general manager of the Detroit Spirits.

This was before the advent of Caller ID, and a strange, forced falsetto voice answered the phone.

"*Hello?*"

"Hello. Is Sam Washington there?"

"*No. Never heard of him.*"

"Sam Washington? The coach of the Detroit Spirits?"

"*What do you want him for?*"

"Oh, this is Charley Rosen with the Albany Patroons? And we just want to know if Sam is interested in trading for Clinton Wheeler?"

"Hi, Charley. I sure would be interested. What did you have in mind?"

Obviously, Sam must have had some dangerous enemies.

Also, whenever the Spirits would embark on a lengthy road trip, Sam's wife would deposit him at the airport. But instead of traveling with the team, he would take a cab back to Detroit and shack up with his mistress of the moment. Meanwhile, his assistant would coach the team, and the radio play-by-play announcer would lead his audience to believe that Sam was indeed on the bench. Then, of course, Sam would rendezvous at the airport in time to meet the team and his wife.

That's why Sam was often called "the Ghost."

This season also marked the first (and second) games that I ever coached from start to finish.

My initiation came after Phil became incensed at a clearly backwards call by a ref named Ralph Lembo that cost us a home game. Phil towered over Lembo, and in the course of his vehement protest, he unloosed a gob of spittle on the ref's bald dome. As a result, Phil was suspended for a game by Commissioner Drucker.

In his absence I directed the Patroons to a lopsided win against the Bombardiers in the Armory.

Later on, we were scheduled to play at Toronto on Christmas Eve, but Phil informed the Patroons brass that he considered the day to be a holy one. So holy, in fact, that working on that day would violate his religious beliefs. He was then given permission to stay home while I drove the van and coached the ball game.

Of course, as soon as Phil was given a pass, Frankie also announced that his religious beliefs likewise forbade his playing on Christmas Eve.

With a short-handed squad, we played a picture-perfect opening quarter and led by 15. But reality soon prevailed and we wound up losing by 15.

When we were in the middle of long road trips, we were often provided by the league with vans and road maps. These cheapo, rented vehicles were usually either antiquated, in need of repairs, or extremely clumsy to handle (especially in high winds).

Phil did most of the driving while I rode shotgun, and our all-night drives tested our stamina and concentration. Our cross-Florida excursion from Tampa to Pensacola, for example, required us to play word games to keep us both alert.

The game of choice was a kind of historical identification quiz. One of us would have a certain historical personage in mind while the other could only ask yes or no questions.

"Is it a male? Is he alive? . . ."

On one such memorable journey, his pick stumped me and my pick stumped him—so the game lasted for the entire four hours we spent in transit.

His guy was Jim Bridger, a wilderness explorer and mountain man well known in rural places like Montana and the Dakotas where Phil grew up. Even after I conceded, somewhere around Leesburg, I had to confess that I'd never heard of Bridger.

Likewise did my selection trump all of PJ's guesses—Judge Crater, a well-known juryman who suddenly and mysteriously vanished in the middle of a busy Chicago street in the early 1930s. When I was coming of age in New York City, "Judge Crater" was a common tag placed on anybody whose whereabouts were unknown.

Of course, Phil had never heard of him.

(Years later, an elderly Italian dentist in Kingston, New York, swore that the foundation that upheld a local municipal building also held Judge Crater's remains.)

Despite our mutual ignorance and confusion, however, nighttime van rides were safer than daylight rides for one reason: Phil was addicted to the *New York Times* Sunday crossword puzzle.

As long as there was sufficient natural light for him to read, he'd spread the magazine page containing the puzzle across the width of the steering wheel and seemed to spend as much time and attention looking at the puzzle as he did on the road ahead.

"Charley, what's a four-letter word for medieval beer? Look here . . . If I can get 51-across, then 39-down will . . ."

"Phil! The road!"

Even though I, and the players behind us, would occasionally cringe with fear, the van never swerved, never went through a red light or stop sign, never precipitously changed lanes, and never slowed down.

"Don't worry, Charley. After driving my motorcycle over mountain passes in Montana in the dead of night during full-blown blizzards, this is a piece of cake."

"It's mead," I said.

I came to believe that Phil was a modern-day, motorized version of Jim Bridger

Extracurricular physical confrontations are not unusual in professional sports. But late that season, certainly the biggest mismatch in sports history occurred (where else?) in the CBA.

At six feet nine inches and 250 pounds, Dave Cowens was the coach of the Bay State Bombardiers. Bill Musselman, the coach of the renamed Tampa Bay Sizzlers, measured about five foot eight and perhaps 160 pounds. Their two teams were involved in a close game in Worchester, Massachusetts, and Musselman thought he was consistently getting homered by the referees.

At one point, Muss made an unflattering reference to the refs being intimidated by Cowens's size and NBA experience—and the two coaches exchanged verbal hostilities. Even as a player Cowens was never known for the evenness of his temper, and he wasn't particularly happy coaching in the CBA anyway. So when Musselman's roosterish defiance became unbearable, the big man made his move.

Stalking over to Muss, Cowens grabbed him by the lapels of his famous blue leather sports jacket, lifted him off the ground, and started to shake the smaller man. Musselman's head, arms, and legs dangled freely as though he were a rag doll. This lasted for several seconds, during which Cowens remained silent—until finally he released his grip, whereupon Musselman dropped to the floor in a heap.

After the game Muss told the assembled media that not only was Cowens a terrific coach but that the two of them were the best of friends.

The Patroons managed to secure the fourth seed in the conference playoffs. It was generally conceded that the powerful Tampa Bay Thrillers would sweep us in four lopsided contests (each series had been extended to best-of-seven). Indeed, Musselman had gathered still another squad of distinguished NBA vets and CBA All-Stars, a cast that included Kevin Williams, Ed Nealy, Rod Higgins, Don Collins, Eric Fernsten, Ron Valentine, Mike Holton, Brooke Steppe, and a future pro wrestler named Rick Lamb. (Frankie Sanders had played in one regular-season game with the Thrillers, and David Magley had played in two games.)

Even though Williams torched us for 42 points in Game 1 and 59 points in Game 6, and Collins registered 45 in Game 5, somehow we managed to extend the Thrillers to a seventh and deciding game. Even more surprising, we were up by 10 at the half. But with Williams notching 37 and Higgins making a surprise reappearance in Tampa Bay after being cut by the Chicago Bulls the night before, the Thrillers prevailed, 118–110.

When we returned to Albany, I was informed that because of strictly financial considerations, the Patroons would be eliminating my job for the 1986–87 season. Not only that, but Phil's new contract would reflect the Patroons' tighter budget: He'd be getting $30,000 plus bonuses of $25 for every quarter-point the team won from game to game. In the event of a tied quarter, Phil's bonus for that game would include $12.50.

More than the grueling schedule, the awful officiating, the constant turnover of players, it would be this penny ante arrangement that would compel PJ to eventually quit the CBA.

So, my three-year apprenticeship with Phil was over, during which I learned my Xs and Os, the organization of practice sessions, and the management of player matchups as well as the game clock. Also how to be firm yet comfortable with players. I imbibed Phil's attitude toward referees—they were cops with whistles, bullies, jackasses, and worse. If I lacked Phil's NBA glow, I could talk convincingly about sacrifice, making the extra pass, and playing the team game.

Here's how Phil summed up my contributions in a passage from *More Than a Game*: "It was Charley who helped soften my sharp edges and enabled me to maintain a workable relationship with the players. Even so, he was no medic, and several of the players chose to do their own pregame taping.

"It's my nature to trust that God will take care of everything in due time, but Charley's way was to prod and press me to deal with issues that had to be resolved immediately. What about this possible trade? Or that one? Shouldn't we give Lowes Moore some time at the two-guard spot? During my fourteen years as an NBA player, I'd never met anyone as obsessed with basketball as Charley was."

11

Keeping My Day Job

Since the CBA season was about four months shorter than the NBA's annual marathon, I continued to write profiles for both *Sport* and *Inside Sports*. Often the interviewing process led to interesting adventures:

• Willy Wise was an All-ABA player for the Utah Stars, and I connected with him in Salt Lake City and New York to get his story. In Utah, I witnessed (and actually participated in) one of the most remarkable games of H-O-R-S-E that I'd ever seen. Since Rick Mount was such a dead-eye set-shooter, any shot that touched or even grazed the rim on its way through the basket was counted as a miss. Even so Mount won easily. Afterward, he put on an absolutely incredible demonstration of jump shooting in which he took long jumpers from various spots on the court, but he shot the ball in such a way that wherever he was the ball bounced straight back to him. It was as though the ball was a living thing that was responsive to his silent commands.

The Stars were practicing at St. John's College in Queens to prepare for a game against the New York Nets. Joe Mullany was the coach (I would encounter him several years later when he coached Pensacola in the CBA), and since several of the Stars' big men were nursing various sprains and muscle pulls, he asked me if I wanted to take part in a scrimmage.

You bet I did!

Once the action began, I nailed an eighteen-foot jumper; recovered and put back an offensive rebound; and set such sturdy screens that Ron Boone called me "Iron Man." It marked one of the happiest days of my entire life.

• Elvin Hayes was suspicious of me, but he basically called Tex Winter (who had coached him in his rookie season) the "anti-Christ" for asking the Big E to pass, set screens, and run plays.

• I flew down to Charlotte, North Carolina, to interview Billy Cunningham, who had just jumped from the NBA to the ABA. He was very polite, centered, and adequately cooperative. He was coaching the Philadelphia Sixers when I ran into him at Madison Square Garden several years later—looking much more frail, pale, and nervous.

"Charley," he said. "Good to see you. Are you still writing?"

"Yes, blah, blah, and blah."

I went on about my business and chanced to encounter him five minutes later leaning in the same spot against the wall outside of the visiting team's locker room.

"Charley," he said. "Good to see you. Are you still writing?"

• It was snowing in Buffalo when I visited with Jack Marin, a dedicated conservative thinker who believed that Bill Bradley and Phil Jackson were both Communists. We had a fruitful connection, but he did scare the daylights out of me when he steered his Porche along a snow-blown highway at seventy miles per hour while digging in the glove compartment to show me something or other—and while controlling the steering wheel only with his knees.

• Julius Erving was playing with the Virginia Squires and had a total game—except for his lack of a reliable jump shot. When I asked why he couldn't shoot, he said, "Because I don't need to."

• I met Calvin Murphy for breakfast at the hotel in New York where the Houston Rockets were staying. When we returned to his hotel room to continue the interview about an hour later, Calvin discovered that he had left his key inside. Unfortunately, Murphy's roommate was Rudy Tomjanovich—and fifteen minutes of banging on the door and screaming blue curses had no effect on the loud snoring that flooded through the door and into the hall. As Calvin's voice got shriller and his pounding more ferocious, the violence of his language also increased.

Rudy T. finally opened the door, groggily claiming that he thought we were thieves or muggers trying to break into the room. For a couple of tense moments, Murphy laid a hot line of electric abuse on his sleepy roommate. Tomjanovich, who had been Murphy's partner for four years, mumbled a few choice nuggets of his own and then fell asleep again before his head hit the pillow.

"That boob," Murphy said. "He could wake up and see somebody stealing his clothes and he'd just turn over and go back to sleep. If it wasn't for me, he'd miss every plane, every game . . . He'd sleep until he'd die of starvation."

• Ralph Sampson was only marginally cooperative. Bill Fitch was the Rockets coach and on the record he called

Sampson "a pussy." The very day that the story appeared, Sampson threw a punch at an opponent.

- When I interviewed Swen Nater in San Antonio, he insisted that his wife always be present. Indeed, he conferred with her before offering an answer to even the most innocent questions, reminding me of a mobster continually consulting his lawyer while being grilled by a congressional committee.

- Dominique Wilkins kept me waiting in a hotel lobby for more than three hours.

- Bobby Knight wouldn't speak to me at all, then called me when the article came out to scold me for several inaccuracies.

- Hubie Brown was remarkably candid, but his most scathing remarks were off the record.

- Louie Carneseca was a bullshitter deluxe.

- Gene Shue was honest and real. As were Red Auerbach, Jimmy Rodgers, Pete Carril, and Mike Riordan.

- Dan Issel was bored. Jim Chones was flattered. Bob "Horse" Kaufman was dull.

- When I alluded to Bill Bradley's being a modern-day Renaissance man and mentioned Sir Phillip Sydney, Bradley knew to whom I was referring.

- Before Red Holzman deigned to speak to me he pointed at my tape recorder and said, "Shut that fucking thing off."

- Mendy Rudolph was probably the best referee in the history of the NBA. In civilian life he was noted for being a slick dresser. I was in my hippie mode when I met him in his office, wearing long hair, jeans, sandals, a

Grateful Dead T-shirt, and peace beads. Even before he shook my hand, Rudolph said this: "Who's your tailor? A blind man?"

- David Stern's father owned a delicatessen and the teenage Stern played for a team sponsored by his dad. "I was only five-nine," said Stern, "but I was a terrific rebounder for my size."

Yet despite being able to rub shoulders with, and eavesdrop upon, basketball celebrities—on someone else's dime— I was determined that my future was in coaching.

12

Georgia on My Mind

The most important qualification for a coach seeking a job in the CBA had little to do with his resume, and since candidates were rarely interviewed, a job seeker's personality and personal appearance were also nonfactors. Indeed, all that counted was the celebrity of those who called the owner or the general manager to recommend any given candidate.

When it was announced that the Detroit Spirits were relocating to Savannah, Georgia, and that Sam Washington had been canned (and would soon pass away), Phil, of course, made several calls to a guy named Robb Larson, the team's rookie GM. Previously, Larson had served in the CBA office as vice president of entertainment and had been the Spirits' director of operations for one season in Detroit. While he was a nice guy and an excellent tennis player, Larson knew next to nothing about basketball. But he loved talking to and being courted by Phil Jackson.

PJ then convinced his ex—college coach, Bill Fitch, to call Larson at my behalf. Then Phil suggested that I contact Jerry West and ask him to speak to Larson for me. Even though neither Phil nor I had any real connection with West—for some reason he agreed.

Years before, I had written an article for *Inside Sports* about the NBA's best sixth men. And as part of my research I had interviewed Red Auerbach, who had developed the entire concept when he placed Frank Ramsey in that role during the 1954–55 season. The article contained a full-page reproduction of a painting depicting Red surrounded by the encircled faces of famous sixth men since then. At Red's request I managed to have the magazine send him the original artwork. Red was so pleased that he told me that he "owed me a favor." And, of course, he'd call Larson.

My most significant competition for the job was an ex-waiter who ran errands for the Lakers' summer-league team and was being promoted by Pat Riley. It was no contest.

Larson was thrilled to schmooze with Phil, West, Fitch, and Auerbach, and therefore he considered me to be a supremely qualified coach by association. I was eventually offered (and eagerly accepted) a nonguaranteed one-year contract that was worth twenty-six thousand dollars.

In the meantime, I left my family in Woodstock and moved into an apartment that the team supplied for me in one of Savannah's outlying islands—only a twenty-minute drive (in a stripped-down but new Chevy that the team supplied) to the arena.

Going about my business in Savannah always brought a tear to my eye and a tickle to my throat. That's because there was a paper bag factory near the airport, and whenever the wind was wrong, the stench was reminiscent of cockroach spray with musky overtones of boiled cabbage. The aroma was particularly overpowering when the factory cranked up on Monday mornings, strong enough to literally cause birds to fall dead from the sky. Strong enough to force the airport to reroute approach-and-departure flight patterns.

When questioned, the locals took deep, defiant breaths and claimed that everything smelled just fine. When pressed further, Savannians declared that the factory employed four thousand workers and lowered real estate taxes all over town. Sure, but I spent my first two months there clearing my throat and coughing, constantly on the verge of bronchitis.

On the upside, the seafood was always fresh, and wonderful restaurants abounded. The recently renovated waterfront area was quaint and thronged with tourists who marveled at the charms of the Southland, studiously ignoring the airborne smell, not to mention the oil slicks and dead fish floating on the Savannah River.

The downtown area was dotted with restored colonial houses and lush pocket gardens, bracketed with wrought-iron fencing and gold-lettered historical markers. The oldest synagogue in America was over on Elm Street. A Revolutionary War cannon sat on Bay Street, aimed inland at the Stars and Bars Bar. There was even an oldies station on the radio, WREB. The city's main traffic artery was entirely shaded by gracefully drooping cypress trees and was called Victory Drive, presumably to celebrate Sherman's decision not to torch Savannah. The air was always wet, and even the trees seemed mildewed.

Savannah's metro population of 150,000 was 52 percent black, yet people of color still felt compelled to cast their eyes to their shoes whenever they passed a white. The crime rate was high—assaults, rape, burglaries—but the average cracker on the street was thrilled that most crimes were black-on-black. Nor did the yokels think twice about casually referring to my ballplayers as "niggers" to their faces.

The team I inherited included only three holdovers from a talented yet undisciplined squad that had struggled to underachieve a record of 24-24: Steve Rambadt was a genuinely good guy but had a perpetually aching back. Alvin "Bo" Dukes was a squat five-foot-six guard who could pass the ball through the eye of a needle and was another wonderful person. Too bad Bo could neither shoot nor avoid being outsized on defense. And Tico Brown, a six-foot-six swingman, was a dead-eye shooter and the league's leading scorer.

Bo, Tico, and I became true-blue friends.

To fill out the roster, I recruited a pair of veterans from the Albany Patroons' heydays: Penny Elliot (whose play deteriorated as the season progressed), and David Ancrum (who would average more than 14 points per game). But Andre Gaddy was married, living in Brooklyn, and felt fortunate to have a job at the main post office in Manhattan—so he turned me down.

Another blast from the Patroons past was Frankie J. Sanders himself. After being cut by Albany after the 1985–86 season, Frankie had played one game for Tampa Bay and sixteen for Maine before being cut and recut. It seems that Phil wasn't the only coach who had problems with Frankie's attitude.

Anyway, I was hoping that Frankie's self-styled "million-dollar jumper" was still intact and that he had learned his lesson, so I asked him to join me in Savannah and he was only too happy to oblige. And he still could play—after five games he was averaging 3 2 points—but he wouldn't pass, defend, or get along with anybody, so I eventually had to cut him one more time.

Virtually every veteran player in every level of competition regards a rookie coach with skepticism. To engender the respect of his team, a newcomer to the power seat must first demonstrate his expertise.

Fortunately, I happened to make a pair of significant on-the-fly decisions that helped to win an early season game at Jacksonville. The first was a half-time spacing adjustment that effectively dismantled Jacksonville's full-court trap. But the clincher occurred during the overtime period.

That's when I spontaneously changed the angle of a down-screen so that Tico wound up with a wide-open three-point shot that he made to win the game.

This was a critical game that made me confident that I could indeed coach at this level, while communicating the same message to my players.

Since suffering three consecutive losses could easily result in a pink slip, it was incumbent upon every CBA coach to seek out and utilize every possible advantage that could help win a ball game. Even food could be a useful tool.

There was (and I hope there still is) a fantastic restaurant in Savannah simply called Mrs. Wilkes. The place had no identifying signage and never advertised. Yet all the locals knew about it, so there were lines around the block for the only two meals they served, breakfast and lunch.

It was an all-you-can-eat establishment and the customers sat at long tables, usually in the company of strangers. Waitresses brought heaping platters of choice southern chow—fried chicken, catfish, and okra. Collard greens, black-eyed peas, mashed this, stewed that. Everything was absolutely scrumptious and there was no way to avoid overeating.

Well, one fine day my good buddy Gerald Oliver brought his Charleston Gunners to town for a game against my Savannah Spirits. A native of Tennessee, Gerald just loved to eat down-home food.

So on the afternoon before we were scheduled to play, I told Gerald about Mrs. Wilkes: great food in unlimited quantities at an incredibly low price. And seeing as how he'd never find it by himself, I offered to join him and his players for a midday repast. Naturally, both Gerald and his team ate much more than they usually did for a game-day lunch. No surprise that they were bloated and lethargic come game time. Nor that the home team coasted to an easy win.

Afterward Gerald could only laugh at my ploy. "You know something, Charley?" he said in a whisper. "Having a meal like that reminded me of how my mother used to cook when I was growing up. You know something else, Charley? Losing the game was almost worth it. Almost."

Shortly thereafter, Charleston visited Savannah for a two-game series, and I delivered a semitruthful scouting report to Stan Kasten, then the general manager of the Atlanta Hawks, that resulted in a pair of slightly tainted—but totally acceptable—wins for the good guys. On the afternoon before the first game of the abbreviated series, Kasten called to say that his second-string big man had just sprained an ankle and he desperately needed to sign a backup in a hurry.

"Who's the best center in the CBA?" Kasten asked.

Without hesitating, I strongly recommended Charleston's Jerome Henderson. I also advised Kasten that the Gunners were in town, and I passed along the phone number of the hotel where they were staying. Within thirty minutes Henderson was on his way to Atlanta.

As a result, the Spirits won both games.

On the flip side was CBA coach Mauro Panaggio, who routinely bad-mouthed any of his players about whom the NBA inquired. No, no, you don't want him. He can't play defense, or doesn't work hard, or stays out late partying, or is hated in the locker room, or smokes pot, or worse. That's exactly what cost Anthony Bowie at least two more years in the NBA.

As for me, I always did the opposite: emphasized my players' upsides while ignoring their shortcomings.

The Spirits' play-by-play radio announcer was none other than Craig "Bibs" Kilborn, future TV star, who was at that time marginally malnourished and chronically broke. Craig was easy to like, always personable and of good cheer, but somewhat arrogant and totally opinionated. We spent a lot of time together, most of it arguing. I was happy to buy him savory meals at least four times a week to augment his twenty-five-dollar per game salary.

At a rangy six foot five, Bibs fancied himself quite the ballplayer and, truth to tell, he wasn't nearly as bad as I wanted him to be. One day after practice, he challenged me to a game of one-on-one, make-it-take-it, eleven wins. Sure. No problem.

But I was more than twenty years his elder and unable to cope with his quick moves, young legs, and general exuberance. Then, with the score 10–6 in his favor, Bibs made a mistake.

"Charley," he said, "do you want me to end the game with a graceful shot from the outskirts or a scintillating drive to the hoop?"

I chose the latter, and as Bibs approached the ring, while ostensibly trying to block his shot I knocked him on his ass and slightly bloodied his lip. After he badly missed his subsequent outside shot, I took over the game—backing him slowly and relentlessly toward the basket and using my face-seeking elbow to keep him away from the ball.

The victory was mine, 11–10, but Bibs complained, "That's not basketball."

"It is in the Bronx." I said.

Phil was still coaching the Patroons, and early in the season the Spirits managed to best them once in Savannah and once in Albany. After the latter loss, the Albany sports media made the ridiculous claim that Phil was an inferior coach without me sitting beside him on the bench.

The Patroons won the remaining four games that our teams played against each other.

Meanwhile, the Spirits were struggling. We started off poorly at 4-10, and our home attendance was just as miserable—1,708 per game, or about 1,300 asses short of the break-even number.

However, since Savannah was exclusively a football town, we wouldn't have attracted many more fans even if we had a better record. Football was king throughout Georgia. In fact, our home court at the Savannah Civic Center housed the only basketball court in the entire city that had a wooden floor.

But there was a savior on the horizon who was supposed to rescue the season, my job, and the franchise itself.

His name was Cedric Henderson, a leansome six-foot-eight, 210-pounder from Marietta, Georgia, who had been drafted by the Atlanta Hawks (second round, thirty-second pick overall) after his freshman season at the University of Georgia. After playing in only two games for Atlanta, he was cut and picked up by the Milwaukee Bucks. Shortly thereafter, however, Henderson failed an illegally administered drug test, was waived by the Bucks, and signed with the Spirits. (Two years later, he would fail a by-the-book drug test and be banned from the CBA from that point on.)

For sure, his total NBA career amounted to only sixteen minutes in eight games, and he was unofficially a druggie, but he still had the NBA glow and was more or less a local guy. Too bad his eyes still looked like pinwheels when he arrived in Savannah.

Cedric was an outstanding CBA player—averaging about 16 points and 10 rebounds per outing—but his jumper was erratic, and if the refs didn't seem to like him, the late Bill Musselman surely did.

Muss was actually one of my favorite citizens of the basketball universe. He was knowledgeable, intense, personable (but only before and after games), honest, and not any crazier than the rest of the coaching fraternity.

The Spirits were battling Muss's first-place Thrillers in Tampa Bay, and the game was close throughout. Led by Tico Brown, Bo Dukes, and Cedric Henderson, we were poised to win the game.

Then disaster struck—in the form of referee Jim Wishmier, who in the space of sixty seconds late in the fourth quarter called three charging fouls on Henderson. Even worse, of the three, not one was legit!

"Jim," I cried out. "What's going on?"

"I can't help it," Wishmier said. "The guy charges every time he drives."

The Thrillers eventually won the game on a buzzer-beating shot by the late "Fast" Eddie Jordan. Instead of celebrating his victory, Musselman followed the refs off the court to their dressing room, screaming that "Henderson was a great player" and that they had "screwed Charley out of the win." He began to kick and pound his fists on the closed door, raging for another ten minutes.

"Muss," I said when he'd cooled down some, "what are you doing?"

"If I can't win a game fairly, then I'd rather lose." Then he shook my hand, patted my back, and was off to congratulate his players.

Granted that according to the vast majority of CBA players the only purpose of young women was to be whammed, bammed, and thank-you-ma'ammed, but Cedric's selfishness eventually disgusted me.

After a few weeks in Savannah, Cedric developed a virulent case of gonorrhea that required intensive medical attention. Even so, he went out of his way to bed down as many Georgia peaches as he could pluck. When I discovered the situation, I scolded him: "Cedric, you selfish son of a bitch! Why don't you keep your dick in your pants, at least until you can't infect anybody?"

He just shrugged and said, "A man's gotta do what a man's gotta do."

I wanted to trade him immediately, but the Spirits' owner, Reggie Henderson, wouldn't hear of such a thing. In truth, aside from the Spirits' woeful record, I was on Mr. Henderson's bad side almost from the beginning of the season.

Mr. Henderson lived in Detroit and ran a chemical-testing laboratory there. The lab was mostly doing blood tests for Medicare doctors, but apparently it wasn't all on the up and up, and Mr. Henderson was eventually indicted by the federal government for fraud. His hobbies were collecting vintage cars, avoiding traveling by air, and hunting big game in Africa. I only met him once, and the results were disastrous.

He had come to Savannah to check me out and also to investigate the books to determine why GM Robb Larson was asking for an infusion of money. Since he hated to fly, Mr. Henderson had traveled from Detroit in a customized van and was accompanied by a cook, a driver/sidekick, and a basketball player.

The player was a six-foot-six defensive ace from Detroit, and Mr. Henderson asked if I would give him a tryout—adding that whatever I eventually decided was totally up to me.

At a practice later that same day, I had the player guard Frankie. WHAM! The first time Frankie touched the ball, the guy stole it away and showcased a spectacular dunk at the end of his breakaway sprint. For an encore, the guy simply blocked two of Frankie's jumpers.

"Wow!" said Frankie. "This guy can play!"

Yes, he could. But to add him to the roster, I'd have to cut someone else. And the only possibility was Regan Truesdale, a six-foot-five guard from the Citadel. Regan was an above-average defender himself and a fairly good shooter—but, more importantly, he was a wonderful person. Modest, quiet, respectful ("Yes, sir."), a hard worker with good instincts, a good teammate, and a pleasure to coach.

He wasn't dynamic enough to entice another team to give up even a draft choice in exchange for his services. And how could I send Regan home?

No way.

So I told the owner that I'd stand pat with my team as is.

"Okay," he said, with a mere shrug of his shoulders, but it was clear that he was very unhappy.

In addition, Mr. Henderson's rather vapid smile told me that I wasn't sufficiently heartless to succeed in the coaching business. And he proved to be a prophet.

After that incident, Mr. Henderson wasn't my biggest fan, so I needed to find a way to somehow convince him that trading Cedric would help the ball club. To do so, I enlisted the aid of Tico and Bo, who had both played in Detroit and were tightly connected to Mr. Henderson. After road games, the three of us would often adjourn to their hotel room, eat pizza, drink beer, and rehash the latest game. This kind of camaraderie was highly unusual and was, in fact, frowned on by most coaches at every level of the game as constituting unprofessional behavior. But we were all older than twenty-one, our relationship was honest and legitimate, they honored and totally supported my authority, we were always respectful, and it seemed to be a natural gathering of friends. Once I broached the possibility of trading Cedric, they immediately agreed. On the spot, they telephoned Mr. Henderson and I was free to make a deal.

A deal that eventually saved my job.

Cedric was sent to Albany in return for Greg Hines, a rebound-eater, and Dominic Pressley, a wild point guard who always operated at warp speed. At the same time, waiver deals brought two more players to Savannah: Steve Woodside, a savvy, laconic, power forward; and Greg Spurling, a raw but willing six-foot-ten rookie from the hills of Tennessee.

With our reconstituted squad, we won eleven of our next fifteen games and quickly edged into playoff contention.

Just as quickly, I saw that Dominic's incredible quickness could very well be his ticket into the NBA. It was just as clear that Bo Dukes, despite his undeniable skills, was too short and too slow to ever graduate into The League. So I made a decision that was unpopular with everybody connected with the Spirits except Dominic and me (although both Bo and Tico came to accept my point of view). No matter what the score or game situation, I began playing Dominic for the entire fourth quarter.

Eventually, Dominic did get his shot at the NBA—but that story will have to keep for later.

After one particular road game, an NBA veteran who was playing with the home team, Leon Wood, joined Bo, Tico, and me in our routine postgame repast. After inhaling a few too many brews, we began discussing the relative demerits of the CBA's refs—several of whom worked split NBA-CBA schedules.

We all agreed that having to work in, say, La Crosse, Wisconsin, immediately after officiating a game in Madison Square Garden made these guys extremely testy. A mild reproach by a CBA player or coach, or even a brow furrowed in complaint was enough for these guys to start handing out technical fouls.

Or were the full-time CBA refs worse? The guys who had to prove how tough they were, and who worked with a palpable belligerence.

We were unanimous in disparaging game officials of every type. They were bullies. Cops with whistles instead of guns. Every one showed some kind of bias—to the home team or to any player or coach who had NBA experience.

"Yeah," said Wood. "Refs are not my favorite people."

Fast forward to the present . . . But you all know the punch line by now.

That's right, once his playing career was kaput, Leon Wood had a change of heart. These days, he's a full-fledged NBA tooter.

I'm not sure about this, but I believe there's something in the CBA by-laws stating that any player who becomes a ref is automatically guilty of treason.

To minimize the cost of lodging for visiting teams, CBA schedules frequently scheduled back-to-back games. And near the end of my rookie season coaching the Savannah Spirits, the usual two games in two nights produced one of the most bizarre forty-eight hours I ever experienced during my nine years in the league.

It all started when we were blown out at Charleston, West Virginia, by a score of 145–121. Gerald Oliver was a friendly, smiley, cornpone guy from Tennessee, and his teams always played with incredible energy.

Hey, sometime you lose and sometimes you win. But what really got me steamed was what transpired after the game was over.

One of the Charleston Gunners' best players was Michael Graham out of Georgetown, who measured six foot nine, 230, and had bona fide NBA skills. Inconsistency and sheer laziness were his downfalls, but when the spirit was upon him he could easily dominate CBA games.

In this particular game, the Gunners had scored just as the buzzer sounded to end regulation play—making a loud noise that easily overwhelmed the cheers of the meager crowd on hand. The home team had won the game by a lopsided margin, and Graham had put on an awesome rebounding, shot-swatting, and dunking performance. But just for the hell of it the Spirits' wonderful point guard, Bo Dukes, threw a fifty-foot pass downcourt to a streaking Johnny Johnson.

Now JJ was one of my favorite players, but I could say the same thing about most of the guys on that team. He was six foot seven, 210 pounds, a product of Tulane, and a minor-league version of Dennis Rodman—but a whole lot saner. JJ could run, defend, rebound, make lay-ups and dunks, but he was a horror show at the stripe—shooting an embarrassing 45.5 percent.

By the time JJ reeled in the pass from Dukes, an additional two or three seconds had elapsed. Still holding the ball, JJ turned his back to the court and started walking to the side-lines, when WHAM! Graham hit him from behind hard enough to knock JJ down and knock him out.

The Gunners' trainer roused JJ after a few tense moments,

but Johnny was still woozy when he finally climbed to his feet. A determination was made to take JJ to the local hospital.

Meanwhile, after checking that JJ had regained consciousness, his teammates calmly headed to the tunnel that led to the locker rooms. If they seemed to be peacefully accepting of Graham's egregiously late hit, I was not.

The entrances to the home and visitors' locker rooms were only a few feet apart, and when I encountered Graham in the hallway, I started screaming at him.

He was a cheap-shot motherfucker! A coward and an asshole!

I was fighting mad, and my grievous insults roused him to the same level of fury. As he took a menacing step in my direction, I ripped off my suit jacket, tossed it to the floor, clenched my fists, and rushed at him. He also put up his dukes and came at me. We were about three feet from being in punching distance when players from both teams intervened. I should note that it took four players to restrain Graham and only one to hold me back.

Afterward we both were escorted into our respective locker rooms and the fracas was over.

Alone with my team, I delivered the most scorching and insulting postgame speech of my entire career. Expletives deleted, here was the gist of my excoriation:

"One of your teammates gets blindsided and knocked out by a cheap shot after the buzzer, and none of you guys got angry enough to take any kind of action? Especially against a punk like Graham? I'm twenty-five years older than most of you, and I had to be the one to retaliate? What the hell is going on here? We've been talking about teamwork and we-are-family all season long—and suddenly it's all-for-one and one-for-one?"

Yes, they clenched their jaws and nodded their heads in shameful agreement. Each one of them took personal responsibility for being so passive.

Then I issued two commands:

"Tomorrow night, I want whoever's guarding Graham to let him dribble past you and beat you to the basket. Then I want the other four guys to converge and smash him. Hit him high and low. Take out his legs. Stick at least one elbow in his nose. If anybody gets fined or suspended, I'll be happy to reimburse you out of my own pocket for whatever money the league takes from you."

It was a deal!

"Next, there won't be any shootaround tomorrow morning. Instead, I want you guys to spend the entire day in your rooms. Send one of the rookies out for food for everybody, but the rest of you should act like you're locked in jail. I'm not going to police this. It's all up to you. I want you to talk to each other and think about what happened, as well as what this can mean to us as a team."

Agreed.

Later that evening, the call came from the hospital saying that JJ had been released, but their examinations had discovered an irregularity in his brain. There seemed to be some kind of tumor or something that couldn't be totally identified without further tests. It should be checked out as soon as we arrived back in Savannah. After a worrisome, sleepless night, I called JJ early the next morning to tell him the bad news.

"No sweat, Charley. I know all about it. I had a head injury when I was a kid and they had to go in there and do some stuff that left some scar tissue. It's no problem."

"So they removed part of your brain?"

"Yeah, but nothing to do with the thinking part."

"It must have been the part that facilitates free-throw shooting."

"Probably was."

So, the guys stayed put all day. And Gerald Oliver called to say that under the circumstances, and to prevent another incident, he would tell Graham to stay home for the game that night.

Hmmm. A clever ploy by Gerald. One that would surely take some of the bite out of my players' intensity.

I tried to ameliorate this by calling everybody's room and giving them an early heads-up. But I could tell by their voices that they were grievously disappointed.

I shouldn't have worried.

We simply annihilated them from the opening tip to the final buzzer. We were totally aggressive and totally unselfish in every aspect of the game.

With Tico Brown scoring 42 points, and Greg Spurling tearing down 14 rebounds, the final count was 150–127.

How good were we?

On our home court, with a little help from the refs, and if the opponents had a subpar game, we played well enough to have beaten the L.A. Clippers, the NBA's worst team.

And that's the truth!

Late in the season, Pete Maravich came to Savannah with a barnstorming team that preached a Christian message. He was heavy and slow as he lumbered up and down the court, but he was obviously having a great time. At halftime, Pete and some of his teammates delivered their born-again testimony.

Before the game, though, I had a sit-down with him. He told me that he was off drugs and alcohol, that Jesus was his Savior, and that he was the happiest he'd ever been. Indeed, his joy and compassion (both for himself and for others) were inspirational.

A few weeks later, he died of a heart attack while playing ball.

The morning after a game in Osh Kosh, Wisconsin, we were driven downstate to catch a flight out of Milwaukee when I came across an old friend—Darryl Dawkins. I'd done a profile on him for *Inside Sports* a few years back and we had stayed connected.

He was with the New Jersey Nets, who had lost to the Milwaukee Bucks the night before and were also en route. I'd already read in the morning's newspaper that Darryl had been tossed early in the game.

"All I did," he explained, "was call the ref a motherfucker and he slapped me with two techs. Hey, a guy his age has to be fucking somebody's mother or else he isn't getting any pussy at all. But I've got a plan. Me and Ham Dick are going to spend the off-season traveling all over the country fucking referees' daughters."

In the tail end of the season the Spirits were still theoretically competing for the last playoff spot when Tico fell and twisted his back in a home game against the Pensacola Tornadoes. As my stint as trainer for the Patroons proved, the players' physical welfare was not among the CBA's top priorities. So when Tico went down, there were no medical personnel on hand, no emergency equipment whatsoever, and he had to be carried off the court lying atop a door that had been hurriedly detached from a storage room—like the mortally wounded Achilles being carried off the battlefield on a shield.

In Tico's place, Regan Truesdale was a total flop. We lost our last four games and finished at 20-28 and out of the playoffs.

In fact, we were 0-8 against Musselman's Thrillers (the eventual league champions) and 20-20 versus the rest of the league. Considering the defensive shortcomings of the team, I thought I had done at least a praiseworthy job.

At the same time, I was well aware of my flaws: the most egregious of these was my being too emotional on the bench, living and dying with each score, missed basket, turnover, and botched assignment. I justified this by convincing myself that my intensity would inspire my players.

But, as with just about everything, I went overboard. I tended to unleash at the referees many of the unconscious resentments I had accumulated throughout my life and ended up leading the CBA in technical fouls. My internal tension was further ratcheted up by the guilt and hostility accompanying the disintegration of my long, unhappy second marriage.

In other words, I was still angry.

Late in the season the Spirits were playing the Tornados in Pensacola, Florida, and as usual I was helplessly demonstrating manic courtside behavior. That was when one of my players, Steve Woodside, casually asked a pivotal question: "Charley, are you having any fun right now?"

I scowled, pointed up at the scoreboard, and quickly said, "If we win, I'll have had fun. But not if we lose."

We lost the game, but I was even more distressed over my inner attitude being unexpectedly exposed. Happiness and suffering recognized only in retrospect. My fundamental well-being entirely based on something I couldn't control. Like a person battling a weight problem, or a TV star addicted to his ratings, numbers alone defined my personal value. I wasn't able to disengage from the multitude of real and imagined off-court worries enough to enjoy the unfolding of the game I loved so much.

The willingness to change is the necessary precursor of change. But I lacked the appropriate tools. My only fallback was to remember the advice of Bill the Ex-Globie: I had to persevere.

The season concluded with a lopsided loss in Tampa Bay. We would be flying out in the morning, but after the game there was still some celebrating to do.

Our rooms were all on the second tier of a rather seedy motel, and after imbibing the requisite postgame beer and pizzas, Bo Dukes instigated a team-wide water fight. Everybody (including me) was running around carrying buckets of water and looking for somebody to douse. The shouts, the laughter—and the moisture—were ubiquitous.

It was round about midnight when the police arrived on the scene.

I quickly identified myself as presumably being in charge

of the mayhem, and I prevailed upon the police to give me a chance to calm things down. But even as I was trying to be imminently reasonable and mature, Bo burst from his room and drenched me with a full pail.

"You're disturbing the peace," one of the cops informed Bo.

"Fuck the peace," was Bo's response as he hurried back into his room to refill his bucket. "There ain't no peace in the CBA."

To their undying credit—and my considerable relief—the cops only laughed at Bo's madcap audacity.

After the law left I managed to gather the players together and warned them that they were in real danger of being arrested if they didn't cease and desist. Plus, they'd have to pay for any damages done. (In fact, we were all docked a hundred dollars each just to replace the soaked mattresses.)

Finally, even Bo simmered down and we all retired to our respective rooms.

And I fantasized that if by some absurdly cosmic quirk of time and space the subject of Leo Tolstoy's masterpiece could be the CBA, he'd have to change the title to *War and War*.

It came as no surprise when I was fired two days after we returned to Savannah. "We're going in a different direction," Robb Larson said.

But my season wasn't quite finished.

I returned to Woodstock ASAP, and Phil called an hour after I walked in the door of my home. The Patroons had finished the season at 26-22 and would be playing the Mississippi Jets in the first round of the playoffs. He invited me to come up to Albany to help him prepare his team for the postseason—and also to sit directly behind the bench for Games 3 and 4, which would be played in the Armory.

Lowes Moore, Derrick Rowland, and Kenny Natt were happy to see me and gladly accepted whatever advice I had to offer. Cedric Henderson had behaved himself in Albany and had developed into a consistent scorer and rebounder, but he wasn't eager to look at me much less pay attention to anything that I had to say.

In a bizarre twist typical of the not-so-wonderful world of the CBA, the Tampa Bay team had relocated to Rapid City, North Dakota, immediately after the regular season ended. After sweeping the Jets, the Patroons next faced the Rapid City Thrillers, who were still coached by Bill Musselman.

For this series the Patroons wound up on the other end of the broom. The last game ended in a 113–112 win for the Thrillers, and the balance was tipped by a horrendous last-second call by one of the refs.

As soon as the final buzzer sounded, Phil's accumulated frustrations overflowed as he grabbed a folding chair and hurled it onto the court. It was his last official act as a CBA coach.

A few months later owner Reggie Henderson was arrested, tried, and found guilty of defrauding the government by overcharging for the requested blood tests. He wound up in jail, Phil wound up being an assistant coach for the Chicago Bulls, and I wound up coaching the Rockford Lightning.

13

King Richard and the Rockford Files

After my debacle in Savannah, another round of celebrity endorsements gained me the coaching position at Rockford, Illinois. Tightly wedged into the very buckle of the Rust Belt, Rockford was once rated the worst city in the country by *Money* magazine. Rockford featured the emptiest libraries in the Western Hemisphere, only two decent restaurants, a highly advanced mall culture, and scores of rabid basketball fans.

The Lightning's owner was Jay Polan, a kindly man who owned a charter bus service in Chicago.

JAY POLAN: *"The operating budget of most teams was a million dollars per season and buying a new or old franchise cost about eight hundred thousand dollars in the golden days of the early and mid-1980s. From the NBA contract we each got about twenty thousand, enough to cover our league dues. There was no TV money and we had to pay for the radio broadcasts of our games by selling advertisements. Some of our income came from signs and banners posted around the arena that we sold to local businesses, ads in our yearbook, team T-shirts, logos, trinkets, and the beer concessions. But*

*our primary source of revenue was gate receipts. At Rockford
our break-even attendance was about four thousand, and our
average attendance was thirty-five hundred. The franchises
in La Crosse, Wisconsin, and Gary, Indiana, usually made
money. The rest of us lost from 250K to 400K every year.
Owning a CBA franchise was either a tax write-off or an expensive hobby. But there were always wealthy businessmen
ready to buy and bring a CBA franchise into their cities because they were positive that the other owners were knuck-
leheads and that only they knew how to turn a profit."*

Polan would wind up in jail two years hence for trying
to bribe somebody on the Chicago City Council into grant-
ing him the most favorable school-bus routes. But because
Polan passed the players illegal bonus bucks under the table, the team's roster always included a sizable contingent
of ex-NBA players.

My first official act as Rockford's new coach in the spring
of 1987 was to prepare for the CBA's college draft. At the
time, the NBA's draft had only three rounds, so there were
still several outstanding players up for grabs.

The fourth overall pick (by Pensacola) was Mark Wade,
an excellent guard who went on to appear in a total of eleven
games for Dallas and Golden State. The eighth pick (by Topeka) was Cedric Hunter, who wound up playing one game
for Charlotte. Other notable selections in that draft were Scott
Brooks (by Albany), who went on to have a long career as
player, assistant coach, and head coach in the NBA, and Eric
Musselman at fifty-eighth overall, who was drafted by Albany, where his dad happened to be coaching at the time.

Rockford's initial selection was the seventh overall, and I
chose Elfrem Jackson from Georgia State, who was cut early

in training camp. My second-round pick was the eighteenth overall, and heeding the advice of Sonny Allen, who had coached him at Nevada-Reno, I tabbed David Wood.

I had never seen Wood play and he turned out to be a gangling yet athletic six-foot-nine, 230-pounder. Trouble was, once training camp began, he had tremendous difficulty learning my offense. For example, I had a box set with an X-call signifying that the play would be initiated on the left side, and a Y-call on the right side. Wood was thoroughly confused until he wrote a big black X on his left sneaker and a Y on his right sneaker.

He made the squad on the basis of his quickness, his hops, his long-distance shooting, and his eagerness to learn. Still, Woody was often wild and out of control, so he mostly sat on the bench. In fact, he was so unpredictable that one of my NBA veterans told me that he didn't want to be on the floor at the same time that Woody was in the game.

Just before I left my home in Woodstock, New York, to arrive in Rockford, I had one more duty: driving down to the New Jersey Nets' training camp to connect with Pace Mannion. A four-year NBA veteran, Pace had played one game for the Lightning in the 1986–87 season before being summoned to finish the season with the Nets.

Should he be cut by the Nets, would he be willing to play in Rockford?

"Absolutely," Pace assured me. "I just want to be playing somewhere."

He was friendly, honest, smart, and a terrific defender, but at six foot seven and with a questionable, low-release jumper Pace was being misused as a point guard by the Nets. Small forward was obviously his natural position.

Having connected with Pace, I then sat back and watched the Nets prepare for practice. I had nearly forgotten that Darryl Dawkins was also on the roster.

The players were lying on their backs as the trainer led them through various warm-up exercises. The arena was silent except for the trainer's occasional directions. Dave Wohl was the Nets' coach of the moment, and he strode through the ranks of the sprawled players wearing a neatly pressed team sweat suit and an air of propriety.

Suddenly the earnest silence was ruptured by a shrill falsetto voice: "Oh, Old Black Joe! Could y'all sing for me one of them Nee-gro spirituals y'all sing so well?"

The faux question was answered with a lazy, sonorous baritone: "Yas'm, Missy Viola. I'se sure be delighted to sing for y'all."

It was Dawkins, of course, who then broke into song: "Ole man ribber, dat ole man ribber . . ."

Wohl was instantly apoplectic. "Let's get serious here! Darryl, practice is no time to be fooling around."

But it was too late. Whatever decorum had been evident was now destroyed as the players convulsed with laughter. Their helpless hysteria was boosted when Darryl responded to his coach's request in the same drowsy, antebellum tone: "Yah suh, Mistah Boss Man."

Rockford's leading holdover player was Richard Rellford from Michigan, known to the Lightning faithful as "King." Rellford was six foot five, weighed about 240, and was a tweener—too short to play a true power game and too slow to play small forward.

Even before the season began I knew that Rellford would be a problem if only because he was the only player I ever heard of who gained weight during training camp. If Rellford loved to eat junk food and hoist up long jumpers, he was disinclined to rebound, run plays, defend, or pass. For obvious reasons I was dissatisfied with his lazy, self-serving game plan—and we often had friendly, but pointed discussions. After all, he was the reigning king and I was a newcomer to his fiefdom. So I settled for periodically reminding him that there was more to the game than just shooting.

Eventually, though, I knew I'd have to go to war with Rellford.

The leader of the team, and by far the best player, was Freddie Cofield, our point guard. Freddie was a veteran of fifty games and two seasons with the Bulls and the Knicks and simply one of my favorite players. He was an incredible clutch shooter (who would eventually win at least a half-dozen games that season with do-or-die treys) of unparalleled intelligence. He was also honest and diligent, and he possessed an incredible sense of humor. Freddie could unilaterally turn a team into a family and, as such, was equally as valuable off the court as he was on the court.

Early in the season we picked up another important player—Pete Myers. In his rookie year with the Chicago Bulls (1986–87), Pete had played only 155 minutes in twenty-nine games. He actually spent most of that season getting abused by Michael Jordan in practice.

At six foot six, 190, Pete was a whippet whose presumed position was shooting guard—actually a misnomer since he had a chicken-wing release and, even in the CBA, was primarily a penetrator and a defender.

In any case, Pete was totally distraught when he was cut late in Chicago's training camp that following year. So overcome with grief was he that he holed up in his hotel room for days. However, after several phone calls, and some encouragement by Phil, Pete was finally convinced to resume his career in the CBA.

Pete was adopted by the always gregarious Cofield. It didn't take long for Pete to abandon his funk and demonstrate what a friendly, vivacious, and all-around nice guy he really was.

Without having to deal with salary caps or guaranteed contracts, I found trading players was an easy undertaking in the CBA. Anybody could be traded for anything—even, as we have seen, a blowjob. It didn't take long for me to engineer my first trade in Rockford.

Anthony Welch was another of Rockford's holdover players, a leansome six-foot-nine small forward. Unfortunately, Welch broke a finger on his shooting hand during a preseason scrimmage and was out of action for several weeks. When he did return to active duty, he took part in a single practice session before suiting up for the opening home game of the season.

Since Welch's timing was still fractured, I gave him only two six-minute rotations—and afterward he was clearly pissed off. In truth, he didn't actually say much to me about his abbreviated playing time but made his feelings known with frowns, shakings of his head, and inaudible mumbles directed at me.

His wife, however, wasn't quite so subtle. As I made my way to the postgame locker room (we'd won by a large margin), she shadowed my every step, loudly cursing me for "screwing up" not only her husband's career but his life and her life as well. I was an "asshole," a "moron," and worse.

In the safety of the locker room, I told Welch to get his wife under control. He just shrugged and said, "She's only telling the truth." And her abuse continued as I reentered the hallway.

My solution was to immediately find the nearest phone, and before I left the building, Welch was traded to Pensacola for the rights to some player who was overseas, or a future draft choice, or a box of jockstraps. I don't rightly remember the deal, and I really didn't care about getting a usable return.

Let his wife go yell at a new coach—Joe Mullaney, late of the Utah Stars. Turned out that Welch was cut just about halfway through the season and never played in the CBA— or anywhere else that I'm aware of—ever again.

Our center was Jim Lampley, a sloe-eyed seven-footer who could do everything—shoot, pass, rebound, block shots, post up—but only when the spirit was upon him. A nice guy with bona fide NBA talent, he had played one solitary game with Philadelphia in 1987—sixteen minutes, 1-3 from the field, 5 rebounds, and 3 total points. Too bad Lamp was so easily distracted.

Carl Henry was a truly exceptional shooter who had bounced around the CBA—playing for Puerto Rico and Cincinnati—while also appearing in twenty-eight games for Sacramento. Carl was also good people, but his defensive shortcomings kept him from starter's minutes.

Our starting power forward was John Fox—six foot ten, 225—who had been the Bulls' third-round draft and had been one of the last cuts in Chicago's training camp. Foxie's specialty was rebounding, and his primary deficiency was a lack of toughness. He was a wonderful young man who palled around with David Wood.

The Bulls general manager, Jerry Krause, asked me to play Foxie as much as possible—which I did.

All told, we had a nice squad. Had King Richard been more interested in banging the boards, we easily might have been among the CBA's elite teams.

Even so, one particular early-season game led me to believe that we were legitimate championship contenders.

Freddie's backup—Bruce Douglas out of Illinois—was simply the best defensive point guard that I ever coached. He was six foot three, 195, and a veteran of eight games with the 1986–87 Sacramento Kings. Douglas had incredibly quick hands and feet, tremendous defensive range, and uncanny anticipation. During his ninety-eight-minute NBA career, he posted 9 steals and 17 assists—not unsubstantial totals given such limited daylight.

However, Bruce's major flaw was his inability to shoot the ball. He was 7 for 24 (29.2 percent) from the field with the Kings, plus 0 for 4 from the stripe. A minor failing was his frequent carelessness with the ball—9 turnovers.

In the CBA, however, Douglas was a dynamic and unsurpassed defender. Even so, Freddie was a better all-around player, leader, shooter, and clutch scorer—so Douglas came off the bench.

We were hosting an expansion team, the Quad City Thunder, which would turn out to be Rockford's archrival. With only 6:22 left in the game, we were down by 26 points. But with Douglas running wild—stealing, deflecting, shot-blocking—we won the game in regulation.

No lie!

Still, I had to cut Douglas about two weeks later.

Why?

Because he never stopped bitterly complaining about the lack of shots that our offense provided for him. Which moved him to fire up long jumpers at every opportunity.

"Bruce," I'd say to him. "You're taking bad shots and you're missing them. Believe me, you're not going to shoot your way back into the NBA."

"You don't understand, Coach," was his riposte. "I've got to prove that I'm really a good shooter."

"No, it's you who doesn't understand. All you're doing is proving that you're a bad shooter."

He just shrugged and kept firing blanks.

His defense was so exceptional, however, that I could easily live with his ill-advised shot selection. But when he began fomenting discord by ruthlessly bad-mouthing all of his teammates to anybody who would listen, then I had to cut him loose.

Throughout the season players came and went—mostly to and from NBA and European teams. We went through "only" nineteen players, while Quad City suited up a total of thirty players.

In-season tryouts were also commonplace, but the one that occurred in Rockford was a standout. The young man's name was Aurang Zeb, he was nineteen years old, he hailed from Pakistan, and he measured seven feet, eight and a half inches.

Zeb's agent, whose name I've long since forgotten, swore that Zeb was the starting center on a team that represented Pakistan's navy. And he was hopeful that a successful tryout with the Lightning would result in a five-year visa that would allow Zeb to attend a university in the United States.

I was anxious to see what the young man had.

First off, he wore a black uniform that was trimmed in white but had no identifying logos. He also wore a pair of strange-looking sneakers, also of unknown origin, that had to be at least size 30. And lastly, he wore a pair of thin black business stockings that were neatly rolled down to his ankles.

With his agent (clad in a rumpled blue suit) chasing down his misses, Zeb undertook to shoot free throws on a side basket prior to a team practice. He shot the ball from his hip and actually showed a decent shot release while making perhaps 70 percent of his attempts.

Then he demonstrated his lay-ups—all of them right-handed and just about all of them true.

"What about a dunk shot?" I asked.

Zeb's response was, "No dunk."

Meanwhile, the other players were running half-speed laps around the court in preparation for their stretching routine. (Never stretch cold muscles!) So I asked Zeb if he would join them.

"No run," he said.

Too bad. Although his agent was too pushy, Zeb seemed like a nice young man. Indeed, he seemed embarrassed by the whole deal. But if he couldn't run, then he couldn't play. Sorry.

No problem, said the agent. They had an appointment in two days to meet with coach Steve Yoder at the University of Wisconsin. Then they'd be on to La Crosse to showcase Zeb to another CBA outfit, the Catbirds. Next on the list was Ohio State.

The agent vowed that their road show wouldn't stop until some coach wiser than me would see Zeb's potential and sign him up.

This was more than twenty years ago. I hope that Zeb has indeed found someplace where he belongs. Someplace where he can be safe, happy, and productive without having to run.

For some reason every CBA team I ever coached was on the road for Thanksgiving. That year, 1987, we were in Rapid City, South Dakota, preparing to play the hometown Thrillers in a nationally televised (ESPN) game on Thanksgiving Day. In order to maximize the audience, the scheduled start was 11:00 a.m. local time.

On the night before the game, I told Pete Myers this: "The Thrillers are the home team, so they're looking forward to a big postgame Thanksgiving feast with their teammates, their friends, whomever. Some of them will also be a little distressed at spending the holiday away from their families—as we all are. Because of all that, and because of the early starting time, it'll be difficult for anybody to be in top form. What you could do, Pete, is to get to bed early tonight and really get yourself psyched for the game. Because it's on national TV, you know that NBA coaches and scouts will be tuned in. Here's your chance to have a bust-out game and get back into The League where you belong."

He agreed.

Turned out that we won the game, 114–94, and none of the Thrillers could come close to matching Pete's intensity. He wound up with eleven steals, and a few weeks later— as soon as the ten-day contracts went into effect—Pete was signed by San Antonio.

All told, Pete played in the NBA for nine seasons (with Chicago, San Antonio, Philadelphia, New York, Miami, and Charlotte), averaging 4.8 ppg, appearing in 377 games, and starting in 100.

This was a sterling example of good things happening to good people—even during a CBA Thanksgiving.

These days Pete is an assistant coach with the Bulls. His defensive expertise is widely renown, but I expect he's not giving jump-shooting lessons to anybody.

During the off-season I had recruited another player from the Albany Patroons' championship season—John Schweitz. Since his time with the Patroons John had played briefly in the NBA with Seattle and Detroit (a total of twenty-two games), and then with the Cincinnati Slammers.

He and his wife lived in Watertown, New York, and they arrived in Rockford with all of their belongings in a small trailer that was hitched to the back of their car.

We had an enjoyable reunion, and I planned to use John as the designated scorer with the second unit. However, his sneakers were much heavier than they used to be, he'd lost his jumper somewhere along the way, and his defense—never terrific to begin with—was downright awful.

After thirteen games, when Alfrederick Hughes became available, I had to cut John. What made the decision even more painful was that John was let go on Christmas Eve and had to drive back to Watertown through a snowstorm.

Not to mention that he left without reimbursing me for the hundred dollars I had previously lent him.

Alfrederick Hughes, who had just been released by a team in Spain, had been San Antonio's first-round draft pick (fourteenth overall) back in 1985. He had been a dynamic scorer at Loyola in Chicago, but he couldn't make the grade in the NBA—lasting only one season, shooting 40.9 percent, and averaging 5.2 points per game.

Upon arriving in Rockford, he instructed the general manager to call him "Al," the owner of the team to call him "Fred," and me to call him "Rick." Unfortunately, although he had a picture-perfect jumper, he turned out to be an extremely unreliable shooter. At least he played better defense than Schweitz had.

Here's the story behind another typically bizarre CBA transaction that the Lightning made that season: It seems that the Wyoming Wildcatters were in deep financial trouble. Their host city—Casper, the Friendly Ghost Town—simply didn't have the population to support a team. Desperate to boost their gate, the Wildcatters' owners decided to run a sensational halftime giveaway.

During the midgame intermission, a band-new Chevrolet was driven out to center court. The deal was this: Both the first page and the center page of every program (sold for two dollars each) were stamped with numbers unique to that specific program. The fans were invited to pull out the center page, fashion it into a paper airplane, stand anywhere they wished along the sidelines, and launch their missile toward the car. The first one that flew through the open sunroof would win the car.

The car dealer had guaranteed that such accuracy was virtually impossible, especially if the arena's ventilation grids were tilted just so and the fans turned on full blast.

Of course, one lucky fan defied the odds.

The team owners were aghast, and so was the car dealer. What could be done?

To refuse the car to the winner would be tantamount to the franchise folding in a flash. The dealer, in his desire to keep the Wildcatters in town, agreed to sell the car to the team for $5,000.

Eventually, the Wildcatters contacted the league's wealthiest team and allowed the Rockford Lightning to buy their best player—center Brad Wright—for the five grand.

Brad was a seven-footer out of UCLA, a classic back-to-the-basket center, an exuberantly friendly guy, and an extremely coachable player. He had previously played with the Cincinnati Slammers and had received a brief (fourteen games) look-see by the Knicks.

Unfortunately, Wright only lasted in Rockford for six games before being called up to the Denver Nuggets. And the Wildcatters continued to operate on a shoestring, losing huge amounts of money before ceasing operations two years later.

Brad had greatly improved his game since he'd graduated and was an extremely effective post-up player in CBA competition, but his most memorable moment occurred in an airport.

The Lightning were traveling from Rapid City, South Dakota, on our way back home. We managed to survive a prop-job puddle-jumper from Rapid City to Denver and were preparing to board a big-bellied jet for the trip to Chicago (where we'd then take a bus to Rockford).

The team and I were at the boarding gate having our passes checked when Brad suddenly said this: "Charley, I can't get on this plane. It's jinxed. I mean it. Something's going to happen before it reaches Chicago."

Wright handed me his boarding pass and said that he would pay his own fare on another flight to Chicago—and then he walked away.

It had been a long, multicity road trip and the flight from Rapid City had departed at 6:00 a.m., so we were all exhausted. Even so, the other players and I were wide-eyed and fearful all throughout the flight to Chicago.

Even though we all managed to conk out during the ninety-minute bus ride to Rockford, I thought it best to cancel the evening practice session I had previously arranged. And when the team convened for a shootaround the following morning, Wright seemed genuinely surprised to see us all.

My relationship with "King" Richard Rellford came to a head during and after a game in La Crosse, Wisconsin.

The day before we bused up to La Crosse, Elston Turner joined the team after being cut by the Chicago Bulls. A native of Knoxville, Tennessee, Elston wound up playing eight seasons in the NBA with Dallas, Chicago, and Denver. At six foot five, 200, he was a lock-down defender with a flawed jump shot. More important, he was honest, modest, intelligent, and an all-around good guy. (He later became a respected assistant coach in the NBA with Portland and Houston.) During the four-hour ride from Rockford to La Crosse, ET studied, and mastered, my thick playbook. In fact, by the time we arrived, he was more familiar with our offenses and defenses than was Rellford.

The game itself proved to be a disaster for us. Nothing seemed to go our way and we trailed by 20 points at the first-quarter break with Rellford's lackadaisical play being a primary factor. That's when I decided to pull all of the starters and give the brothers of the pine a long look.

To no avail.

We lost the second and third quarters by sizable margins, and with our deficit approaching 30 points, I once more made wholesale substitutions and kept the starters glued to the bench for the entire fourth quarter. The final score was 139–90.

In the postgame locker room, I was about to begin a heated harangue when Rellford beat me to it.

"I know what you're trying to do to me, Charley," he shouted.

"What's that?"

"Break me down. Destroy me. That's the only reason why you didn't play me in the fourth quarter."

"Richard," I said, trying my best to control my anger and my disbelief. "We got stomped in every quarter you played in, so what makes you think that the fourth quarter would have been any different?"

"It would've been because I'm the best player on this team."

"That's your opinion."

"Anyway, I'm not gonna let you beat me, Charley."

My last word was "Whatever."

Just as we left the locker room, ET took me aside. "This is the craziest thing I've ever seen. What have I gotten myself into?"

I could only shrug and say, "I ask myself the same question every day."

After getting mauled in La Crosse, we arrived the next morning in Albany to play that night against Bill Musselman's league-leading Patroons—which consisted of once and former NBA players such as Tod Murphy, Scott Roth, Tony Campbell, Derrick Rowland, Michael Brooks, Scott Brooks, Eric Fernsten, Lowes Moore, and Michael Ray Richardson. Truly an outstanding ball club.

Because of Rellford's outburst after the La Crosse game, the King started the game on the bench and only played about ten total minutes. And with ET feeling more comfortable, we played inspired ball.

In fact, the game wasn't decided until the final play. We were ahead 108–107 and the Patroons had the ball. Musselman's win-or-lose call was to run a clear-out for Roth.

So there it was: Roth dribbling at the top of the key looking for the game-winning score. Unfortunately for Roth, he was being guarded at close quarters by Elston Turner, who had been an extraordinary defender during his long NBA career. No matter how many fakes and jukes Roth attempted, ET refused to be suckered out of position. The startled look in Roth's eyes showed how confused he was by Turner's stubbornly adhesive defense—and Roth eventually responded by backing away.

By now the game clock was about to explode, and Muss was screaming his brains out from the Patroons bench. "Go! Go!"

Roth stayed clear of Turner and wound up taking a weak fadeaway jumper that barely scraped the rim as the buzzer sounded.

Musselman was still steaming as our paths crossed in the vestibule outside the locker rooms.

"I know what you did, Charley! You can't fool me!"

Say what?

"How many points did you lose by in La Crosse last night?"

"Forty-nine."

"Don't tell me I'm lying, Charley, but you tanked that game. You threw it. You deliberately lost it."

"Why would I do that, Muss?"

"To lull my players into a false sense of security. If you dumped the game up in La Crosse, then you'd do the same thing here. I ought to report you to the commissioner. Hell, I ought to report you to the FBI."

Then he stormed away.

Craziness on top of craziness.

Of course, the next morning I traded Rellford to Wyoming for a player to be named later.

Home and away, I must have coached in at least seventy-five different venues during my nine-year stint in the CBA. If the arena in Cedar Rapids, Iowa, eventually proved the most troublesome for me, I still retain the fondest memories of the Wharton Field House, where the Quad City Thunder played.

The old Tri-Cities Blackhawks played there in the early days of the NBA, and it was a stately redbrick building situated in Moline, Illinois. Inside, the fans were right on top of, and right behind, both benches and were always passionately involved in the games—even more so because of the intrastate rivalry between the Thunder and the Rockford Lightning. However, as vigorously as the fans cheered the good guys and booed the bad guys, they were still well behaved.

The Thunder was coached by Mauro Panaggio, a wily veteran of the CBA, whose teams always played hard. And because he was forever altering his rosters and his offenses, preparing to play one of Mauro's teams was always a difficult task.

There was a hint of friction between us only because Mauro had coached the Lightning two seasons before I arrived in town. Even so, our relationship was as friendly as the circumstances made possible—at least for a while.

The main objection I had to the Field House was the court itself. Whereas professional courts are mandated to be ninety-six feet long, the floor in Wharton was ten feet shorter. Mauro, of course, took advantage of this shortcoming by employing various highly effective full- and three-quarter-court presses.

After my first visit to Wharton, I chanced to opine to the gathered postgame media that playing there was akin to playing in "a telephone booth."

The next time I brought the Lightning to town, a full-sized telephone booth was wheeled out to center court during a time-out. Subsequently, the phone rang and the bizarrely dressed Thunder mascot exited the booth, wobbled over to me, and handed me the receiver and a microphone—while the public address announcer blared, "It's for you, Charley."

I went along with the gag, took the receiver and the mike,

and ordered a pizza to be delivered to the visitors' locker room at halftime.

Henceforth, whenever the Lightning visited the Field House, the Quad City management always had some kind of telephone bit to entertain the local fans—and me, too. Sometimes the paid customers would receive miniature telephones, and when a loud ringing was broadcast over the PA system, they'd point the phones at me and say in unison, "It's for you, Charley!" Sometimes they'd go through the same routine even if phones were not distributed.

Also, pregame ads in the local newspapers promoting any upcoming Lightning-Thunder games at Wharton invariably featured some cartoon rendition of a phone booth and me.

It was all great fun.

That is, until one particular night when everything turned mean.

There was an extremely narrow aisle separating both teams' benches from the first row of bleacher seats behind them, and the aisle was covered with a long flimsy strip of rug that was always wrinkled.

Even worse, the entrance to the visitors' locker room was immediately adjacent to an exit door.

It happened that after losing an extremely close and aggravating game to the Thunder, my players rode the rushing tide of the quickly exiting crowd and approached our locker room. However, the door to our space was locked, which meant that my sweating players had to stand in the hallway about a foot from the exit door waiting for someone to arrive with the proper key.

To add to the problem, standard procedure in the CBA was for a team's warm-ups to be taken from the bench to their locker room minutes before the game ended. This was done to prevent theft.

Worse still, the outside temperature was several degrees below zero. And because of the migration of the capacity crowd, the outside door stayed wide open.

Plus, the jamming of the crowd through this one door created a solid wall of wrong-way traffic that prohibited the players from battling their way back into the relative warmth of the court itself.

Freezing winds on bare sweating skins. I had visions of team-wide pneumonia.

Because I was trailing my players, I succeeded with great effort in making my way back to the scorers' table. With as much restraint as I could muster—which wasn't much—I explained the situation to a security guard. His reaction was to shrug and claim he had no idea who might have the key.

I got the same reaction from the official scorer, who was still at the table collating the game stats.

By now I was irate. Pounding my fist against the table, I started shouting: "Who has the fucking key!"

Nobody knew nothing.

Intent on kicking down the locker-room door, I quickly wheeled around . . . and tripped on a huge wrinkle in the cheapo rug, lost my balance, and was about to fall headfirst into the first row of bleacher seats.

But there was somebody sitting in my landing spot. A young boy, perhaps seven or eight, holding a plastic telephone. "It's for you, Charley," he said with a big smile.

To avoid crushing the boy, it was all I could to stretch out my arms so that they straddled the boy as they crashed into the seats. I suffered severe bone-bruises on the palms of each hand, and I couldn't prevent myself from slightly brushing the boy with my left shoulder.

The boy, of course, was frightened and started to cry.

"Sorry," I said. But I was distracted when a maintenance man hurried past me with the key in hand.

Okay, no harm done.

Right?

Wrong.

Headlines in the local newspapers and the local telecasts claimed that I was raging mad after the loss. I was so angry, in fact, that I had assaulted a young boy in the stands.

The league, of course, was ready to fine and suspend me. But I went unpunished when I told my side of the story.

In my subsequent visit to Wharton, the fans weren't quite so friendly.

After another "It's for you, Charley" routine, one loud-mouthed fan yelled this: "It's the state police, Charley! They want you to coach the team in Attica!"

Bill Klucas was a solid, professional coach with old-time values and years of experience in a long alphabet list of minor-league basketball teams. His Xs and Os were exemplary, and his talent evaluations were sound. However, Bill's major problem was being a bit too dictatorial to suit the moods and personalities of the modern players.

Bill's Rochester Flyers, in Minnesota, featured ex-NBA players like David Thirdkill, McKinley Singleton, and Jose Slaughter—but the players and their coach didn't have the right mix for success.

The Lightning visited the Flyers at the tail-end of the 1987–88 season, bringing with us a record of 33-15, which was just about the reverse of the home team's record to date. No surprise, then, that we dominated the first half. That's why I didn't have much to tell my guys during the intermission.

However, the locker rooms of the two teams were separated by a thin board of plywood that was situated at the back of the showers. Just as I began my "keep up the good work" spiel, we heard loud and distinct curses coming from the Flyers' side of the plywood wall.

"Don't tell me what to do, motherfucker!"

Immediately, my players and I hustled over to the thin wall and pressed our eager ears against it. And the argument continued with even more gusto.

"I'm the goddamn boss here!"

"You ain't shit!"

Then some scuffling followed by generic shoutings and various thumps and bumps—before everything quieted down.

In the second half of the game we completed the rout, eventually winning by the score of 101–83. Rockford was led by Jim Lampley's 22 points and 16 rebounds, while Rochester's leading lights were Thirdkill (25 points) and Brian Christensen (9 rebounds).

Shortly after the game, we discovered what the halftime fuss was all about.

It seemed that the home team had a soda dispenser in their locker room, and during Klucas's halftime excoriation of his players' effort, David Thirdkill walked over to the apparatus and started filling a paper cup with soda. Seeing this, Klucas freaked out. Because of their miserable performance, there'd be no soda for his players.

That's when the frustration of their losing season boiled over.

Thirdkill ignored his coach's order and continued filling the cup. Whereupon Klucas stormed over, reached out, and knocked the half-filled cup to the floor.

Thirdkill reacted by grabbing Klucas in a headlock and threatening to punch his face in.

The other players took a few moments to consider what they should do about the turn of events. Eventually, a few of them interceded and broke up the melee before Thirdkill could actually start punching away.

Klucas was fired later that night. And guess who the interim coach was: David Thirdkill.

After winning one game, Thirdkill was replaced by Scott Carlin, who was too nice to be a successful coach at this level. And the franchise was transplanted to Omaha after the 1989–90 season.

Late in the season, we picked up a lifetime CBAer, Ron Spivey, a six-foot-seven, 220-pound power forward out of Louisiana Tech—and one of my all-time favorite players. He was an intelligent, extremely aggressive player who was a total stopper on defense. If he wasn't much of a shooter, he rarely took shots he couldn't make. And if he would have been two inches taller and twenty pounds heavier, he certainly could've been an NBA player.

But sometimes his intensity got the better of him.

The Rockford Lightning were concluding a practice session and we were huddled in the lane while I reminded the players about our upcoming road trip. *Be at the airport at such and such a time. We'll be gone for eight days . . .* Even as they shuffled their feet and tenderly fondled basketballs, the guys were paying as much attention as they could muster.

Suddenly, Spivey took a step toward the basket, jumped, and violently slammed the ball through the basket. Then he caught the ball on a high bounce, leaped for the sky, and re-dunked with the same awesome energy. He repeated this routine five times, six times, seven times . . . again and again and again. Working up a running sweat, he worked in total silence, not even grunting with the effort.

After perhaps a dozen slams, he suddenly stopped, and casually resumed his spot in the loose huddle.

The rest of us were speechless, until I finally asked, "Ron, what was that? Why did you do that?"

He looked at me with his calm brown eyes and said this: "Do what?"

As the regular season dwindled down to a precious few games, we visited the La Crosse Catbirds, a powerhouse team under the direction of Ron Ekker that eventually finished at 40-14, the second-best mark in the history of the CBA.

With twenty-four seconds left in the game, we trailed by six and as the players gathered around me in the huddle, I crouched and repeatedly banged an open palm against the floor, saying, "We're gonna win this game! We're gonna win this fucking game!"

Then I called Freddie Cofield's number for the ump-teenth time that season. "Freddie," I said, "we need a three-pointer."

"Okay," he said.

"Good. After Freddie knocks down the three, we want to foul Chris McNealy as soon as possible. Got it?"

When play resumed, Freddie dropped the trey, and Mc-Nealy was fouled as he caught the inbounds pass. Heading for the foul line at the far end of the court, McNealy gave me a surprised look. After all, hadn't he already played 108 games with the Knicks over the course of three seasons? Hadn't I treated him with the utmost respect when he played for the Patroons? And did I really think the pressure of a game in What's-Izz, Wisconsin, would get to him?

Yes.

And it did.

After he missed both freebies, I burned my last time-out and called for Freddie to stage a repeat performance.

Which he did—at the buzzer.

We wound up winning, 115–108, in overtime, with Freddie scoring 49 points.

The game was so discombobulating to the top-seeded Catbirds that they were eventually upset in the opening round of the playoffs, 4-2, by the fourth-seeded Wyoming Wildcatters.

David Wood's heart-felt acceptance of Christianity resulted in a minor miracle during a game in Casper, Wyoming. That's when Elston Turner went down with a twisted ankle that appeared to be as serious an injury as I'd ever witnessed. Racing onto the court, I feared that ET's ankle was fractured and that his playing career was over. My fears were increased when it was obvious that the otherwise stoic Turner was in excruciating pain.

However, hot on my heels was Woody, who proceeded to lay his hands on ET's ankle, softly recite a prayer, and ask for healing. Almost immediately, the relaxation evident in ET's face proved that the pain had suddenly eased.

Turned out that x-rays were negative and that Turner returned to action in about ten days.

My fourteen-year-old son, Darrell, accompanied the team on that particular trip to Wyoming, and Freddie Cofield took a liking to him. During a stopover in Denver on our way back to Rockford, Darrell had to visit the men's room. "Me, too," said Freddie. Then he turned to the rest of us and said, "I'm gonna teach this young man the secret of life."

A few minutes later Darrell burst through the swinging door with a wide grin on his face and Freddie following close behind. Darrell obviously had something he couldn't wait to say in front of the gathered players.

Wiping his hands together, this is what Darrell finally blurted out: "Bitches ain't shit!"

Even though Elston Turner was re-signed by the Bulls late in the season, the Lightning finished the regular season at 37-17 and prepared to meet the Thunder in the first round of the playoffs. The morning that we were scheduled to bus our way to the Quad Cities to begin the series, I got a call from Pace Mannion, saying that he'd just been cut by the Milwaukee Bucks. He added he would immediately set out on the two-hour drive to Rockford and arrive in time to board the bus.

Okay. But his imminent arrival meant that I had to adjust the roster.

So I called Alfrederick Hughes and told him that he was being cut. Hughes was always a nice guy and we'd had a strictly businesslike relationship. He was glum, but he understood the realities of professional sports.

Next up, I called the CBA office and spoke to the commissioner, Jay Ramsdell, who also happened to be a good friend and a reasonable man. Ramsdell recorded the roster change—Hughes was out and Mannion was in.

However, just a few minutes later, I got another call from Mannion. There was some kind of delay with the paperwork in Milwaukee and he had two immediate options: arrive in Rockford a half-hour or so after the bus was scheduled to depart, or show up in Rockford later that evening.

Whoops!

So I called Ramsdell and explained the situation. What I needed to do was rescind the roster move—keep Hughes and forget about Mannion—just to make sure that we'd have a full roster. Ramsdell fussed for a while. The "do-over" was highly illegal, but since he wasn't a fan of Mauro Panaggio, Quad City's coach, and since the original transaction hadn't yet been officially released, he acceded to my request.

Next up was another call to Hughes, advising him that he was back on the team. He was puzzled but didn't say much.

The other players knew that something was afoot when I, who had a reputation for always adhering to timely departures, had the bus idle for thirty minutes just in case Pace did show up. But he never did arrive, so we left.

Guess who was waiting for us at the Wharton Field House in Moline?

Pace Mannion.

A quick call to Ramsdell and the original transaction was reinstated. Now I had to face Hughes and tell him that he was indeed being cut—which he'd already figured out once he saw Mannion.

Again, Hughes was disappointed but accepting of his fate—and he simply vanished into the night.

After downing the Quad City Thunder in seven pulse-pounding games—with Pace having a terrific series—the Lightning then squared off against Cazzie Russell's Wildcatters in the Eastern Conference finals. Unfortunately, Mannion broke a bone in his shooting hand in Game 5 and we headed back to Rockford down three games to two.

Game 6 turned out to be one of the most exciting contests ever.

Wyoming's stalwarts were Kenny Natt, Ron Cavenall, Steffond Johnson, Todd Mitchell, and Michael Phelps, guys who had already, or were destined to, log some time in the NBA. Also on Wyoming's roster was Richard Rellford.

In the initial five games, Rellford had hurt us by hitting a number of clutch-time jumpers. *Ouch!* But, despite their 3-2 advantage, the Wildcatters were undergoing some internal difficulties. The primary one was the fact that the players had totally tuned out their coach, Russell. Indeed, after listlessly listening to his comments during huddles, the players would rehuddle on the court and formulate their own strategies.

Nonetheless, we were trailing by double digits and playing uninspired basketball when we retreated to our locker room during the halftime intermission. After making some strategic tweaks in our game plan, I spoke to Freddie Cofield in private.

Before sending the team out for the second half, I glanced at the stat sheet and saw that Cofield had scored only 6 points.

"Freddie," I said, "you've got to be more aggressive on offense or we're done for."

"Got it," he said.

And he surely did get it. Behind Freddie's determined point-making, we staged a dramatic rally to send the game into overtime. The first overtime, that is.

There was also a second OT, and a third, but the game wasn't decided until the fourth extra period. After sixty-seven minutes of thrilling competition that featured an abundance of clutch shooting, spectacular plays, and foul shots (Wyoming shot twenty more free throws than we did), the deciding factor was a bogus call by Steve Javie.

The Lightning was up by 134–131 with only twenty seconds remaining. One defensive stand and the game would be ours. Our immediate game plan was to switch at all crossings, pressure perimeter shooters to prevent open three-ball attempts, and send them to the basket. However, with the clock ticking down, David Wood had overreacted to ball penetration by Phelps and left his man, Steffond Johnson, unattended along the left baseline.

Woody made a valiant attempt to attack the shot, but from my vantage point (which was about eighty feet away but on the same side of the court) it was clear that his flailing hand missed touching either the ball or any part of Johnson's body by at least twelve inches. The shot barely grazed the rim. Nevertheless, Javie tooted his tooter, called the foul on Woody, and sent Johnson to the line. He stepped up and converted all three of his free throws.

Phil Jackson happened to be on hand for the game and was sitting courtside just a step away from the action. "I had a great angle on the play," Jackson told me afterward, "and there was about sixteen inches of daylight between Wood and Johnson."

Even more convincing was Wood's testimony. David was (and is) a devout Christian whose honesty was beyond questioning. "Coach," he said to me during the next time-out, "I never came close to making contact. That was the worst call I've ever been a part of."

How could a referee, who's currently considered to be one of the best in the NBA, botch such an easy call?

Because most of the CBA's refs were contracted to also work several dozen NBA games over the course of the season—Javie being among them. Accordingly, once having experienced the NBA glow, too many of these guys viewed anything to do with the CBA with disdain. As a result, CBA coaches and players who had previously played or coached in The League always got the benefit of the doubt against CBA lifers. Johnson was already a veteran of one full season with the L.A. Clippers, while Wood's NBA days were still ahead of him.

Javie's ruinous call was based more on status and wishful thinking than on reality.

Oh, well.

Even though the score was now knotted at 134, we never scored again—mainly because Curtis Green missed a lay-up. The final was 137–134.

Cofield played all sixty-eight minutes and finished with 51 points. The Wildcatters went on to lose the championship to Albany—but they did so without the services of Rellford, who was called up to San Antonio immediately before the finals. Rellford's NBA career lasted four games and his stats were admirable—5-8 from the field, 6-8 from the stripe, 7 rebounds, 4 turnovers, 4 blocks, and 4.0 ppg in only forty-two minutes—but his defensive ineptitude did him in.

Two days after the aggravating season-ending loss, I was driving down State Street, Rockford's main drag, and still replaying the game. I was barely paying attention to my driving and was shocked back to reality when a cop stopped me.

"You were doing 60 in a 30 zone," he said. Then he recognized me and said, "Oh, I guess you're still thinking about the game, huh? You know, I was sitting right near the play and I could've walked sideways in the space between Woody's hand and Johnson. You know what, Charley? I'm gonna let you go with a warning. Keep your mind on your driving. Okay?"

I was effusive in my appreciation. But I would have traded a speeding ticket plus a week in the slammer for a righteous call from Javie.

14

The Pacer, the D-Train, and Mr. Animal

A few short weeks after the 1987–88 season ended, I signed on for my second season as Rockford's coach. My salary was now up to thirty-five thousand, plus a rent-free house, and a brand-new Audi to use for the duration of the season. As a special bonus, all of my technical fouls would be paid for—which would come to about three thousand dollars.

Dick Bavetta was a ref with a reputation for making biased calls, and just before the opening of training camp, I learned firsthand that he was indeed a jerk. As the senior NBA referee, Bavetta was addressing a preseason meeting of the CBA's coaches to go over some new rules and new interpretations of some old rules. When he was finished, he asked for questions.

It seems that several of my players had been complaining for years about some of the CBA refs' after-game activities. Given the relatively small cities that hosted CBA franchises, there weren't many appropriate nightclubs and bars to choose from where the players could party after the games. Those refs who were likewise interested in the same nocturnal pursuits were faced with the same limitations and subsequently frequented the very same venues.

Given all the available alcohol and female companionship, there was bound to be rivalries and confrontations between the players and the refs—edgy face-offs that the players swore subsequently influenced the refs' on-court judgment.

So I brought the subject to Bavetta's attention, emphasizing that it was never a healthy situation when refs and players tried to romance the same women. Didn't Bavetta think it would be best if the CBA refs were prohibited from frequenting these venues?

Bavetta's response was to start laughing. "What's the matter, Charley? One of the refs got a girl you were after?"

Everybody joined in the laughter, and that was the end of that.

Early in the subsequent season one of my players moaned when he saw that a certain ref was working the game. "Charley," the player said, "last week that guy was drooling all over the girl I was with at a club in Tampa Bay, and I had to get up in his face to make him go away. I'm telling you, man, it's gonna be payback time."

Sure enough, when the player merely shook his head after the ref tooted him for a charge that clearly should have been a block, two back-to-back toots signified a pair of technical fouls and banishment.

"What did I tell you, Charley?" the player said as he headed for the locker room.

The other team converted both Ts, and we eventually lost the game by one point.

Thanks, Dick.

A few games later, during a time-out in an away game,

one of the refs was called over to the scorer's table where he began an earnest conversation with the home team's radio guy. Barely containing his subsequent laughter, the refs approached me with the good news.

It seemed that one NBA ref had just taken a punch at another NBA ref. The good news became even better when the ref said this: "I sure hope that it was Dick Bavetta who got clocked."

And it was!

In the previous spring, Gerald Paddio had been the Celtics' third-round draft pick (seventy-fourth overall) out of UNLV, and when he failed to make the grade in Boston his rights reverted to Rockford. Paddio had all of the physical attributes to succeed in pro ball—he could run, jump, and hit long-range shots fairly reliably.

In fact, Paddio eventually went on to have an erratic three-year career in the NBA with Cleveland, Seattle, Indiana, New York, and Washington. That's 129 games divided among five teams in three seasons—an indication of how much physical potential Paddio possessed. Too bad he was unwilling to pass, defend, and execute plays that didn't end up with a shot for him. Plus he was incredibly immature.

He succeeded in demonstrating his adolescent mind-set even before the CBA season began when the Rockford management arranged a gala Meet the Players party for the Lightning's season-ticket holders. Paddio had had a promising training camp and was penciled in as a starter—but as the fans moseyed around the room, glad-handing the players and getting autographs, Paddio made himself unavailable.

Instead of socializing, he was curled up in a far corner of the room with his girlfriend where they were blatantly fondling each other. If what they were doing wasn't exactly R-rated, it was at least PG-13.

So I walked over for a little chat.

"Gerald," I said, "I don't think that what you're doing is appropriate. What you're supposed to be doing is making nice-nice with the fans. They're the ones who pay your salary."

(In Rockford, his surprisingly decent hotel accommodations were paid for by the Lightning, he'd get $20 per diem on the road, and his weekly paycheck came to about $350.)

Without ceasing to explore his girlfriend's most obvious charms, Paddio laughed and said: "This CBA is nowhere, man. I'm an NBA player and this is a hick town. And don't be telling me about my salary. I got paid more money at UNLV than I'm getting here."

A few days later I traded him to the Rochester Flyers— where he averaged 13.9 ppg for a sad-sack team that set a CBA single-season record for fewest wins on the road. Zero.

Which was approximately the sum total of what resulted from Paddio's considerable talents.

We opened at home with a 92–80 drubbing of Cedar Rapids, winning every quarter and coming away with all seven available standing points. Ron Spivey had the game of his life—23 points and 8 rebounds. But one of my players was distraught—Kenny Green, a six-foot-seven forward out of Wake Forest who had spent the past two seasons in the NBA. With Philadelphia and Washington, Green had averaged 10.1 minutes in sixty games, shot 41.2 percent from the field, had three times as many turnovers as assists, and tallied 4.4 points per game.

Like his NBA coaches, I was unhappy with his inadequate handle, reluctance to pass, and nonexistent defense. So he came off the bench in Rockford's season opener, logging eleven minutes, 9 points, 6 rebounds, 1 assist, and 2 turn-overs—excellent overall production for his limited playing time. My intention was to use him as the backup to both Lampley and a sensational shot-blocking rookie named Derrick Lewis.

But immediately after the game Green cornered me outside the locker-room door and assailed me for not giving him enough daylight. "I'm an NBA player," he said. "I should be starting in this bullshit league."

"Be patient," I said. "Things will sort themselves out."

"Later for that. I want out of here now."

So I got on the phone and traded him to Topeka that very night. Subsequently, Green played four games for Topeka before he was dealt to Quad City. After seventeen games, Green then wound up in Tulsa (twenty-two games). The next season he competed in a few games for Cedar Rapids and has not been heard from since.

Once the season got rolling, this edition of the Lightning soon developed into my favorite CBA team. Pace Mannion and Freddie Cofield were not only superb players, but they kept everybody laughing—plus they both were able to cajole Lampley into playing as hard as he could for as long as he could. Derrick Lewis was a wonderful young man. Dwayne McClain evolved into an explosive scorer and was always smiling with genuine good cheer. Jose Slaughter was a three-point specialist and defensive ace off the bench. Kenny Natt kept to himself but was usually agreeable. And David Wood was scrappy if still somewhat wild on the court, but forever virtuous outside the lines.

Everybody got along like brothers. The long bus rides were extended celebrations of laughs, good-natured teasing, and fondly remembered players, coaches, and games. They partied hard and played hard, and I never had to institute any kind of curfew. CBA teams spend so much time together—on long bus rides, waiting in airports, eating in the same restaurants—that the close relationship that can develop between all members of the traveling party is unique. This is in dramatic contrast to NBA teams where everybody moves in his own sphere of influence.

So we were mutually respectful and supportive, there were no cliques on the team, and we thoroughly enjoyed each other's company.

Even so, because Pace was absent-with-leave due to a pair of ten-day contracts with Atlanta and Detroit; because after thirty games Freddie opted to sign a significant contract with a European team; because Lamp suffered a late-season broken hand; because Wood went to Spain just before the playoffs began; because Ron Spivey was wearing himself out with nonstop partying; because a player was caught stealing money from his teammates' lockers and had to be cut . . . we suited up a total of twenty-two players throughout the season. One of whom came up with the best excuse I have ever heard for missing a practice session.

I'd thought I'd heard them all:

"The dog ate my sneakers."

"I had an argument with my wife and she hid the car keys."

"Today's Tuesday? Oh, man. I got wasted last night and I thought today was Sunday and we had a day off."

But here's what this guy came up with:

"I was out all night with a babe I met at a club. There's no question that my wife is freaked out because I didn't come home, and she was sure to come looking for me at practice. Man, the screaming and the cussing would've been incredible. And I would've been totally embarrassed in front of all the guys! The only way I could've maintained the respect of my teammates would've been to slap her around, and she definitely would've called the police. So I missed practice to stay out of jail."

And the guy was right! His wife had stormed into our practice session, searching for him in the locker room, the bathroom, and even under the stands.

So I fined him fifty dollars and the team put him up in a cheapo motel for a few days.

Then he came up with this:

"Me and my wife had it out, but we were okay when I promised to give her all of my next paycheck. But when she saw that it was fifty bucks short, she accused me of going out clubbing without her. She doesn't believe that you fined me. You could save my marriage, man, if you wrote out a note saying that I was fined for practicing without getting my ankles taped or for losing my practice jersey, or something like that."

No problem.

Except that after our next home game, his wife got into my face about stealing their money over stupid rules. Leaving me no choice but to trade the guy (and his wife) ASAP.

Early in the season we were in Charleston, West Virginia, preparing for a game that would be televised on ESPN, when the color commentator, Kevin Loughery, asked me to sit down for an interview.

"What do you think about the CBA's quarter-point system, Charley?"

"I hate it, and here's why . . . Because the end of each quarter is so critical, you have to have your best players on the court, which means that they wind up getting too many minutes. Also, for the same reason, you can't employ a normal rotation, which would be having your subs in for the last four minutes of the first and third quarters, and then for the first few minutes of the second and fourth quarters. The entire idea that each quarter is a game unto itself is unnatural and makes absolutely no sense. It's like giving a baseball team extra points for winning an inning. Whatever excitement it's supposed to generate is phony excitement."

A few minutes later, Loughery approached me again. "The director says that what you said was way too negative. Do you think we could do it again with you emphasizing the positives this time?"

Sure.

"I really like the quarter system because it hastens the education of young players. By that I mean they're forced to concentrate at the end of a close quarter as if the entire game were up for grabs. It also teaches them that every single play is important. The drama, of course, is also very appealing to the fans."

"That's great, Charley. Thanks."

Yeah, great. How could I be such a hypocrite, such a sophist? Was the CBA killing my soul? Or was it dying all by itself?

A coach's courtside manner is extremely important.

Some coaches are prowlers who spend most of the game on their feet. This gets them closer to the action but can also have tactical implications. Henry Bibby, for example, liked to toe the sideline and wave his hands whenever his team was trapping an opponent in the immediate vicinity—making the trapee feel that he was being triple-teamed, thereby increasing his anxiety and raising the odds that he'd make a foolish pass.

Within the restraints of the coaches' box, stand-up coaches have more mobility and can get close enough to the refs to engage in quiet personal debates. Which is usually fine with most refs—as long as the prowler is guard-sized.

Many refs are discomforted when taller coaches roam the sidelines, especially when they loom over the refs to communicate their grievances. That's why stand-up bigs are more liable to be T'd up than sit-down bigs.

Being six foot nine, I mostly stayed seated except when I was unusually (and frequently) outraged by what I deemed to be an egregious miscall. My penchant for keeping my seat led to a highly unusual circumstance during a game played in Topeka, Kansas, early in December.

The home-standing Sizzlers were the worst team in the CBA (finishing the season at 14-40), and the Lightning was one of the best. So my players and I had a lighthearted attitude both before and during the ball game.

Topeka went through two coaches and twenty-nine players during that season, and when we arrived in town, the roster included such once and future NBA players as Jim Rowinksi, Perry Moss, and Carlton McKinney. The soon-to-be-fired coach was Art Ross, who had gained much of his experience coaching in Scotland and England and was a CBA rookie. As such, Ross had a perpetually dazed and confused look about him.

The game was a rout from start to finish with Rockford winning 123–97. That's why I remained seated throughout.

As it was still relatively early in the season, there were slightly more than a thousand fans on hand. Just as the second half commenced, there was a shrill cry from the stands directly adjacent to the visitors' bench. This was immediately succeeded by a loudly wailing young child—perhaps eighteen months or so—in the act of stumbling down the aisle and on the verge of falling onto the court.

I instinctively reached out and grabbed him, saving him from being trampled by still another Lightning fast break. As soon as I perched the toddler on my lap for temporary safekeeping, he stopped crying and actually began to gurgle with happiness.

His mother was there in a flash, prolific in her gratitude and her embarrassment. But as soon as she picked up her son, the boy started wailing again even louder than before.

When the child was replaced on my knee, the crying stopped and the happy gurgling resumed.

With the mother's consent, I continued coaching with the boy on my knee. When I lifted him to consult with my team during time-outs, his good mood wasn't altered.

The boy fell asleep midway through the fourth quarter—apparently bored by the lopsided game—and was quickly rescued by his mom.

The crowd responded by giving me a standing ovation, and when I stood to acknowledge their applause I noticed a small pee stain on my pants leg.

As a result of the malodorous consequences, my players made me sit by myself in the back of the van on the ride back to the hotel.

Shortly after this anecdote was posted in my column at Foxsports.com, a good twenty years after the incident, the following message was e-mailed to me:

> Uncle Charley: That toddler you rescued from his mother was me. My name is ———— and I am now twenty-two years old. I am inmate number ———— at ———— State Correctional Facility. I'll be out in fifteen years. I owe you a new pair of pants.

On December 31, 1988, the Rockford Lightning hosted the CBA All-Star game. Since the game was to be telecast on ESPN, the league was determined to put on a show that would impress everybody concerned.

The day before the game, with all of the players shunted off to a local greasy-spoon buffet, a gala dinner was given for the media, the team owners and their sidekicks, the league's executives, and the coaches (me and George Karl). The scene was a cordoned-off and ribbon-bestrewed waiting room at the Rockford Airport.

To further celebrate the upscale event, each guest found a gift as part of his or her dinner setting. These were small straw baskets overflowing with colorful strips of tissue paper and crepe paper curlicues.

After much digging through the packing, we finally uncovered our gifts—which, we were told, were provided by one of the local sponsors of the dinner. And which turned out to be small bags of potato chips. Very small bags.

The CBA sure knew how to throw a party!

We won the All-Star game, 103–97, against a squad that featured several onetime NBA players—Bryan Warrick, Andre Turner, Bill Jones, Vince Askew, Carlton McKinney, Ron Rowan, Jerome Henderson, and Ken Johnson. But the star of the game was Dwayne McClain, likewise an NBA veteran, who was 9-12 from the field and tallied a game-high total of 18 points in only twenty-one minutes of daylight.

Although he never got another shot at the NBA, from then on Dwayne became one of the CBA's most proficient point makers.

Throughout my CBA career I've had contentious relationships with the fans of certain teams. Like the boosters, for example, of the Cedar Rapids Silver Bullets.

The team's primary sponsor was the Coors brewery, and the progenitive Silver Bullet was a can of beer. It was not surprising, then, that many of the hometown fans were appropriately juiced before and during ball games. As a result they were particularly foul-mouthed and nasty, throwing beer cups, candy wrappers, popcorn boxes, and whatever else they could find at both me and the visiting players on the bench.

No doubt they might have been prompted by my own overly excitable responses to frequent calls by the refs that I considered to be evidence of their bias in favor of the home team. Still, the fans reaction was over-the-top crude and insulting.

My penchant for being too honest and less than diplomatic also served to stoke their ire. For example, after one particular game in which the fans were even more outrageous than usual, I responded to a local sportswriter's question by saying this: "The behavior of the Cedar Rapids fans is the ugliest that I've seen in any other arena in the league."

Somehow my quote was twisted to indicate that the Cedar Rapids fans were the ugliest-looking in the league.

The president of the Silver Bullets was a young man named Kevin Krause, whose father had purchased the team to give him something to do. Previously, Krause's claim to fame was being the costumed mascot at the University of Iowa when he was a student there. The mascot's name was Herky the Hawk, and that became Krause's nickname throughout the league.

In any case, the next time I brought the Rockford Lightning to Cedar Rapids, Herky had dreamed up and executed quite a fanciful publicity stunt. Each fan at the game was presented with a life-size head shot of yours truly, with the (my) eyes cut out and the whole deal mounted on a stick.

When I was introduced before the game, and during every time-out, all of the fans stood up, held a Charley Rosen mask in front of their faces, and cheered when the public address announcer said, "Now we're really ugly!"

I thought it was kind of cute—and I still have a couple of the masks at my home in some closet somewhere.

But my next visit to Cedar Rapids produced a series of "stunts" that were not so amusing. Just a few weeks after the Charley Mask promotion, the fans adjacent to the visitors' bench seemed to be more amped up than usual. As I headed to the locker room for the halftime break, I saw a red-faced, rowdy fan in the row immediately behind the bench holding a cup full of beer in one hand and a Charley mask in the other.

He started cursing me in a loud voice, which was fine. As they used to say back in the Bronx: "Yer pays yer money and yer makes yer choice." But then he cocked the cup and initiated a motion that would undoubtedly end in his dousing me with the beer. There was no question whatsoever that this was his intent.

In self-defense, I reached my long right arm up and strategically ticked the cup just as he was bringing it forward. As a result the fan was splashed with the beer instead of me.

I just laughed and went about my business.

The next day I was informed that the fan had complained to the league office that, without any provocation, I had grabbed the cup from his hand and poured the beer on him. Even after I told my side of the story, the CBA's publicity director wasn't entirely convinced that I'd acted in self-defense. Surely, I must have done something to provoke the fan.

Yeah. Like falsify a quote in the local newspaper, then distribute several thousand Charley masks, and have the PA announcer incite the fans during every time-out? Yeah. It was all my fault.

The league's bigwigs insisted that I was indeed to blame. What I should have done was allow myself to get drenched, and then point out the fan to the arena's security personnel.

Okay. Next time I find myself in the same perilous spot, that's exactly what I'll do! Even though the incident was highly publicized in the Cedar Rapids' media, and I could expect to be subjected to a waterfall of beer on the Lightning's next appearance in Cedar Rapids.

"I have a better idea," I said. "Next time I'll bring an umbrella to the game."

The initial verdict was to fine me $100 and demand that I make a public apology to the complainant. When I refused to do so, the fine was increased to $150.

With Freddie gone over the waters, I traded for Dominic Pressley and installed him at the starting point guard slot. His jumper was vastly improved, he already knew my offense, and although he had a touch of tendonitis in both knees, Dominic was still as quick as a wish.

When Jim Lampley broke his shooting hand, I engineered a trade for Mike Richmond, a six-foot-eight lefty with a soft shooting touch.

But, from game to game, I called dozens of isos for both Pace and Dwayne and we were still a powerhouse ball club.

Not long ago, Kenny Natt became the head coach of the Sacramento Kings after spending several years as a highly valued assistant coach—all of which is somewhat of a surprise to me.

Back in Rockford the Natt-Man was a shoot-first-and-ask-no-questions guard. He was a little less plump than he is now, didn't wear glasses, and sported at least a sprinkling of hair atop his dome. He was also slightly bow-legged, so that when he ran he had a crablike gait. He never played much defense, nor was he interested in passing—but, man, oh man, could he shoot.

As an NBA coach I'm sure Kenny was personable and hardworking, but somehow I have doubts about his basketball acumen. As ever, there's a story behind this:

During one of Pace Mannion's ten-day call-ups, the Lightning had just been blown out for the third consecutive game.

Over the course of those games, Kenny was a combined 33 for 99 from the field—numbers that were as shocking as they were easily remembered.

Back at the hotel after the third game, Kenny approached me, saying, "Charley, I know why we're losing so badly."

"Why?"

"Because I'm not getting enough shots."

And the kicker was that he wasn't joking.

Coaching in the CBA always involved a certain degree of risk.

For example, after a game in which the Rockford Lightning happened to beat our archrivals from Quad City, one of the losers was extremely upset that his autocratic coach, Mauro Panaggio, had singled him out for criticism in the postgame locker room. So much so that the player grabbed his coach's necktie and lifted up as high as he could. Unfortunately, Panaggio was only five foot nine while the player was six foot six, and the necktie was still fastened around the coach's neck.

Eyewitnesses reported that Panaggio's face turned blue and his feet left the floor before he was rescued.

Like any self-respecting CBA coach, Panaggio's response was to trade the player that same evening.

Overnight lodging on the road was always an iffy business in the CBA. There were top-notch hotels in La Crosse, Wisconsin; Rockford, Illinois; Rapid City, South Dakota; and sometimes in Cedar Rapids, Iowa. On the other hand, low-rent motels were SOP in Lancaster, Pennsylvania; Sioux Falls, South Dakota; and Pensacola, Florida, with the worst accommodations being in Grand Rapids, Michigan. That's where there was always at least a four-inch gap between the bottom of the outside door and the threshold—allowing snow and/or frigid air free entry into the room. Plus, the heating system would bang on and off all night long. Indeed, the difficulty in getting a good night's sleep on the road was one important reason why many CBA teams were virtually unbeatable on their home court.

But perhaps the best hotel was the Hilton in Albany—classy, cozy, with excellent restaurants and snack shops on the premises, and situated only a short walk from the arena.

However, one fateful morning, a CBA coach, who had played in the NBA and was also infamous for his skirt chasing, had breakfast in the Albany Hilton and created a triple-X dilemma for the entire league.

It seems that the coach in question was served his meal by a beautiful waitress. When she didn't respond to his slightly suggestive verbal come-ons, he left her a huge tip plus a note scrawled on a paper napkin. The note boasted about his sexual prowess in no uncertain terms and included his room number.

Turned out that the waitress was the daughter of Albany's archbishop! The result of the ensuing hullabaloo was that all CBA teams were banned from the Hilton. Instead, visiting teams were housed in still another drafty, noisy, filthy motel on the outskirts of town.

A few weeks later this very same coach begged me to volunteer to take a surprise pregame drug test that the league mandated that either of the coaches must submit to.

"I did a little too much partying last night," he said. "Heh, heh, heh."

It was only after I'd agreed that he asked me if I was "clean."

The abuse of illegal drugs was a perpetual scourge in the CBA with anywhere from five to ten players being annually banished due to failed drug tests.

Besides the womanizing, party-hearty coach already cited, several other of my colleagues sought relief from the pressures of their job in inappropriate ways.

- Like the coach (and ex-NBA player) who was suspected of being a chronic pot smoker, but was a nice enough guy that the CBA's commissioner, Jay Ramsdell, arranged for a special drug test that would clear his name. Too bad the coach decided to settle his nerves on the taxi ride to the test by chain-smoking innumerable joints. After failing the test, he could only find employment coaching teams in obscure Middle Eastern countries.

- And like the coach (and ex-NBA player) who had to drink himself into oblivion in the bar across the street from the arena before every home game.

Coaching in the CBA had its good aspects: I learned the game from the inside out. I learned how to evaluate players not only on the basis of what they did but also on what they were supposed to do. I met scores of interesting, knowledgeable, well-connected people, both good guys and lunatics. It opened up a world I would never have seen otherwise.

On the flip side, while I never resorted to drugs during the season, the special pressures that came with the job brought out both the best and the worst in me. The foremost characteristic in the latter category was a tendency to erupt in sudden rages—usually instigated by an unjust call by a referee.

The worst example of this was evidenced after the Lightning lost a home game to the Rapid City Thrillers, who were coached by Eric Musselman.

I was in a bad mood even before the game began, primarily because of an article in one of the Chicago papers that claimed I was a cinch to replace the recently fired Johnny Bach as a Bulls assistant coach. I knew the story was erroneous, but the public mention of just the possibility filled me with a resentment born of frustrated ambition.

Anyway, we lost the game on a last-second bogus call by some ref or other, so I felt doubly cheated as Eric and I chanced to meet in an otherwise deserted passageway under the stands.

My opening remarks set the tone of our dialogue: "You didn't deserve to win the game."

Eric vehemently disagreed and our conversation quickly became combative. So much so that I grabbed him by his neck and lifted him off the floor (I'm about a foot taller than he is), spewing curses at him all the while. Whereupon I squeezed his throat for a few seconds until I let him fall.

It was really a shameful performance on my part. My anger had exploded for no real reason. Eric was an innocent victim and I was the foul-mouthed bully.

Later, upon sad reflection, I was filled with remorse.

That night I got a call from Eric's dad, Bill. Before I had a chance to apologize, this is what Bill said: "Both Eric and I admire what you did, Charley. It proved to us that you're a true competitor and that you want to win at any cost."

"Umm, thanks, Bill."

Even though Bill had taken me off the hook, I had one more reason to believe that I was in the wrong business.

Since then, my relationship with Eric, a.k.a. Musselboy, has been absolutely friendly. One reason for this was that each of us had an appropriate sense of the absurd.

On one fateful day late in the season, Eric had suspended an NBA veteran named Wes Matthews for conduct unbecoming of a rational human being. Unfortunately, later that very same day, three of Rapid City's players were called up to NBA teams—Fennis Dembo, Shelton Jones, and Clint Wheeler.

That left the Thrillers with only six available players as they faced off with the Thunder in Moline. Because CBA rules state that seven players had to suit up for games, Matthews was forced to don a uniform and sit on the bench. But because Matthews was angry with Eric, he refused to tie his sneaker laces.

Nobody fouls out in the CBA—every foul over six is penalized by a bonus free throw—so Eric felt that six players would be sufficient.

Unfortunately, the game went into a third overtime.

After the initial fifty-eight minutes, all of his six players were exhausted and Eric had no other choice except to immediately unsuspend Matthews and send him into the game.

Out of spite, Matthews didn't bother to tie his sneaker laces. Even so, he dominated the action—running up and down the court with his laces flying and flapping, and screaming curses at Eric every time he managed to score.

Turned out that Matthews registered 13 points in the third overtime and won the game for the Thrillers.

"If something like that had happened anywhere else,"

Eric told me, "it would have won awards for being the craziest episode in the history of sports. But in the CBA, crazy basketball was the name of the game."

There were many times when I thought that even the referees were borderline crazy.

In my third season as a head coach, I managed to maintain my position as the league leader in technical fouls.

Most of my T's resulted from my constant nagging and constant abuse of the refs, although I did receive a T from Duke Callahan in Wichita Falls, Texas, when he mistook a fan's loud, drawling complaints for mine.

Danny Crawford rang me up in Omaha, after my team yielded six consecutive offensive rebounds, when he misheard a jocular remark I had made to him: "It's like a hockey game. We can't clear the puck back across the blue line."

Similarly proving that some refs are deaf as well as blind, Bill Spooner once booted me from a game in Albany, New York, when I questioned his concentration by saying, "You're missing a good game." Later I was informed that Spooner thought that I had called him "gay."

After the CBA and I were done with one another, however, I encountered several refs who said that my constant comments from the bench had helped them to focus hard on every play. Glad to have helped them out.

After joining the Lightning late in the season, Ken "The Animal" Bannister manned the middle with power, belligerence, and creativity, plus being equally intimidating in the low post or at the high post. I called him Mr. Animal. He also provided whatever semblance of discipline the team required. For example, if any of the players was less than fully attentive during a huddle or a team meeting, Bannister would whomp the guilty party upside his head and order him to pay attention. He never had to tell anybody twice. Indeed, Ken was such an overwhelming physical presence that he scared both opponents and referees into submission.

Best of all, he was extremely coachable.

With Bannister a menace in the middle and Mike Richmond backing him up, Lampley's extended stint on the injured list was hardly noticed.

However, while Lampley's broken hand was mending, he did nothing to keep himself in shape. No running. No exercising. No attendance at team practices. And a complete avoidance of the regularly scheduled rehab appointments the team had set up.

When the soft cast was removed from his hand, Lamp simply showed up at practice one day and announced that he was not only ready to play but also ready to reclaim his starting spot from Bannister. Never mind that Lamp's legs were jelly. That his timing was atrocious, that he'd gained at least ten pounds, or that Bannister was a better player. When I explained to Lamp that he'd have to work his way back into meaningful playing time, he was personally affronted.

Too bad the trading deadline had come and gone.

We finished the regular season at 34-20, and two days before the playoffs began, David Wood left to play in Europe, and Dominic Pressley's tendonitis had reduced his blinding speed to a fast limp. Dom's backup was Brent Carmichael, a pint-sized ball hawk who had trouble putting the ball through the basket.

So there was ample reason for concern when we opened

the playoffs by losing two games on the road to Mauro Pa-naggio's Quad City Thunder. Then, after falling behind by 18 at halftime in Rockford, I delivered a blistering, insulting ora-tion—and we won the next four games to cop the series.

Next up was the Rapid City Thrillers, under the direc-tion of Flip Saunders and featuring a host of NBA veter-ans—Todd Mitchell, Milt Wagner, David Henderson, Con-nor Henry, Chris Engler, Sidney Lowe, Kevin Williams, and Jim Thomas. We lost the first game, 116–115, and immedi-ately thereafter Bannister was signed to a ten-day contract by the L.A. Clippers.

But with Pressley (whose limp was getting even worse), Mannion, and McClain stepping up their games, and with Lampley getting Bannister's minutes, we managed to upset the Thrillers in six games.

That set up the championship series—Rockford versus the Tulsa Fast Breakers, who were coached by the redoubt-able Henry Bibby.

The ensuing series would prove to be the most dramatic, most bizarre sequence of games I'd ever seen.

In Tulsa, Bibby had put together a talented team that featured several ex-NBA players: Peter Thibeaux, Wes Mat-thews, Dexter Shouse, Gary Voce, Tracy Moore, and Duane Washington. The roster likewise featured several once and future druggies.

The series opened in Rockford, and prior to the first game, Bibby drove his team to a shabby outdoor court on the wrong side of the tracks. "This," Bibby said, "is where the Light-ning has arranged for us to practice."

This was an obvious absurdity, and his team was actually scheduled to practice at the Metrocenter where the games would be played. Nevertheless, Bibby's players felt dissed and subsequently played with untoward belligerence.

We lost the first game 109–103, and we were all surprised by the visitors' demeanor. Trash talking with a vicious edge. Fouling after every whistle. Unmitigated arrogance.

"If Bannister was still here," said Pace Mannion, "these guys would be trembling in their sneakers."

But Mr. Animal was sitting on the L.A. Clippers' bench—and failed to make an on-court NBA appearance during the CBA finals.

At halftime of the second game, we were trailing by one, 56–55—but Lampley chose to pause to talk to a woman in the stands instead of coming straight to the locker room. When he did make his appearance, he was ten minutes late.

And I blew up.

In his defense Lamp barely lifted his sleepy eyelids and said only that he "had business to take care of."

Business!?! Basketball was, and should be, his only business!

He just shrugged, then I really went off. Cursing him up, down, and sideways. I even had to be restrained from physically attacking him. Just before we had to get back on to the court, I informed Lamp that he was suspended without pay for what was left of the season.

He simply shrugged once more.

After battling for all we were worth for the third quarter, we were routed in the final period and lost 117–104.

By now Dominic Pressley was doing an inadvertent Fred Sanford imitation as he hobbled up and down the court. He scored only 9 points in the game, on 3-15 shooting.

The next day, just as I was leaving for the airport, I got

a call from Phil Jackson. At the time, Phil was an assistant with the Bulls.

"Jerry Krause just signed Dominic Pressley to a ten-day contract," Phil said.

"That's ridiculous. The guy can't run. If he was a horse they'd shoot him to put him out of his misery. Didn't he send anybody over here to see him play? Why didn't he call me?"

"Jerry has his own way of doing things," is all that Phil said.

Actually, Carmichael did an excellent job in place of Dom—scoring a total of 40 points and shooting 16-35 in the remaining games. But Pressley's leadership was sorely missed.

Turned out that Pressley played seventeen minutes in three games for Chicago, shooting 1-6 and scoring a total of 2 points. Even worse, the Chicago fans and media ridiculed Krause for calling up "a crippled player."

Meanwhile, back in Tulsa I foolishly made public reference to the "shady pasts" of several of the local players—and the local media had a field day. Plus, the Tulsa players went out of their way to cuss me out during the subsequent games.

My bad.

It should be noted, though, that shortly thereafter several of the Fast Breakers were booted from the CBA for failing drug tests.

Anyway, without Bannister and Pressley we had no chance in Game 3, losing 124–107.

Before Game 4, I filled the blackboard in our locker room with the following reasons why we'd win the game at hand: "Pride. Courage. Resiliency. Talent. Togetherness. And, above all, love."

Corny, for sure. But all valid points.

When I came back to the locker room after checking out the identities of the referees, the word *love* had been erased and replaced with the following: "Two more days of per diem."

It had to have been Pace's doing. And we all laughed together.

Despite our being overmatched, it took a three-pointer at the buzzer by Wes Matthews to close out the game, 114–111, the series, and the season.

Afterward, Derrick Lewis (bless his heart) wept, and we all hugged one another. A sad ending to an otherwise happy season.

Even though we were swept, we did outstat the Fast Breakers in one category: they had six technical fouls for the series (three for Bibby, two for Matthews, and one for Shouse),and we totaled nine (three each for Mannion and me, one each for Jose Slaughter, Lewis, and Lamp).

A week later, I was still boiling mad. The best pickup game in Rockford was at a local Catholic high school, so I climbed into my gear and showed up. But it was Lampley's game, and probably because I couldn't wait to get out there and knock him on his keister, I was constantly told that someone else had "next." After an hour, I left.

Immediately after the season ended, the CBA announced that an All-Star team would participate in a tournament in France. Since Tulsa and Rockford had played in the finals, Bibby was named the head coach of this squad—and I was asked to be his assistant. Bibby, though, reserved the right to handpick the members of the team.

All expenses paid for the ten-day trip, and I could even bring my wife.

However, since I wasn't exactly a fan of Bibby's, I passed. My wife (ex-wife now) went nuts. How could I not go? Was I crazy? I must be crazy!

Of course I was crazy, but that was beside the point.

I simply didn't want anything to do with Bibby's on- and off-court philosophy in which the ends always justified the means. Plus he was a hypocrite, an avowed Born Again who remained a notorious womanizer. His penchant for backstabbing anybody who got in his way was likewise proverbial— when he was named an assistant coach at USC, everybody who knew him said that it wouldn't be long before he'd either get fired or be hired as the head coach. Indeed, within a year he was USC's head coach. The same prognosis was made when he was named Mo Cheeks's assistant; this time he was fired before he could stab Cheeks in the back.

My decision to stay home was vindicated when Bibby named his All-Star team. Several of the shady characters from Tulsa were included, plus a CBA player who'd once played in the NBA and was currently supplementing his basketball earnings by dealing drugs.

The CBA team finished with a 3-3 record in the tournament but reportedly wowed the local media with their nonstop partying.

All these years later I'm still in touch with Pace—who does the pregame, postgame, and halftime studio analyses for the locally televised Jazz games. I saw Brent Carmichael while on a book tour. And, by all reports, Jim Lampley is still living in Rockford.

However, barely fifteen years later, the most disturbing news came from several usually reliable sources—that Dominic Pressley had passed away! A diligent search of the Internet failed to locate any specific time, place, or cause.

It's hard to imagine a world without Dom's buoyant good humor, indomitable spirit, and funky jumper.

15

In the Jailhouse Now

Two weeks after the NBA held its draft, plans were finalized to hold the CBA college draft in Columbus, Ohio—home of the Horizon. The proceedings would be televised and shown live in all of the other currently extant CBA franchises. However, a tragedy of major proportions occurred the day before the draft was scheduled to commence.

On July 19, 1989, United Airlines Flight 232 crashed at the Sioux City, Iowa, airport after losing all hydraulics. Of the 296 passengers and crew on board, it was eventually determined that 112 had lost their lives. The passenger list included Commissioner Jay Ramsdell and Jerry Schemmel, the CBA's deputy commissioner. In the immediate aftermath of the crash, dozens of passengers were still unaccounted for, with Jay being among them.

Was he alive? Seriously injured? Or dead?

For me, and for many other coaches, team owners, and league officials gathered for the draft proceedings, Jay was a voice of sanity in a crazy business.

Jay had first made contact with the CBA as a ninth grade student in 1978 when he interviewed Frederick Haer, the owner of the Maine Lumberjacks, for an article in his high school newspaper. Jay was so impressive that he was asked to "help out" the team on opening night. As the game began, Jay was assigned to the scorer's table, and by the end of the game he was the Lumberjacks Statistical Crew Chief. Seven days later Jay received another promotion, becoming the team's director of public relations.

He remained with the Lumberjacks until his high school graduation in 1982, when he was hired by the CBA's league office as an administrative assistant. Within a year he was the league's director of operations, and before his twenty-first birthday he became the CBA's deputy commissioner.

Jay returned to Bangor, Maine, to serve as general manager for the Maine Windjammers for the 1985–86 season. When the franchise folded in the spring of 1986, Jay returned to the CBA front office (which was located in Conshohocken, Pennsylvania, not far from Jim Drucker's home) and his post as deputy commissioner.

Shortly thereafter, Drucker resigned to pursue other business interests and was succeeded by Carl Scheer, and the league office was moved to Denver. After one season Scheer quit and was replaced by Mike Storen, who likewise lasted only a single season.

Having run out of ready, willing, and able candidates, in 1988 the Board of Directors made the twenty-four-year-old Ramsdell the youngest commissioner in the history of professional sports.

Having come to his maturity in the CBA, Jay was well aware of the league's precarious financial status, importance, charm, and above all inherent insanity. He was smart, personable, reasonable, and also compassionate.

Except for his being a Boston Red Sox fan and my being a New York Yankees fan, Jay liked the same players, coaches, and owners that I did, and we also shared a common dislike of an additional cast of characters.

Although it was universally assumed that Jay had perished in the crash, I believed that it would be unseemly to go on with the draft as scheduled while his fate was still unknown. My view was supported by a loose consensus of those present, but the owner of the Columbus Horizon—Dr. Seymour Killstein, a proctologist who was always behind in his league dues—refused to cancel the draft extravaganza only because so much money had already been shelled out for hotel reservations, the ballroom rental, and so on.

On Saturday morning, Jay's charred body was finally found and identified.

Thoroughly frustrated and disgruntled, I wanted to lodge a protest by refusing to draft anybody, but I was discouraged from doing so when the Board of Directors threatened to fine both me and the Lightning.

Then my old nemesis, Mauro Panaggio, said he was interested in obtaining my sixth-round selection. Mindful of Jay Ramsdell's sense of the absurd, I offered the pick in exchange for a Quad City sweat suit, size XXL. And the deal was done.

Somewhere up in commissioners' heaven, I knew that Jay was chuckling. But I also knew that he was laughing loud enough to shake the heavenly rafters when I finally received the sweat suit, and it was size L—the pants barely reaching below my knees and the shirtsleeves dangling above my elbows!

Soon enough—too soon!—Jerry Schemmel was named the new commissioner, and the CBA's championship hardware was christened the Jay Ramsdell Trophy.

In recent years Rockford and Albany had been the CBA's model franchises, but even before my third season with the Lightning there were ominous signs that the golden age was over. Over the summer, Jay Polan, the Lightning's enlightened owner, had been tried, convicted, and jailed for having bribed some Chicago politician in an attempt to procure the city's most lucrative routes for his bus company. While Polan served his time in a minimum security joint in California, the team was run by the minority owner, his dim-witted, cheapskate, and racist buddy—who was referred to by all of the wise guys in the organization as Palie.

Before the season began, it was discovered that one of the Lightning's best holdover players was in trouble with the IRS. To rectify the situation the government put a lien on his salary—raking off 30 percent of his weekly paycheck to pay his delinquent tax bill and the penalties. The player was more than happy with this outcome. "I can still live well on what's left," he said, "and it's much better than having to play basketball wearing a striped uniform."

However, Palie wasn't quite so delighted. It seems that he, too, was worried about some potential IRS problems—and he had one solution. "If we let those tax guys poke around our finances, who knows how much they'll dig up? Charley, you got to trade him ASAP."

The player who would be the focus of my offense? One who was committed to playing in the CBA and who had no chance of going overseas or being called up to the NBA (because he'd already failed there)?

Yes. That was an order.

So I scratched around, made hundreds of phone calls—and came up with a semiacceptable deal. Although he wasn't nearly as dominating as the guy I had to trade, the player I would get in return was another CBA veteran, Barry Mitchell, whose superior defense and all-around hustle could make a huge difference in my team. Trouble was, he was currently playing in South America and wouldn't be coming back to the States until the CBA season was halfway finished. Still, it was the best bargain I could make.

Eventually Mitchell returned to the States and was eager to play for me, but his agent demanded a salary of six hundred dollars per week. "No way," Palie said. "The most you can pay him is five hundred dollars."

"But . . ."

"No way. Hey, you could find some schvartzer hanging around on any street corner in Chicago who could do the job for a lot less money."

"But . . ."

"That's final."

Unfortunately, the agent was just as stubborn. "Six hundred or he's not going to play." I offered to pay the extra hundred dollars out of my own pocket, but the agent still refused.

Turned out that a few years later the guy I traded away had an All-Star season and led his team to the CBA championship. Also, Mitchell stayed home for the rest of the season.

During the off-season in Chicago, Doug Collins had been canned and Phil was promoted from assistant to head coach. For a while I sparkled with the hope that he might be able to bring me in as an assistant.

But no. Jerry Krause still had a veto in the hiring of the scouts and coaching staff, and I was the spirit of Woodstock Past, an embarrassing reminder of Phil's heyday as a hoop-o-hippie. Krause even called me to say that he thought I was well qualified but that Phil's assistants had to be former NBA players.

"Those are the only guys today's players have any respect for," Krause told me. "I give you my word, Charley. I'm forced to hire an ex-player."

Shortly thereafter, Jimmy Rodgers was hired, an outstanding and experienced NBA assistant who had never played pro ball at any level. And I was left to wonder exactly what the "word" was that Krause had given me. "Bullshit"?

I'd never really harbored the belief that Phil would someday be able to bring me into the NBA. I had even told him that there was no obligation for him to do so if and when he got a head-coaching job. I was pained, however, by the fact that although neither Phil nor I had much respect for Krause, it was Krause who called to tell me the bad news. I had a tough time forgiving Phil for allowing that to happen. For, at least, not manning up and telling me himself.

In *More Than a Game,* Phil, of course, expressed his own take on this issue.

PHIL JACKSON: *"When I succeeded Doug, there was a glimmer of a chance for Charley to join my staff. I respected Charley's eye for the game almost more than anybody else's, and I wanted him there with me. But I also knew that bringing such a close friend on board the Bulls' coaching staff might be seen as compromising my integrity. It was a hard decision for me, and Charley had a tough time accepting it. I could certainly understand his anguish and disappointment.*

Our friendship became strained and we didn't talk to each other for several months. In fact, it wasn't until a couple of years later, when we were both pallbearers at Eddie Mast's funeral, that we became totally reconciled.

"Years later, I told Charley that I'd probably made a mistake by ever encouraging him to abandon his primary calling in order to become a basketball coach. Although I can't exactly say when I fully realized this, I always had the feeling that Charley had more to offer our society through his talents as a writer. It's generally acknowledged that he's the sport's greatest champion when it comes to translating the game of basketball into words that capture its spirit. But at the time it was not an easy thing for our friendship."

So it was with no hope of ever working in the NBA, and with the realization that my latest career was headed toward a dead end, that the Lightning's 1989–90 season commenced. It seemed only fitting, too, that many of my best (and my favorite) players were gone.

Pace Mannion, Dwyane McClain, Jim Lampley, Dominic Pressley, Jose Slaughter, Derrick Lewis, and Ken Bannister were all playing elsewhere. Bobby Parks averaged 26.4 points per game, but he left after thirteen games to play in the Philippines. Orlando Graham, who had played for Wyoming in the 1984 championship series against the Patroons, recorded 22.6 points and 11.2 rebounds over twenty-one games before opting to play in France. Darren Guest, a powerful rookie center, failed a drug test in midseason. Gary Massey, a talented wingman from Villanova, tore up his knee in early January.

On the plus side, Freddie Cofield was back for the entire

season. He scored 24.1 points per game, but the magic was gone and he couldn't knock down a win-or-lose shot to get into heaven. Elston Turner also returned to Rockford, but he pulled a thigh muscle and missed nearly as many games as he played. Brent Carmichael was as quick around the ball as ever before but still couldn't shoot. And Steve Woodside, who had played for me in Savannah, added his wry intelligence to the mix.

No surprise, then, that after we split our initial twelve games the season went downhill in a hurry.

I was desperate to turn the season around.

How desperate?

Jim Lampley had signed with Pensacola, and before a game on his new home court, I walked over to where he was rehearsing his free throws. And then I asked him if he would consider returning to the Lightning. A trade, after all, could easily be arranged. Actually, I didn't really ask him. I practically begged him.

He smiled broadly and was delighted to turn me down. Then he tallied 23 points to lead the home team to victory, and smiled again each time he trotted by my bench.

Shame on me.

How desperate? Several of the many scouts I consulted reported that Lewis Brown (!) was tearing everybody up in a highly competitive semipro league in L.A. Even after getting such short shrift several years ago in Albany, Brown was nevertheless happy for another chance to break into the CBA and swore that he was in terrific shape. So arrangements were made for him to meet us in Columbus, Ohio, just in time for him to participate in a game-day shootaround.

Brown suited up with the rest of the team, but he was running with a noticeable limp. "I've got a bad leg," he said. "Had it for several years. So I can't really run."

Immediately after the shootaround, Brown was driven to the airport, given a few bucks, and sent back home. This episode also lasted for about twenty-four hours.

In the Crazy Basketball Association not-so-instant replays constitute business as unusual.

Here's the most unethical action I ever undertook in the CBA:

One of the most important duties of a CBA coach is to keep track of players leaving the States to play overseas and also those who are returning. Many of these players were free agents and if their whereabouts could be ascertained they could be signed by either the highest or the earliest bidder.

One such player (let's call him James Smith) had recently returned from France and had arrived at his mother's home in Mississippi just two days previous. There were (and are) several reasons why players are released from their out-of-country contracts: they aren't scoring enough points; they can't adjust to the alien culture, the alien style of play, and/or the alien coaches. Perhaps the team's paychecks are either significantly late or else made of rubber. To absolve themselves of any responsibility, the teams often claim that the released player has failed a drug test; this is true in maybe one of three cases. Indeed, Smith's team had made this charge against him.

Anyway, Smith had played extraordinarily well in the CBA several seasons back. He was six foot six with a deadly jumper, a big heart, and excellent defense. The day after I called him, Smith met up with us on the road in Pensacola.

CBA rules required all in-season newcomers to undergo immediate drug tests, but Smith had a plea to cop.

"Charley," he said, "I had no idea that I would be playing here until you called. So the day before you did I was at a party and snorted a few lines of coke. I need at least another day to clean out before I could pass a drug test."

So here's what I did: I postdated his contract, did not inform the league office that he was with the team, flew him to our next stop on a separate flight, and kept him stashed in the hotel while we played our next game in Birmingham. It wasn't until three days later, when we returned to Rockford, that his contract was faxed to the league office and he was officially added to our roster.

Naturally, he passed the ensuing drug test with no problem whatsoever.

And for the next two weeks he mostly performed like he belonged in the NBA. Single-handedly rallying us from a 20-point deficit against the always tough La Cross Catbirds, he then made the clutch shot that put us over the top. Sure, Smith had one or two bum games as well as a couple of lethargic stretches in other games. But he was a definite plus on the court and in the locker room.

Then his name was randomly selected to undergo one of the league's surprise drug tests—and he failed.

Good-bye James Smith, who never again played professional ball in any country.

And good-bye to my own integrity and also my self-image as a good guy in a ruthless profession.

My only consolation was that my sin was a minor one compared to what some other coaches were doing. For example, there was a guy coaching in the CBA that season who had previously coached in a rural high school, in a sad-sack summer pro league, and overseas in the lowest level of international competition. He'd also been an assistant coach at several midlevel colleges. And he'd been fired after serving for one year as a part-time scout for an NBA team.

He seemed well on his way to oblivion, primarily because it was well known that, according to a veteran CBA coach, the guy "couldn't coach his way out of a paper bag."

But then out of nowhere he was hired to be a head coach in the CBA!

How did this come about?

Not because of his expertise, nor his previous experience, nor a barrage of top-flight recommendations. No, sir.

What happened was that the guy slept with the wife of a CBA team's general manager and had her convince her husband that he was right for the coaching job.

If crime supposedly doesn't pay in the real world, adultery certainly does in the CBA.

P.S. The guy lasted less than two seasons before being fired. Overall, the teams under his direction finished well under .500. At last report, the guy was employed as a physical education teacher in a midwestern high school—and trying hard to get the head-coaching job there. Unfortunately for him, the principal of the school is a bachelor.

CBA teams were still doing most of our traveling in vans and, especially on the way back home after road games, this was often a problem.

During their long drive home, a certain CBA team was celebrating a significant road win by inhaling large quantities of beer. Indeed, the coach (not me!) was even more inebriated than the players. They laughed, they yowled, and in their over-the-top exuberance they bounced around in their seats.

Only the driver of the van was stone sober. He was the last man on the squad, a rarely used point guard whose primary attributes were long-distance shooting, good decisions with the ball, and a maturity level not normally found in the CBA.

It was past midnight when a state trooper noticed the van rocking from side to side even as it headed on a beeline down the highway. As the trooper flipped on his pursuit lights, the alarmed players opened all of the windows, hid their beer cans, and splashed aftershave lotion all over themselves and the interior of the van.

This was standard operating procedure in the CBA.

At the side of the road, the trooper took a quick whiff of the interior, then asked the driver to step outside. As instructed the substitute point guard qua driver touched his nose with his fingers in the proper fashion.

"Okay," said the trooper. "Now let me see you walk a straight line."

"I can do much better than that."

Whereupon in rapid succession the driver proceeded to perform two front flips and two back flips.

The trooper was so impressed that he sent the team and driver on their way.

The coach was so impressed that the driver started the next game.

Forget about Michael Jordan and "the Shot." Disregard all of Kobe Bryant's game-winning baskets. Pay no attention to the end-game heroics of Jerry West and Reggie Miller. As told by a veteran CBA coach who, at the time, was working for a team in the CBA's Eastern Division, here's an account of the best clutch performance in the history of the game.

"My best player had a wife and two kids in Denver, but he'd left them home during the CBA season. In their absence he was screwing as many of the team's groupies as he could. So he came up to me in the locker room just before a home game to say this: 'Coach, I'm absolutely beat. I've been fucking these two twins on a regular basis and we were up all last night. There's no way that I can play my usual forty minutes tonight. What if I fake an injury early on? Or get into early foul trouble?'

"The guy always played his heart out for me, so I really didn't mind him taking a night off. But I thought foul trouble would be the less complicated way out. Okay. That was our plan.

"But guess what? Just as the team took to the court for their pregame warm-ups, the guy's wife was there.

"'Honey!' he said to her. 'I'm so happy to see you. What a great surprise!'

"They feverishly embraced at courtside and told each other how horny they were. Then he came over to the bench, summoned a gofer, dashed into the locker room, gave the kid fifty bucks and the key to his motel room, and instructed him to clean up the mess and get rid of the panties and bras that were strewn around the place.

"Naturally, our pregame plan to limit his minutes was inoperative. So he played forty-three minutes, scored over 30 points, and we won the game. Afterwards, he looked like he'd just survived the Bataan Death March.

"But, wait. His most transcendent clutch performance happened later that night when he managed to convince his wife that he was sex-starved. All in all, it was a Hall-of-Fame achievement."

After six years in the CBA, I thought that I'd heard every possible bogus excuse for guys being late or missing a practice. But this one floored me.

In Rockford, the unmarried players had free lodging in a motel in town (the rent was subsidized for the apartments that the married guys occupied). The team also provided two cars to be shared by the motel-based players—a dark blue Oldsmobile and a pink Lincoln. However they divvied up the driving time was strictly their business, and apparently everybody was happy because nobody complained.

Until one day when four of the single guys were a half-hour late for practice.

What was their collective excuse? Somebody had slashed all four tires on the "stinkin' Lincoln."

Say, what? How could that be? What could motivate someone to do that? None of them claimed to have a clue. It sounded like a fishy story to me, so I fined them all.

A few days later, I rescinded their fines when I finally discovered what had really happened. It seems that one of the guys had a hot date and was allowed to use the car. However, it turned out that his date was the wife of a local contractor—and since the Lincoln was so easy to spot, the illicit get-together was quickly discovered by the outraged husband, who took his revenge on the car.

For the sake of total justice, and to hide the whole story from the team's ownership, I wanted to fine the backcourt adulterer the exact amount that it would cost to replace the tires. But the player in question (who'd spent some time in the NBA) made a deal with a local tire distributor, trading a batch of complimentary tickets for new tires.

Stumped, I let him slide with a hundred-dollar fine for being responsible for wasting a practice session.

But there's more to this tale.

My standard operating procedure was to use all of the collected fines as prize money for various shooting games. At our very next practice, one hundred dollars were at stake for a three-point shooting contest. And guess who won!

The moral is that, in the CBA, crime did pay.

In his second season in the CBA, Eric Musselman still couldn't get used to the league's residual crazies.

ERIC MUSSELMAN: *"That was the year I had Jarvis Basnight from UNLV. All season long he was complaining about some kind of health problem. There was a pain in his head, a pain in his shoulder, a pain in his chest, and he was a total pain in the ass. He had doctor's appointments every other day and the team was spending lots of money for all of the prescriptions that were ordered. It got to the point where his medical bills were higher than his salary, and that's when the team's owner, Pat Hall, stepped in.*

"Pat told the team's trainer to get a bunch of sugar pills and to make sure that they were of different colors. Once Basnight started taking these placebos, he experienced a miraculous healing."

The eccentricities of other players were more predictable and more understandable. In seasons to come, John Starks would be idolized in New York for several reasons:

- His rags to riches story of graduating from being a bagger in a supermarket in Tulsa to the NBA
- His exceptional play with the Knicks against the league's weaker teams
- His in-your-puss dramatic dunk that posterized His Airness

But I knew him when he played for the Cedar Rapids Silver Bullets:

- When he routinely ate peanuts or popcorn while sitting on the bench
- When he was only interested in scoring to the extent that he'd dribble and fake for up to twenty seconds until he could create a shot—and when there was no shot to be found, he'd pass to a teammate who'd then have to throw the ball at the basket to avoid a shot-clock violation

So I was not at all surprised when he totally choked against Houston in the seventh game of the 1994 NBA finals—shooting 2-18, including 0-11 from beyond the arc.

Losers eventually lose the big ones.

Speaking of Cedar Rapids. The inability of the Lightning to develop any semblance of continuity really had me down. Depressed by the constant losing, missing Jay Polan, constantly irritated by Palie's tightfisted ignorance, I was an accident looking for a place to happen. And that place turned out to be Cedar Rapids.

It was Christmas 1989, two days before we were scheduled to play at Cedar Rapids. Whereas Jay Polan had always presented me with a holiday bonus of seven hundred dollars, Palie gave me a small jar of strawberry preserves. A very small jar.

Also, since the bus ride from Rockford to Cedar Rapids took four hours, we had always been allowed to travel there the day before a game. Palie, however, insisted that we leave at 8:00 a.m. the day of the game. "You'll get there in time for a noon shootaround," he reasoned, "and I'll save a day's per diem and a big hotel bill."

I begged Palie to reconsider. "This is what'll happen if we do what you want: the game will be close for three quarters, then our players' legs will turn to rubber, and we'll get blown out in the fourth quarter."

"You're the coach," Palie said. "It's your job to make sure that doesn't happen."

The night before we left for Cedar Rapids, I received a disquieting phone call from the coach of the Rapid City Thrillers, Eric Musselman. It seemed that the Thrillers had just played a game at Cedar Rapids against the homestanding Silver Bullets, coached by a notorious jackass named George Whittaker (and owned by "Herky the Hawk"). Eric's complaint was that late in the fourth quarter, with the Silver Bullets ahead by 24 points and in full control of the quarter-point, Whittaker had ordered his team into a full-court press.

"It was like he was kicking us when we were already down and out," Eric told me. "Like he wanted to beat us by 100 points if he could. It was humiliating, and my guys were really upset. I had to stop a couple of them from going over to the other bench and punching Whittaker's lights out."

In my fourth continuous season of employment, I was the CBA's senior coach, and as such Eric asked me to speak to Whittaker and explain the error of his ways.

No problem.

We did indeed arrive in Cedar Rapids just in time for our appointed shootaround, and just in time, too, for me to catch up with Whittaker as his team was leaving the court. He was a round-faced young man with Shirley Temple curls. When I repeated Eric's accusations, Whittaker appeared to be insulted. Yes, such a tactic was deplorable, said Whittaker, but he pleaded his innocence.

"I don't even have a full-court press," he insisted. "And even if I did, Charley, I would never do anything as disrespectful as that."

Okay. Fine. Terrific. Thanks, George. You're a helluva guy.

The game that night played out exactly as I'd anticipated: We lost each of the first three quarters by one point before getting our doors blown off in the last quarter. Then, lo and behold, the score was 112–89, with 1:17 on the game clock, when I distinctly heard Whittaker shout out, "Red! Red!"—thereby ordering his team into a full-court press.

Jumping up from my seat, I glowered downcourt to where Whittaker likewise stood in front of his bench. "That's bullshit," I yelled at him.

"Fuck you!" was Whittaker's response. Then he waved his hands, challenging me, beckoning me to approach him. "Come over here and do something about it!"

And I couldn't take it anymore. The game. The CBA. My life. "YOU MOTHERFUCKER!" Some last vestige of self-control snapped, leaving me wild and bellowing, a wounded beast suddenly turning on the hunter, charging downcourt, out of my mind with rage, intent on obliterating Whittaker, who moved to hide behind his bench players. I think I could have actually killed him.

But thankfully one of the referees, Jim Kinney, grabbed me in a bear hug from behind, pinning my arms and swooping me off my feet. "It ain't worth it, Charley," he said in my ear. "Calm down. It ain't worth it."

"It is! I'm gonna kill the fucker!"

Slowly Jim increased the pressure on my chest so that I had to gasp for breath. "It ain't worth it." He literally carried me toward the baseline, where the desperate need to breathe, to inhale, to live, suddenly overrode my anger.

"I'm okay," I said. "Thanks, Jim. I'm okay. Let me down."

He released me gently. "I have to call a couple of Ts," he said, almost apologizing. "You're ejected."

"I understand. I'm okay."

So I walked slowly off the court, the fans in an uproar behind me, hurling abuse, paper cups, and crumpled newspapers as I entered the tunnel that led to the basement staircase, thinking, hoping, that this fiasco would motivate my players for our next game. Then, just as I reached the top of the stairs, gathering my body for the rhythmic descent into the basement, a hand seized my right forearm from behind.

"What?"

It was a cop. About five foot eight, a solid 170 pounds, wearing his play-hat with its shiny black brim, a badge on his hat, a badge on his chest. The nameplate above his right breast pocket said, "G. Murray." His eyes were gray, almost colorless. There was an oversized six-shooter strapped to his waist.

Now his other hand also locked onto my forearm. "Let's go," he said. The force of his grip nearly tilted me headlong down the steps, and he had to yank me back to right my balance.

"I'm going," I said, then shook him loose. "Get the fuck off me. This has nothing to do with you."

He clutched at me again, and I repeated, "Get the fuck off me."

When we arrived at the bottom of the stairs, he pushed the small of my back, propelling me toward the locker room. "Get away, leave me alone." Then he shoved me into the locker room and slammed the door behind me.

I proceeded to kick every dented, rusty locker in the narrow room. Right then, at that moment, everything that had happened was someone else's fault. Palie's. Whittaker's. Murray the minicop's. I was the outraged innocent.

But then I realized that I was thirsty, so I ventured into the hallway to find a water fountain. And that's when all hell broke loose.

Evidently the game was over, because here came Whittaker, bopping down the stairs and happy to be a winner, feeling invincible, knowing that he was a genius.

I instinctively rushed toward him, and suddenly we were face-to-face. I clenched my right hand. Instead of moving to defend himself, he stared at me, speechless, apparently shocked at my riotous fury, his mouth twisted into a vacant grin. I no longer wanted to hurt him, yet some red-eyed, swaggering compulsion moved my fist in a threatening arc. Whittaker never retreated as I swung weakly and missed his face by at least a foot.

All at once something grabbed at my neck from behind. My legs were shoved forward, and I tumbled to the floor. I found myself on my back, with the minicop jamming a forearm against my throat and a knee into my chest.

By then, my players had arrived. "Get off him," one of them shouted, and another said, "Let him up."

The cop backed away, and I was helped to my feet, but suddenly the cop was at me again, his left hand poking my chest, his right hand balled into a fist.

"It's over," one of my players said. "Let him alone. We'll take him into the locker room."

The players slowly formed a circle around me and Officer Murray. Large black men closing in behind him, cutting off his only avenue of escape. The cop's right hand moved slowly toward his gun, carefully unsnapping the strap on his holster.

"How many of us can you shoot?" I asked him. "How many bullets do you have?"

Now the cop stepped back, holding his hands open in front of his chest, allowing the players to hustle me back into the locker room.

Inside, nobody knew quite what to do. So we moved in an aimless circle, waiting for the music to stop. We had the feeling that we were all under siege, and none of us was eager to leave our sanctuary.

But then the door burst open and a dozen cops poured into the room. The biggest one—six foot five, 240 pounds— the one with the angriest face—said to me, "Come outside; we want to ask you some questions."

"Ask them in here," I said.

"Come outside," he insisted. Officer F. Jablonski.

"They're gonna bust you," a player said, and the entire team surged forward to shield me. But the cops waved their nightsticks, and the players quickly retreated. Then Jablonski grabbed my necktie, yanked me through the doorway, and slammed me facefirst against the wall. My arms were pulled behind my back, and my wrists were cuffed. The peace officers swarmed around me as Murray stepped up close in order to bang his nightstick against my legs and thighs.

"You fucking cowards!" I shouted. I would have said more, but the handcuffs were immediately ratcheted a notch tighter.

I was pushed up the stairs, outside the arena, and into the backseat of a squad car. A photographer flashed his gizmo as the car door slammed shut.

Officer Half-Pint drove while Jablonski rode shotgun. In the cramped backseat with my wrists tightly manacled, I couldn't twist or angle my legs without some part of my body suffering. Jablonski recited my rights in rapid-fire delivery. I couldn't understand most of what he said, but I didn't dare ask for clarification. I was a prisoner.

"What happens now?"

"You'll get booked," Murray said without a trace of hostility. Just doing his job. The law-abiding citizens of Cedar Rapids could rest easy tonight.

"What's the charge? Did Whittaker file charges?"

"No," said Murray. "We'll file charges. Resisting arrest. Just cooperate and behave yourself."

"You know something?" I said to G. Murray. "You'd make a terrific referee."

Built to withstand attack, the station house was only a short jaunt from the arena. Inside, everything was as neat and sanitized as a hospital, and I was led through a bewildering maze of corridors and remanded to the custody of another uniformed officer. This one wore a brown cardigan sweater that hid his nameplate, and floppy slippers instead of shoes. I was a prisoner in Mr. Rogers's neighborhood!

"No funny stuff?" he asks.

"No. I'm done."

So he unlocked the cuffs and asked to see my driver's license. Both my wrists were pinched and still bleeding. Did Mr. Rogers care? He took my watch, wallet, belt, necktie, and shoes and stashed them in a large canvas pouch. He hung my jacket on a hook. He signed something. I signed something and was handed a receipt.

When my mug shots were taken, I couldn't help saying "Cheese." Then Mr. Rogers held my fingers firmly for the printing and it was all somehow reassuring. Crime will never, ever pay.

Mr. Rogers told me I had been charged with "simple" assault and also resisting arrest. In truth, I verbally resisted being taken from the locker room to answer "some questions," but I never had the capability to resist arrest. In any event, my bail was four hundred dollars, payable in cash or certified check only.

"I haven't got that kind of money on hand."

Did I want to make a phone call? No. The guys would be back for me when they had finished showering (and eating?).

So I padded down another carpeted corridor, bent through a door, and found myself locked into a cell by Mr. Rogers. There was a sink and a toilet made of stainless steel. The walls were cinder blocks painted institution gray. On top of a low cinder-block bed, there was a thin plastic mattress, also in gray. The floor was cold and bare. The ceiling was white and the only light was recessed overhead behind a wire grid.

I was alone in a jail cell. No TV. No books. Not even to-night's stat sheet. My entire life had led me to this place, this moment. Should I cry? Pray? Lord, just get me out of this one and I'll be good forever?

Should I fine-tune my excuses? Whittaker had no right to . . . Perhaps I should get my story straight. First he did that, then I did this. . . .

I was alone. Totally. At least the ancient mariner had the sea to look at, the sky, the ship, the dead bodies sprawled on the deck. All I had was my own bottomless, wordless despair.

And, yes, I did pray, and I did weep. Because in the clutch I could not fool myself. "Vanity of vanities . . . all is vanity," sayeth the Preacher, and his finger pointed at me. There were absolutely no extenuations that might excuse me. *Mea culpa.* I was utterly responsible for my own life.

After a while (an hour? two hours? a lifetime?) Mr. Rogers returned my belongings and led me to the front room, where a couple of the guys were waiting. I was informed of my "plea" date, then I signed a few more documents and was free to go.

It seems that the players had chipped in for my bail, and back on the bus, they had a sack of Mickey D's best for me.

"You're always hungry when you get out of the slammer," one of them said.

When I climbed into the bus, they all applauded and hooted and treated me like a hero. I had "stuck up" for them.

Then they regaled me with their own personal testi-monies.

"Being arrested ain't no big thing. Most brothers, if they

live in a big city, have been in the joint some time or other. Me? Yep. I had a fight with some dude in a bar. I stayed in jail overnight, and the school got the charges dropped."

"I got caught drunk driving when I was in school, and they also got the charges dropped."

"I beat up some girl the year after I got out of school. She let me stay in jail for two days, then she dropped the charges. The day I got sprung, I moved in with her."

"Not me, man. I've never been busted. My momma would kill me if I even got a parking ticket."

A short, bouncy clip of the original hassle in the corridor with Officer Murray made it on to the TV news in most major cities. As well as a shot of my being shoved into the squad car. Another clip of Whittaker also got national exposure.

"Charley should stick to writing poetry," he claimed with a smug grin. Then he denied having put on a press. "I don't even have a press."

For the rest of the season, several players from opposing teams would come up to me and say that they appreciated what I'd done for my players. I was suspended for six games, and my return to the bench happened to coincide with a return match with the Silver Bullets in Rockford. After we trounced them Whittaker approached me to apologize. We shook hands and swore to let bygones be gone.

And one of his players privately informed me that Whittaker did, in fact, put on a press, and that they were hoping that I would have punched his lights out.

But Palie was not impressed.

The immediate cost to me was reimbursing my players for the four hundred dollars' bail money they had collected among themselves, plus having to serve the suspension (without loss of salary). Eventually, I also had to shell out three hundred dollars for a local lawyer who negotiated a three-hundred-dollar fine with the Cedar Rapids court that had the relevant jurisdiction.

But the story didn't end there.

I was confined to the hotel the next time Rockford engaged the Silver Bullets on their home court. Some late-game heroics by Freddie Cofield won the game for us.

But, hold on, there's more.

The very next season I was coaching the OKC Thunder, an expansion team. I was not at all surprised when my appearance on the court (my first since the brouhaha) elicited more out-loud abuse from the Cedar Rapids fans.

Okay, I couldn't say that their reaction was undeserved.

They were especially delighted when their hometown heroes routed my guys from tip to buzzer. But guess what Whittaker did with only ten seconds left in the game. With a 26-point lead, and with the quarter point well in hand— he called a twenty-second time-out!

This time, I managed to confine my reaction to using all of my remaining time-outs after the refs signaled the resumption of play. Oh, yes. I also called about three or four additional time-outs, thereby earning a tech for each one that was beyond my legal quota.

Afterward, Herky the Hawk stopped by to apologize for his coach's unseemly time-out call. And within a week, Whittaker was fired.

Several years later I got the word that Whittaker was substitute teaching at a junior high school somewhere in West Virginia.

I hope that instead of coaching basketball, Whittaker is spending his spare time writing poetry.

In any event, I wasn't exactly shocked when Palie fired me the day after the season ended. After all, not only had I been arrested, but also the team's record was a lowly 22-34.

It was small consolation when Jay Polan's son called to tell me that his father was so disgusted with Palie that he bought out his erstwhile buddy, who then retired to Arizona. I was also informed that had Polan been consulted, he would have insisted that I be rehired.

Oh, well.

Even though I had lost my enthusiasm for coaching any-where—especially in the CBA—I still had a family to feed. So I embarked on yet another round of phone calls to CBA general managers, trying once more to find a proper balance between begging and bragging. And I canvassed every NBA acquaintance who I hoped would give me a recommendation.

As it turned out, Phil had just won his first championship with the Bulls, so his word was gold—and my new job was to coach an expansion team in Oklahoma City.

16

Blocked Shots, Bricks, and Barbecued Baloney

OK City . . . The wildest West, where even the shortest drink of water proudly wore a ten-gallon hat. Where barbecued anything (including bologna) was treasured as being top-of-the-line eats. Where the airport was named after Wiley Post, who perished in an airplane crash.

Chip Land was the general manager, a refugee from the oil bust, who hired me primarily because I swore that I would produce a winner. But I was officially welcomed to town by Abe Leamons, the legendary cornpone coach of Oklahoma City University, who said, "So you're the Jew coach from New York that's going to set this town on fire?" And it went downhill from there.

Simply put, by then I was burned out, depleted, exhausted, bored, and in it only for the money. The CBA version of the game held no charm for me anymore, and my only goal was to survive the season without getting fired. Which I did. Barely.

As soon as I got there, my "exploits" were used to sell tickets. My likeness was plastered in the newspapers, on TV, in promotional leaflets, with the following motto: "BIG ACTION COMES TO TOWN."

My arrival coincided with a local extravaganza called the Festival of the Horse. The festivities included the showing of some kind of rare breed of horse flesh at the Cowboy Hall of Fame, a concert by Tony Bennett, and a H-O-R-S-E contest at one of the malls.

Land was eager for me to participate in the shooting competition and I readily agreed. However, he insisted that I dress for the event in a business suit replete with necktie and civilian shoes. When I protested, he said that since highlights of the event were to be featured on all the local TV stations, I had to be properly attired. And he refused to back down.

So there I was, matching shots with sneaker-clad opponents in my shirtsleeves (he ultimately agreed that I could abandon my jacket and loosen my tie) and slippery city shoes. Even worse, the temporary basket was installed on a highly polished tile underfooting. It was all I could do to keep my balance while launching my corkscrew jumpers, but the necessary concentration and awkward physical contortion quickly exhausted me.

By some miracle I won three rounds before being soundly trounced in the finals by a local sportscaster.

My shirt and long pants were drenched with sweat as I accepted the second-place trophy. Even so, Land was irate. After all, I was the coach, and my losing made the Cavalry look bad.

I told him that I would have had a much better chance of winning had I been allowed to compete in sweats and sneakers.

"You don't understand, Charley," he insisted. "It's all about image and class."

Oh. My bad.

That season I wheeled, dealed, and wheedled, and I used the expansion draft to assemble a semirespectable ball club.

At the outset, the cast of characters included some respectable players:

- Anthony Frederick, an NBA veteran of forty-six games with the Pacers, was a terrific guy and a terrific scorer. Too terrific, since he was called up to Sacramento halfway through our season.

- Luther Burks severely sprained his ankle in our eighth game when we were 5-3 and hopeful. He didn't bring his 25.4 points per game average back onto the court until the last eight games of the season.

- Kelsey Weems was as quick as Dominic Pressley but lacked any court awareness whatsoever. Take the time we had possession with the score tied and only twenty-four seconds left in the game. During the time-out I carefully explained our game plan at least four times— Kelsey was to dribble the ball until I signaled him to attack the basket (which happened to be the one nearest our bench). I'd be standing in front of the bench, holding up my arms in a surrender position, then I'd bring them down to my sides and shout "GO!" when it was time for him to start his move. However, he took off as the clock registered ten seconds and missed a wild shot. Naturally, the bad guys got the rebound, scored an unopposed fastbreak lay-up at the other end, and won the game. His excuse? He didn't remember the play, and he didn't see six-foot-nine, 235-pound me.

- Alvin Heggs was a six-foot-eight muscleman with an overpowering jump hook. Blame me for not starting him until the season extended into the New Year. Eventually, Alvin had a cup of coffee with the Houston Rockets before winding up overseas.

- Ozell Jones had played seventy games over the course of two seasons with the Spurs and the Clippers. At seven feet, 260 he had NBA size and talent. Too bad he was even lazier than Jim Lampley.

- Perry Young was a wizened CBA veteran who had his NBA shot five years previous. He was a solid citizen nearing the end of his ability to play acceptable defense.

- Bob Henige was a small-college star who was too slow to compete.

- Mark Plansky had started for the Villanova squad that had played a perfect game in besting Georgetown in the 1989 NCAA championship game. But he was even slower than Henige.

We went through twenty players that season. Some of the late comers included the following:

- Steve Burtt, one of my all-time favorites, had played bits and pieces of four NBA seasons with the Warriors, Clippers, Suns, and Bullets. But at six foot two he was categorized as a shooting guard in a point guard's body. Steve was also deemed to be too confrontational to peacefully coexist with his coach of the moment. But I found him to be friendly, savvy, cooperative, and appreciative, plus he played NBA-quality defense and could shoot well enough to average 27.6 ppg. Eventually he went to Europe, but Steve should have had a long and successful career in the NBA.

- Willie Simmons was an elongated shot-blocker who had no other viable physical presence.
- Dennis Williams was an erratic shooter who kept both teams in the game.
- Orlando Graham could rebound, but he couldn't shoot or execute the simplest of plays.
- Royce Jeffries was a muscular, mild-mannered, sky-walker out of Antliers, Oklahoma, and OK State—a joy to know and a pleasure to coach.
- Darren Sanderlin had survived a local tryout camp and made up for his talent limitations with a superb attitude and endless hustle.
- It should also be noted that I traded one player—over Land's vehement protests—when I discovered that he was dealing drugs.

Two other players joined the team late in the season and deserve special mention, primarily because they were respectively the most threatening and the most obnoxious guys I ever coached.

- Ron Moore measured a legitimate seven feet, 265 pounds, and he had split fourteen games with the Pistons and the Suns in 1987–88. But he wouldn't rebound, pass, defend, or shoot anything but turnaround jumpers. In short, he played as though he was about six foot five. But he sure was a scary dude. Every time I criticized him for playing so small, he just glared down at me with murder in his eyes. After he showed a particularly weak effort in Sioux Falls, South Dakota, I was fed up with him—and he knew it. "If you cut me, Charley, I'll kill you." I did cut him, over the phone and just hours before we left OKC for another road trip.

- Leroy Combs had a reputation for being a bad actor, but he was born and raised in Oklahoma City, played at OK State, and had spent 1983–84 with the Pacers. I wanted nothing to do with him, but since our season was already down the tubes Chip Land insisted that we sign him. During the first practice that Combs attended, he voiced his disdain for my offense and ordered his new teammates to disobey me and listen only to him. He also insisted that he play forty-eight minutes per game, that every offensive possession should run through him, and that he should be responsible for making substitutions. Before long, our only dialogue consisted of mutual insults—and, knowing that my days were numbered, I suspended him for our last two games in San Jose. But he sat behind the bench and we continued to curse each other during every dead ball. The following season, Henry Bibby replaced me on the Cavalry's bench, and Leroy signed on as his assistant.

With this roster of erratic characters, it should come as no surprise that the season was a disaster from the get-go.

For example, our chartered bus ran out of gas about halfway through a three-hour trip to Wichita Falls, Texas. We had to stay put for another three hours before another bus appeared and our journey resumed.

We arrived in Wichita Falls about fifteen minutes before the scheduled tip-off, but the refs (if I remember correctly Duke Callahan was one of them) refused to delay the starting time. We got dressed in a rush, then warmed up for all of two minutes.

As you might expect, the home team (the Texans) broke out to a quick 10-point lead and routed us from wall to wall.

Also as you might expect, I rode the officials so furiously that I got ejected before halftime.

Apparently CBA refs didn't get paid by the hour.

On the occasion of my fiftieth birthday, the Cavalry was engaged in a home game at the Myriad Center. There had been a questionable call made at the end of the second quarter that favored the visiting team, so as I headed for the locker room I barked at the officials.

Imagine my surprise when I was greeted with a birthday celebration as I approached the team bench prior to the start of the second half. One of the cheerleaders presented me with a clutch of several helium-filled Happy Birthday balloons, which I grabbed with my right hand. Another pair of cheerleaders then presented me with a birthday cake.

The cake was contained in a pan that was about three feet long and two feet wide. But the rack in the oven must have been tilted because the cake came out somewhat lopsided. With the balloons in my right hand, I accepted the cake with my left hand while the fans serenaded me with the Birthday Song.

What a wonderful, thoughtful surprise!

Unfortunately, while the fans were singing, I was having trouble balancing the cake with my left hand (which had been slightly gnarled by gout). Just as the last note resounded through the arena, I felt the cake slipping out of my tenuous grip. Instead of releasing the balloons, however, I tried to flip the cake as far away from me as possible so as not to get my suit soiled with whipped cream and sweet goo.

The cake traveled only a few feet and landed harmlessly near midcourt, about twenty feet from the nearest sideline and about thirty feet from where the refs were standing. But both the fans and the refs reacted to my clumsiness with kindness and rousing good cheer.

Fast forward a few weeks.

A writer and photographer from *Sports Illustrated* arrived in Oklahoma City to do a lengthy profile on yours truly. He spent several days shadowing me, asking questions about writing fiction, as well as the vagaries of coaching in the CBA. He was quite respectful and seemed genuinely curious about my literary opinions.

Another of our topics concerned the long life of the CBA, which was three months older than the BAA-cum-NBA. Among several other observations, I suggested that the longevity of the CBA could be compared to the famous endurance of cockroaches, which have survived famine, pestilence, hail, and floods. I meant this as a positive equation, even quasi-biblical in tone.

However, unbeknownst to me, the prearranged angle the writer secretly sought to explore was whether Charley Rosen was a lunatic or a genius. While witnesses were quoted on both sides of the issue (many more on the former than on the latter), Chip Land's observation was especially painful: "Everybody likes to hate Charley Rosen." In the end the incident with the birthday cake was cited as being the deciding factor in my general lunacy.

According to the writer, because of my disagreements with the officials at the close of the first half, I had deliberately tossed the cake at the refs in protest—and narrowly missed hitting them. The writer added that I had accompanied this misdeed with a round of searing curses.

Say what?

The point being that, in the madcap world of the Crazy Basketball Association, even top-notch journalists are apt to lose their minds

Meanwhile, as we continued to lose games, local TV ads claimed that I was really eight feet two inches tall! Accordingly, a full-length photo of me in a Cavalry sweat suit was greatly enlarged and mounted on a stiff cardboard cut-out. The whole apparatus was then installed in the lobby of our home court, the Myriad Convention Center.

The fans gawked at the photo with many becoming convinced that I was actually eight two—which is fifteen inches taller than I really am.

And I can't count the number of times when I was stopped in the streets, and at courtside, by otherwise rational folks who looked me up and down, then said this to their companions: "See? I told you he was really eight foot two!"

Which only goes to prove that everything is always bigger than real life in OKC.

Kelsey Weems had played under Jim Valvano at North Carolina State and was under the impression that several of his teammates were shaving points in league with gamblers. Midway through the season, ESPN-TV was in the process of investigating this very possibility and brought a crew to Oklahoma City to interview an "anonymous player."

In the eventual broadcast, this player was shown in silhouette and his voice was electronically altered to presumably protect his true identity. And, yes, he claimed that "several" of his teammates had turned tricks for a number of bookies and high-fliers on several occasions. However, Kelsey's profile was extraordinarily memorable—resembling a cartoon character named Jiminy Cricket. So no one who had ever seen him in person was fooled.

Still, throughout the remainder of the season, Weems had to deny that he was the shadowland informer several times every week. No wonder the young man was perpetually distracted.

Money was usually in short supply in the CBA, but just as often priorities were absurd. Like the time when the Cavalry was in dire need of a backup center. I contacted Abdur Rahiim al-Matin, who had played for the Albany Patroons a few years back when I was Phil Jackson's assistant. He was a six-foot-eight star-toucher who could rebound, block shots, and get along with everybody. And he agreed to play in Oak City for a reasonable paycheck.

At the time, Rahiim (as he was called) lived in St. Louis, which was a two-hundred-dollar flight from Oklahoma City. A small investment, I thought, for such a vitally needed player.

But Chip Land disagreed. Besides, he had another plan for his limited budget, one that he assured me would uplift the team's morale and be more useful than a backup big.

Like what?

Like buying new bras for the cheerleaders!

We finished the season at a dismal 18-38, and for the sixth consecutive year I led the CBA in technical fouls. Despite this dubious accomplishment, I happened to witness with great envy the T'd-up antics of one particular coach.

The Cavalry was being stomped by the Albany Patroons, who were coached by George Karl. At the time, the Patroons had relocated their home court to a sixteen-thousand-seat venue called the Knickerbocker Arena—it later became the Pepsi Arena, then the Capitol Arena, and is now the Times-Union Arena—and only the lower stands were made available for the CBA games.

Despite having a 20-plus-point lead late in the final period, and with the quarter-point well in hand, Karl was angered by an out-of-bounds call occurring in front of his bench that went against the Patroons. The miscall was totally meaningless and had no bearing on the game. Yet Karl, with the ball in his hands, stepped onto the court and began to loudly curse the refs, their ancestors, and their progeny.

ZAP! He was hit with a quick T, but that didn't stop him.

Calmly, and with admirable focus, Karl punted the ball high, wide, and deep into the upper deck! When the second T was inevitably tooted, Karl simply turned and walked peacefully and silently toward the locker room.

But what a kick! In an open field it would have traveled fifty yards or more! Man, was I impressed. In fact, I was so impressed that after the Cavs had returned home, I lingered after one practice session until there were no witnesses on hand. Then I attempted to duplicate Karl's incredible feat.

Alas, the best I could do was kick either line drives into the courtside seats or high pop flies that landed on the court.

That's what I got for growing up in the crowded streets of the Bronx where nobody was silly enough, or rich enough, to punt any kind of ball into passing traffic.

The *Sports Illustrated* article about me was printed late in the season—March 3, 1991—and my "cockroach" metaphor was emphasized. I didn't think anything of it—wasn't any publicity a positive thing for the league? Especially in a widely read, internationally distributed magazine?

However, the CBA Board of Directors, that is, the franchise owners, took exception and fined me four thousand dollars.

I was allowed to defend myself during a conference call, wherein I explained that cockroaches were really clean, courageous, and versatile creatures. My arguments only succeeded in cutting my fine in half. But I remained outraged.

It came as absolutely no surprise when I was canned two days after the season. As soon as I returned home to Woodstock, I began my revenge—writing a novel that was peopled with real players, coaches, and team executives under assumed names. About 90 percent of all the happenings in the novel were likewise copied from actual events. The title of the novel was *The Cockroach Basketball League*.

Since then, the CBA has become extinct. But my novel is still in print, and the twelve hundred different species of cockroaches are still going strong.

However, my CBA career wasn't quite over.

17

Down and Eventually Out in Albany

A new owner, Joe O'Hara, had taken over the Albany Patroons, and he'd decided to arrange for a revival of the franchise's glory years. That's why I was hired to coach, Lowes Moore was my assistant, and Derrick Rowland was still on the active roster.

I was only in it for the lucre, so I was happy to agree to a fifty-thousand-dollar contract in which only the first thirty thousand was guaranteed. However, the additional twenty grand would be inexorably mine if I was still employed by game number 45.

Unfortunately, the Patroons' most recent past was more influential than the good old days. That's because, while I was in Oklahoma City, George Karl had coached the Patroons to a record-breaking 50-6 regular season before losing in the conference finals. Never mind that the best players from the previous season were gone—Vincent Askew, Snoopy Graham, and Mario Elie were in the NBA; Albert King and Pete Myers were overseas; Clinton Smith was playing in Fort Wayne. The only returning players of note were Jeff Sanders and Derrick.

Sanders was supposed to be the Patroons' best player, and I turned down several trade possibilities to bring him back to Albany. He was a six-foot-two, 240-pound power player who had been a top draft choice by the Chicago Bulls in 1989. But after disappointing stints with Chicago and Charlotte, Sanders's next stop was Albany, where he'd averaged 20.5 ppg and 9.5 rebounds for Karl. Too bad Jeff and I never really connected.

One reason was that, out of sheer boredom, I decided to abandon my favorite flex offense for the triangle.

During the summer, I had studied Tex Winter's seminal text, *The Triple-Post Offense*; relentlessly questioned Phil Jackson; and pored over a Bulls' training film that Phil had given me. It was all I could do to learn the basic formation, the key passes, and a few specialty plays. But if I knew the parts, collating them into a cohesive overview was beyond my capabilities. Turned out that my half-baked version of the triangle was a series of plays in which I signaled the key pass. It was an execution offense played station to station with absolutely no continuity.

After his rookie season in Chicago, Sanders certainly knew the triangle much better than I did. But I felt too insecure to ask for his help, and to establish his standing as the franchise's VIP, he didn't volunteer.

After limping out of the gate with a record of 2-6, I trashed the triangle and reinstated the sturdy flex. For a time, at least, this move gave me the upper hand over Sanders.

But our ever-shaky relationship was irrevocably rent when Sanders complained to the local media that I was hurting his chances to return to the NBA by "messing" with his minutes. He actually said this even though he was playing nearly forty minutes per game, an average that included his being tossed from a game in Columbus, Ohio, for protesting a ref's call in the opening minutes.

Things came to a head when the Patroons were scheduled for a Thanksgiving game against the Rockford Lightning. Our flight terminated in Chicago the day before the game, where a van was made available for the sixty-mile drive to Rockford. But Jeff Sanders had a suggestion.

Since he still maintained an apartment in Chicago, why didn't we stop over at his place, enjoy a Thanksgiving feast there, and then proceed to Rockford?

Everybody liked the idea, including me.

Turned out that Jeff's luxurious digs were in a high-rise somewhere near the lake. He flipped on some music, put a video in each of the two huge TVs, and left to pick up the food. He was gone for nearly two hours. Meanwhile, the music was too loud and too rappish for my taste, there was plenty of beer in the fridge, one of the videos was heavy-duty porn (too gross even for me), and the other was *Coming to America* with Eddie Murphy, which I'd already seen in a hotel in Moline.

Everybody wandered from room to room, drinking beer, laughing at this and that, but too embarrassed to linger too long in the porno room.

Jeff finally returned and, after buzzing from the lobby to summon help, brought several huge aluminum pans full of delicious holiday goodies—from turkey to sweet potato pie and everything in between. It was a glorious repast.

Then, just as we gathered ourselves to leave and resume our drive to Rockford, Jeff pulled me aside. Was it okay if he stayed the night there? He promised, he swore, that he'd be on time for tomorrow's shootaround.

In the face of his generosity, how could I refuse?

But, of course, he never showed for the shootaround.

He was even late to arrive at the game that night. His only excuse was a vague one. "Personal problems."

I was irate, but my options were limited.

Since he still had plenty of NBA money at his command—I'd witnessed Jeff's spending twenty thousand dollars in a men's clothing store during a prolonged layover in the Atlanta airport—fining him a couple of hundred bucks would be ludicrous. Suspending him would be a gross overreaction.

So I decided the most appropriate punishment would be to have him start the game on the bench and then limit his daylight to about twenty minutes. Needless to say, he wasn't very happy—and when we lost to the Lightning by 20, neither was I.

Shortly thereafter, Jeff informed me that his agent had arranged a gig for him in Europe.

"Good luck, Jeff. I hope you can work your way back into the NBA."

"Good luck to you, too, Charley."

In truth, though, we were both happy to be rid of each other.

Christmas on the road wasn't much better: We arrived in Moline, Illinois, on Christmas Eve, the day before we were scheduled to play the Tri-City Thunder. Most of the players in the league were extremely friendly with one another, having previously crossed paths in college competition, common hometowns, summer leagues, preseason NBA camps, or on other professional teams—so members of the host team gladly opened their homes and their parties to visiting players.

Coaches were not nearly as friendly. Especially the Thunder's Mauro Panaggio and me, who had a history of public confrontations both verbal and physical.

So I was left to my own resources at an old, drafty hotel with some kind of Nordic theme. Without a car and with the weather too cold to be roaming around a strange city, I stayed in my room, read, watched TV, read, napped, and read some more. My Christmas was a buffet consisting of dried pieces of salmon, chewy turkey, and tasteless trimmings.

Whatever.

As long as we beat Panaggio.

The game turned out to be fiercely contested, and my guys played their hearts out. It all came down to this: The score was tied and the Thunder had possession with only ten ticks left on the game clock. A. J. Wynder was a solid player and all-around nice guy who was destined to have a cup of coffee with the Celtics—and he was totally in control of the situation as he brought the ball upcourt.

In the previous time-out, I had called for a tight, switching defense and warned my players to ignore fakes, stay on the floor, and, since we were already over the limit, avoid fouls.

However, even before Wynder crossed midcourt, his defender (who shall remain nameless because he, too, was a terrific player and a wonderful person) deliberately fouled him!

Say what!

Wynder calmly sank both free throws—and, of course, our last-ditch effort to tie the game ended up with the wrong guy taking the wrong shot and slamming a brick off the backboard.

I went berserk in the postgame locker room, especially after the fouler offered no viable excuse. He was a shy young man and was actually one of my favorite players.

No, he hadn't misread the scoreboard, or misunderstood my instructions, or anything. It just "happened," he shrugged. "I don't know why."

When I got back to my hotel room, I called the league office and unceremoniously cut the offending player.

Leaving the two of us with precious little to be thankful for.

The only good news was that I re-signed him a week later.

As the season progressed I altered the roster to include several players I had previously coached elsewhere: Jose Slaughter (who played in only nine games before leaving for the Philippines), Ken Bannister (who played in only seven games before failing a drug test), and Royce Jeffries. Also Derrick Lewis's younger brother, Cedric. And because of various injuries, Lowes had to play in a handful of games.

But nothing seemed to be working well enough as the Patroons flirted with the .500 mark for most of the season.

Johnnie Hilliard was a high-scoring rookie, who, after Sanders left, became the focus of the offense. My buddy Gerald Oliver was coaching the Fort Wayne Fury and was eager to make a trade for Hilliard—and he did have a player whom I also lusted for.

Clinton Smith was an NBA vet who played point guard to perfection and whose infectious enthusiasm had a way of uniting his teammates and raising everybody's morale.

Smith's only downside was his habit of borrowing money and then vanishing.

But since our first-round draft pick—Marc Brown from Siena—couldn't defend a fire hydrant and couldn't make a shot on the move, I agreed to the swap.

Gerald and I agreed to make the deal official after the Patroons played that very night. But Hilliard proceeded to erupt for 36 points! So the trade was off.

Gerald had been around the CBA too long to be unduly upset by the turn of events, so we wrangled for a while, then came up with another deal that finally brought Smith to Albany. As soon as he arrived, the Pats began playing like world-beaters. Indeed, after sweeping back-to-back games in Grand Rapids, I even entertained hopes of winning a championship.

But after fourteen games, Smith reprised his disappearing act, and when the Animal failed his drug test, our season was officially doomed.

I finally reached my freak-out point in Birmingham, Alabama. The management of the home-standing Bandits had made high-priced seats available that were situated right next to the visiting team's bench. Sitting beside me during this particular game was a dude who came equipped with a fat butt, a western-cut suit, a ten-gallon hat, and a pair of pointy-heeled cowboy boots.

Soon enough, he became greatly annoyed at my habit of jumping up and shouting my complaints at the refs—even to the point where he forcibly tried to shove me out of his line of vision. And when I was seated, he was constantly elbowing me, trying to gain more space for his oversized behind in his small seat.

But not long into the game I began cursing—the refs, the scoreboard, several missed lay-ups, the inept defensive sequences by my players, and, above all, my own destiny—in a voice not loud enough for anybody to hear except him and my players. That's when the good ole boy really got irate. So much so that he lifted the leg that was pressing against mine and stomped the pointy heel of his boot into my instep.

Man, did that hurt!

But I didn't say anything, nor did he.

My reaction was to jump out of my seat and stand directly in front of him, moving to my left or right as he tried to peer around me. That's when he started kicking me in the back of my legs.

I turned around and called him "a fucking asshole" and he said, "You, too!"

I became so focused on devising ways to make this guy's life miserable that I lost track of the game. What was the score? The time? The matchups? I surely didn't know.

Maybe I could pull out the sides of my suit jacket like a pair of wings so as to further limit his sight lines. Or I could crouch in such a way that he'd be face-to-butt with me.

We lost by 137–133, and I went overboard in excoriating my team afterward. "I'll trade any of you guys. Hell, I'll trade all of you!"

I was fired one home loss later. After forty-one games, the Pats' record was 19-22.

My replacement, Herman Kull, finished up at 5-10 and failed to make the playoffs.

In truth, I wasn't anything more than a fairly good CBA coach. Although I had only five or six offensive sets at my command, I was better at that end of the court than I was coaching defense. The weakest part of my repertoire was designing sophisticated half-court traps and double-teaming patterns. And I could never seem to avoid being unnecessarily distracted by the referees. But I did have a good feel for a game in progress and my in-game adjustments were usually effective. My practices, though, were often too general and were often necessarily devoted to making newcomers familiar with my team-of-the-moment's game plan—except immediately before and during the playoffs.

Watching game tapes to scout opponents was difficult because most of the footage was taken by a single camera located somewhere in the upper reaches of any given arena. Plus, Flip Saunders was the only CBA coach who was allowed to take a tape machine with him on the road. When the conditions were appropriate—for example, in preparing for playoff series—my tape work was excellent. Studying these tapes also expanded at least my recognition level of Xs and Os.

By the same means, I came to understand not only the importance of what a player did but also the importance of what he was supposed to do within the context of his team's offensive and defensive designs. Moreover, I learned to appreciate the benefits of watching what the players did when someone else had the ball—which constitutes 90 percent of the game.

I was also fairly accomplished at scouting college players and predicting what kind of pros they would become.

And my scouting reports on individual opponents were likewise first-rate.

I also got along extremely well with the guys who wanted to win, and not so well with the players who were only interested in padding their own numbers. But whether I had good guys or bad guys to coach I was considered to be very much a players' coach. My lifetime record was 150-159, with my win total good enough to qualify as fifteenth best on the all-time victory list. And by coaching in 309 regular-season games, I placed thirteenth on that list.

More important, after getting fired three times in six years, I was compelled to realize that coaching was not my path. For me, coaching was too public, too competitive, too ruthless, and too life-consuming. I finally had to face it—I was a writer. I needed to edit reality, over and over again, until I got it right.

Here's how several other coaches and players describe the education that the CBA provided for them:

After working in the CBA, Eric Musselman went on to coach the Golden State Warriors and the Sacramento Kings.

ERIC MUSSELMAN: *"The experience gained by coaching in the CBA for one season is equivalent to five years' coaching in the NBA. That's because a CBA coach always had to be extremely flexible. We had to coach the available personnel, and be prepared to adjust our game plan to suit the most unexpected circumstances. So the most important skill that I brought with me into the NBA was concentration. No matter what happened, no matter how crazy things got, I was able to concentrate on the next play, the next substitution, the next game. Once I got into the NBA, things like injuries, personnel changes, and wacky players acting out didn't faze me that much. After coaching in the CBA, the NBA is a piece of cake."*

Certainly, being flexible has different connotations for different coaches.

PHIL JACKSON: *"Coaching in the CBA made me a much more flexible coach in the sense that I had been too rigid in my player rotations and too obligated to players who had performed well for me in the past. A crucial part of my development was learning how to go with the flow of a ball game."*

The harsh realities of CBA travel also contributed to the coaches' education: NBA teams routinely travel by chartered flights whose arrivals and departures can be tailored to fit any eventuality. Plus, everybody's luggage is transported by hirelings from the appropriate hotel rooms in one city to the appropriate hotel rooms in the next city, while traveling secretaries are responsible for arranging any additional intracity transportation (chartered buses or limos) as well as scheduling practice sites and medical appointments for injured players who require treatment. In the CBA, however, the head coach was responsible for confirming everybody's reservations on their commercial flights (usually 6:00 a.m. departures since they're the cheapest fares), for confirming the normal triple-flight itineraries that land in places like La Crosse, Wisconsin, or Wichita Falls, Texas, barely an hour before game time. Likewise, they are responsible for shepherding players and their luggage through the airports, for ensuring that airport-hotel-arena transportation is in order, for distributing meal money, for keeping track of players' fines and locating AWOL players.

Moreover, since most CBA players only earned from three hundred to five hundred dollars per week, a van provided by the home team and driven (for insurance requirements) by the visiting coach was the most convenient and affordable means of getting around in foreign cities—which meant that the coach and the players also generally ate cheapo meals together, whiled away downtime together in the local mall, and saw the same movies en masse. This allowed for plenty of face-to-face contact between a coach and his players. Lots of time to gossip, bullshit, complain, reminisce, compare shared acquaintances and experiences, and relate on a personal, nonbasketball level.

FLIP SAUNDERS: *"I liked the camaraderie of being around the players so much and getting to know them. Because we all had the same goal of getting into the NBA, we realized that we needed each other to get there, and that brought us all very close together. It gave me a model of behavior that I try to implement in the NBA. Also, the CBA was where a coach could experiment and try out different concepts without the multimillion-dollar NBA pressure of having to win every night."*

Jim Sleeper was a twenty-year man, having coached the Grand Rapids Hoops, the Maine Lumberjacks, the Bay State Bombardiers, and the Sioux Falls Skyforce. JIM SLEEPER: *"For all its quirks, the CBA game was more real, more human, and much more fun than the NBA's dumbed down, arrogant, me-first version. Notice, too, that the only teams playing an inter-*

esting, intricate style of basketball in the NBA *are all coached by* CBA *refugees."*

Jason Sasser played briefly for the Seattle Super Sonics after a lengthy stint in the CBA. JASON SASSER: "*All these* NBA *guys are spoiled rotten. They should be forced to play in the* CBA *for a week just so they could appreciate what a privileged existence they have here."*

Pete Myers has been a Chicago Bulls assistant coach for several years. PETE MYERS: "*I played in the* NBA *for eight years and I found that most of my coaches (except for Phil Jackson) were very aloof from the players. Like we were the reluctant schoolboys and they were the righteous principals. But when I played in the* CBA, *I discovered that most of those guys were so hands-on and fun that we were eager to follow their instructions. That's when I decided that my future was to become a coach. And the kind of coach that I wanted to be was modeled after the guys I played for in the* CBA."

However, by 1990—concurrent with my season in Oklahoma City—the golden age was defunct, and the entire tenor of the CBA had changed. Players were increasingly desperate to shoot their way into The League, coaches were routinely fired after losing three consecutive games, and owners were pinching pennies tighter than ever.

HERB BROWN: "*Nobody wanted to be there. Not the coaches, not the players, not the referees. That's why we were all pissed off all of the time."*

Within sixteen months after Joe O'Hara fired me, he moved the Albany Patroons—once the bellwether of the CBA—to

Hartford, Connecticut. And the frantic game of musical franchises sped up.

The CBA didn't last much longer. In 1998 Isiah Thomas bought the entire CBA for approximately $8 million! He knew that the NBA was planning to establish an officially sanctioned player development league (which later became the National Basketball Developmental League), and Thomas's scheme was to sell "his" arena leases, administrative staffs, and so on, to the NBA for a profit of millions.

While he negotiated with the NBA, Thomas visited every CBA franchise and promised regular appearances to help promote them all. But when the NBA offered Thomas only $9 million, he withdrew his support from the CBA and left the longest continuing professional basketball league in a shambles. Largely due to Thomas's machinations, the CBA went bankrupt in 2001.

Shortly thereafter, a small group of businessmen in and around Boise, Idaho, bought the CBA name and logo and operated a regional nine-team bus league. After fifty-five years, the CBA had reverted to its origins.

In 2006, however, the CBA experienced a brief revival. Jim Coyne was back in charge of the Albany Patroons. Under his influence, the city spent nearly $7 million to purchase the old Washington Avenue Armory from the U.S. Army and to refurbish the joint. But the revival didn't last very long.

After fielding teams in nearly 150 different cities since the league's inception, the CBA was down to five teams as the 2008–09 campaign commenced—until Pittsburgh dropped out less than a month into the season. The survivors struggled on for another ten weeks before deciding to pull the plug.

- The league's abbreviated sixty-third season terminated in a three-game series starting on February 5 between the two best teams, Albany and Lawton–Fort Sill, for the "championship." Fewer than five hundred fans turned out in Albany to witness the visitors winning what was most likely the last CBA game ever played.

- Immediately thereafter, there was some brave talk out of the league office about reorganizing and expanding the CBA in time for the 2009–10 season. But that was clearly wishful thinking.

Why, then, was the CBA on life support for so many seasons? And why did it perish?

For one, the various CBA commissioners made perpetual efforts to convince the NBA to form a farm system similar to the long-established relationship between major league baseball teams and their minor league affiliates. But the NBA Players Association just as perpetually fought this—simply because a farm system would result in each NBA team unilaterally controlling the fates of too many players.

Since individual CBA teams were unable to negotiate profitable TV contracts, the only available sources of income were gate receipts and merchandise—not nearly enough to balance out the roughly $1 million annual budgets required to field a team.

Back in the halcyon days of the 1980s, the only universally televised NBA games were those that were broadcast on the networks. Some CBA franchises that were in proximity to an NBA city could also receive regular game telecasts: the Bulls in Rockford, the Celtics in Worcester, or the Sixers in Lancaster. Aside from local high school games or the rare presence of a Division I college team, the CBA provided the only game in many towns. However, once cable TV became established and the NBA Package was available, it was easier (and cheaper) for a fan to stay home and watch the best players in the world from his or her easy chair.

Once the D-League became the feeder for the NBA's in-season replacement players, the best available talent either played there or shipped overseas. Consequently, there were no over-the-hill NBA vets to juice up CBA rosters and the overall level of competition took a nose-dive.

And most recently, of course, the bottom falling out of the economy was the immediate reason for the CBA's death throes.

Joe O'Hara provides the most fitting epitaph for the Crazy Basketball Association: "Here's how to make a small fortune . . . Start with a large fortune and buy a CBA franchise."

18

The End of Regulation

Now that my CBA career was history, I was able to resume my playing career on a full-time basis. The Woodstock Joneses convened on Tuesday nights and early Sunday mornings at Red Hook High School, where Rod Chando was coaching the boys' varsity. These were serious confrontations and the very best competition in the area.

Another primo game in which I often participated took place on Thursday night above the firehouse in nearby Saugerties as well as Saturday mornings at Saugerties Junior High School. These runs were clean, good-natured, and always energetic with an emphasis on playing unselfishly.

In my early fifties I still had barely enough gas to accompany my usual teammates to play in various local prisons—with the best run always being in Green Haven.

The colossal stone walls surrounding the Green Haven Correctional Facility were cold to the touch, even in the summertime. Located near Stormville, New York, Green Haven was (and is) a "max joint," so the machine gunners in the turrets took casual aim at every visitor.

The forty-foot front gate rumbled open and slowly slammed shut. Like all visitors, my teammates—Greg Dodge, Ron Chando, Dennis Odle, and Al Dufty—and I were subject to body searches, ultraviolet hand brands, and the lonesome clanging of the gates. Inside, all the breezes smelled like rust.

Lying only two hours north of New York City, Green Haven sheltered 60 percent of all lifers in the state and had New York's only wired electric chair. The population was 2,100, 95 percent of whom were black or Hispanic, but the vast majority of the security guards were from redneck neighborhoods farther north. That's why the time was hard at Green Haven. It was said that ten years upstate in Clinton was quicker than five years here.

There was always a certain underlying air of tension inside the walls. But our presence made the edge sharper than usual. We'd never lost to the GHCF hoopers even though our team always consisted of five old and slow white guys—the inmates called us the Cracker Attack—but we could all shoot, pass, and play with discipline.

The guards informed us that the morning line favored us by 10.5 points. The stakes were cigarettes, pushups—fifty at a time, due right after the final buzzer—or the overnight "use" of the participating bettors' "sweet boys."

The GHCF varsity used to play thirty games each season—against other local squads from Newburgh and Poughkeepsie, with special guest teams from Harlem—but their schedule was greatly reduced when an inmate dusted a guard in 1981.

The guards wished us luck as we passed through the inspection process. "Kill the nigger motherfuckers!" was their common refrain.

The gym was empty of spectators, but wired canisters of tear gas could be seen mounted near the ceiling. The court was made of some kind of long-lasting rubberized compound. Most hues of the rainbow were prohibited for prisoners, but here they could eschew the hated pine green institutional clothing. All fifteen of the home-standing players were waiting for us, proudly attired in their "jazz red" uniforms neatly trimmed in white.

These guys represented the best from Green Haven's extensive intramural leagues. Most were culled from the Mau Maus or the in-house dynasty, the African Warriors. The privileged All-Stars normally shared chow and yard, and several of them inhabited the same cell block. Their leading scorer was Burton Jones, a lean, six-foot-seven center and convicted arsonist who played seven feet tall. Next best was Benny Bates, number 3869639, serving a "big-time bid" for homicide.

Virtually all of the GHCF inmates had been in the system for years, so their youthful wildness had long since been burned out. As such, it was axiomatic that an "old jacket's" best friends were Jesus and Basketball Jones.

As the game got under way, the home team showed its pent-up impatience, driving to the hoop, trying to force every play to a speedy and spectacular conclusion.

We were ahead 16–7 midway through the first quarter, when the afternoon count in Cell Block B concluded and five hundred inmates suddenly filled the gym with a raucous energy. Most of the prisoners had bulging bodies and massive arms—there were thirty thousand pounds of weights available and all of the workout stations were outdoors. The inmates grunted in the rain, in the blistering heat, and in the frigid snows.

"You fucking chumps gonna lose again?" shouted a muscle-bound lifer, and the roiling crowd screamed abuse at the home team.

One player responded by clearing his teammates out of his way with a disdainful wave of his hand, then he faked, juked, and spun hoopward to miss a backhanded lay-up.

"Give up the ball!" yelled the coach, a broad-chested jewel thief named B. Nice.

But the player was offended, saying, "Hey, man, it's my main move. And it's money!"

Before long, we had gained even firmer control of the game.

In one corner of the stands, two white-haired convicts played chess, oblivious as Burton Jones hacked me and the referees sucked their whistles as I missed the ensuing lay-up. Actually, we played much more physically than they did, because should there be a fracas in the stands or on the court, the basketball season would be defunct.

We led 62–46 at the half. In a small storage room off the gym, we gulped the house beverage, orange Kool-Aid, and discussed strategy.

Despite our lead, our only hope would be to build a huge lead that would stave off the varsity's inevitable run, for speed, depth, and conditioning are the home team's advantages.

Lights out was 2200 during the week, 2300 on Fridays and Saturdays, and the wake-up bell rang promptly at 0700. The inmates ate three nourishing meals daily, smuggled drugs and alcohol were costly, and even in their sequestered situation AIDS had made many of them wary of casual sex. The varsity hoopers ranged in age from twenty-six to thirty-four, yet prison time was famous for preserving the appearance of youth and they all resembled schoolboys.

Across the corridor in the gym office, the prison players savored their Kool-Aid and tried to rouse themselves to victory. "Run faster!" commanded their coach. "Run the legs off them old men!"

But the nice advice was ignored as the second half began. Our lead was growing when the refs signaled an "official time-out" to let a fat, homely, middle-aged woman cross the far side of the gym. She wore a midnight-blue administrator's uniform, and wolf whistles and lecherous howls followed her. After she closed the door behind her the rowdy invitations turned to insults.

With 5:44 remaining on the game clock, the varsity finally launched its counterattack. Bates stole a wayward pass and led Jones for an elegant stuff. Chando gambled by throwing a long pass to me—I was open only because I couldn't get back on defense in a timely fashion—but it was overthrown by ten years. Suddenly the game got wild. Another jumper for Bates. A tip-in by Jones.

We had horded all of our time-outs to use in the fourth quarter, but the rampage didn't abate.

Another steal. More fastbreak dunks. And Green Haven suddenly ran away with the game, winning by 142–133.

They jumped around and hugged each other, as jubilant as if their sentences had just been commuted.

In their hearts, they knew that they wanted the game more than we did. They needed it more. Somehow the victory put them in touch with the outside world. For the moment, the walls were made of smoke and perfect justice prevailed.

Then another bell rang, and the prisoners were herded back behind bars.

As for us, we hustled out of there without showering, eager to break open the beer on ice hidden in a cooler in the trunk of Chando's car. Yes, we lost, but it was a good run.

Shortly thereafter, Chando got a phone call from Arnie Spadafora, Green Haven's recreation director. It seemed that just three days after his basketball heroics, Burton Jones returned from practice to discover that his cell had been torched. For reasons of economy, Jones decided not to pay protection to a gang working Cell Block B.

Immediately, Jones was placed in protective custody, where he would remain until his sentence was served. That meant no hoops for the next twelve and a half years to life.

Not long after that, I played in the last structured game of my career.

I was recruited by some hoopers I had met while I was coaching the Patroons to compete in something called the Huntsman Chemicals World Senior Games. Nobody involved ever knew—or cared to know—precisely what those chemicals were. In any case, for a not outrageous entry fee individuals over the age of fifty could compete in track-and-field events, swimming races, and team basketball competition. (There was also an over-fifty-five classification.) The fifty-plus double-elimination basketball tournament was supposed to be fiercely competitive.

The games were held in St. George, Utah, which boasted of being the summer home of Brigham Young. We were the Albany Golden Bulldogs, and my teammates included Howard Dewey, Jim Zullo, Billy Romer, Paul Visconti, Dan Smith, Bob McCarroll, JD Walko, Ed Shepard, and Fritz Showers. And a nicer bunch of teammates I've never had.

NBA veteran Barry Kramer practiced with us on several occasions, but he was unable to make the trip. The rumor was that his wife wouldn't let him go. Nevertheless, we opened the series by beating a team from Detroit, 79–29, wherein I was guarded by a big-boned woman! I was reluctant to shoot and only tallied 10 points.

Next up was a feisty team from North Utah, whose players made sure that every one of their fouls was a nasty one. Even so, we cruised to a 79–34 victory. Because of the lopsided score, once again I concentrated on rebounding and passing and wound up with a mere 6 points.

Now came our toughest opponents—the defending champs from Portland, starring the late LeRoy Ellis, a six-foot-eleven-inch veteran of fourteen NBA seasons (1962–76). The game was tight for most of the first half—we led 28–20 at one point—until the resident refs made several outrageous calls against me.

One of these resulted when Ellis slammed his left elbow into my chest as he went up for a jump hook, then knocked me to the floor on his way down. Yet the foul was called on me.

I was also called for a phantom moving screen, and a wild attempt to block one of Ellis's shots that missed hitting anything by at least a foot nevertheless hung another foul on me. Even worse, in another sequence, when I left my feet and unloosed my own version of a jump hook, I was clearly hit by Ellis as I released the ball—which made the net dance on its way through the hoop. The ref couldn't help but call a foul—but he also said that the basket didn't count. I was so irate that I split the resulting free throws. Ellis also disappointed me by lobbying the refs for a foul call every time he shot the ball.

I picked up my fifth and final foul on a highly dubious charging call with 7:50 remaining. Portland was nursing a 5-point lead at the time and the outcome was very much in doubt. However, my vehement protests earned me a pair of techs—and the game was effectively over. The final score was 68–42, and I finished with 5 points.

The very next day, we participated in a one-night, four-team playoff with the winners to receive bronze medals. We beat a local team from St. George 84–70 (I had 10 points), and immediately returned to action against a team from Chicago that featured six-foot-ten Bill Chmielewski, who had been the MVP of the 1962 National Invitational Tournament for the Dayton Flyers.

All of the games that night were reffed by a single official, and he did a wonderful job. I had my best performance of the tournament as we won 64–57 in overtime. My stats in the last game I ever played in a basketball uniform amounted to 26 points, including 8 for 8 from the stripe in the extra period.

When I returned home, I was eager to resume my career at various pickup games at the local YMCA and at the Woodstock Joneses' twice-weekly runs. However, while I was able to match the quickness (or lack thereof) of the players at the Senior Games, I suddenly discovered that my legs were gone. Apparently, I had used up all of my diminishing resources in St. George and if my spirit was willing, my wheels were wobbly.

So it was that during one particular midday pickup game at the Kingston Y, a thirty-ish six-foot-five, 230-pound opponent and I were in a race to rescue an important loose ball.

It looked like he'd beat me to the right spot by about a half step, so I tried to slow him up by applying the Elbow of Experience to the side of his head.

BANG!

However, he shook off the blow as though I were made of straw, grabbed the ball, and executed a nifty pass that led to the winning basket. I mean, the kid didn't even rub the point of contact!

The next morning, when my elbow was swollen to the size of a large grapefruit, I decided to hang 'em up.

Which I did.

And that was the ignominious termination of my daze as an active player. For the rest of my life I would be a mere civilian.

Even so, still understanding that coaching is the next best thing to playing, I became the women's coach at a D-3 college only a half hour's drive from my home in Woodstock.

We were only 8-18 during my initial season but had qualified for the postseason playoffs—as the eighth seed—for the first time in the school's history. And, of course, we got shellacked in the opening game.

Yet despite the relative success we'd achieved, my rookie season wasn't much fun. Because of the good-old-boy clubbiness in the athletic department, the women athletes were treated as second-class citizens. So we had to practice at six o'clock in the morning. And sometimes we had to convene at halftime of our games in the remnants of a basement bowling alley while the men did their pregame stuff upstairs in a classroom.

Also, the department at large and many of the coaches of

the men's teams were guilty of some financial hanky-panky, including such innovations as these: a slush fund filled with leftover money from deliberately overbudgeted items; kickbacks from sporting goods stores; having three players share a motel room on the road instead of two—with the coach and the hotel clerk splitting the monies that had been allotted for the empty rooms; and coaches keeping meal money for players who didn't make road trips because of injuries, term papers due, and so on.

After nine years in the CBA, the actual coaching was rewarding but also frustrating. I liked the fact that the women didn't define themselves as being basketball players, so they were open to learning and they always played hard. But the talent level was so low that my coaching chops weren't fully utilized. And the referees couldn't be any worse than they were—or so I thought. Too many of them had a superior attitude, as if it was beneath them to be working a D-3 women's game.

In any event, I agreed to come back for a second season primarily because my daughter, Alexandra, would be on the team. A legitimate six-footer, Alexandra wasn't much of a player—but she could make an occasional lay-up and set crushing picks, even when playing against men. Indeed, late in the season she converted a pair of clutch free throws that clinched a tight road game for us.

However, here's the game that effectively ended my coaching career:

Late in the season we traveled to New York City to play against Hunter College. Since I'd been admitted to Hunter's athletic hall of fame several years back, I was looking forward to the game as a kind of homecoming.

Hunter had a top-notch team, but it was obvious from the get-go that one particular ref was a blatant homer and, unfortunately for us, he was making virtually every call. Every time he tooted his tooter we got a raw deal.

Okay. That's what happens on the road. So my protestations were rather mild, even as Hunter built a double-digit lead.

But what eventually pushed me over the edge was when this knucklehead started laughing at every miscue that my players made. Misdribbles. Botched passes. Bricked lay-ups.

"Hey," I finally shouted out. "What're you laughing at? They're working harder than you are."

That triggered my first technical foul.

Okay. In the CBA (and NBA) coaches sometimes deliberately got themselves T'd in hopes of "buying" more favorable calls. But this jerk started making calls that were even more biased than before, while his partner continued to suck on his whistle.

"Yo," I said to the silent ref. "Doesn't your whistle work?"

Tech number two.

We were behind by 17 at the half, but I made a rousing locker-room exhortation and we began the second half playing like gangbusters. Our flex offense was working like a clock. Our shots began to fall. We played terrific position defense and controlled our boards. In a matter of minutes we trimmed the lead to 7 and had possession—when the lead ref made an atrocious charging call that was compounded by an imaginary hacked-in-the-act call at the other end.

In quick succession, another bogus charge and still another invisible foul went against us. Suddenly we were down by 12, our enthusiasm was depleted, and it was clear to me that the offending ref simply would not let us win.

"You should be arrested for stealing the game, you jackass!"

Tech numbers three and four. And automatic ejection.

We lost by about 20, and I happened to be waiting in the corridor when the refs exited their dressing room.

"You guys are an embarrassment to the game and to yourselves!"

It was when I started cursing them that they flinched and ran out the door.

The next day, the athletic director called me into his office. Complaints had been filed. My behavior was unacceptable. But if I wrote a letter of apology, all would be forgiven.

And I did write the letter—a craven, humiliating mea culpa. Why? Because, despite the hardships and frustrations, I truly loved coaching, and because I wanted to coach Alexandra for at least another season.

Anyway, after the season concluded, the AD presented me with a choice: regardless of the letter of infamy, I could either resign or get fired. Clinging to what I deemed to be my last and only vestige of self-respect, I told him that he'd have to fire me.

Of all the games I've lost because I didn't play well, missed critical shots, or made faulty decisions on the bench, the most painful I-wish-I-could-do-it-over basketball memory that still haunts me to this day is my writing that letter.

But I've got no complaints. Sometimes all's well that doesn't end well.

19

Beyond Basketball

Nowadays, I only touch a basketball once every year—during a summertime weekend workshop ("Beyond Basketball") at the Omega Institute in upstate New York.

"Omega" is the twenty-fourth and last letter of the Greek alphabet, yet it was employed in an inspirational context in the writings of Teilhard de Chardin, a twentieth-century mystic and philosopher. Teilhard used the word to describe the point within each of us where our inner, spiritual nature meets our outer, worldly nature. Teilhard believed that in the synthesis of these two manifestations of our being lay the greatest challenge—and the greatest hope—for human evolution. The Omega Institute in upstate Rhinebeck, New York, was established and designed to create an environment in which this synthesis could more easily take place.

The Omega Institute first opened its doors in 1977 at a time when holistic health, psychological inquiry, world music and art, meditation, and traditional forms of spiritual practice were being adapted to the modern American experience. Taken all together, this New Wave was rapidly becoming a vibrant part of the country's subculture.

Omega's cofounders were Dr. Stephan Rechtschaffen and (his then wife) Elizabeth Lesser. Both were students of Pir Vilayat Inayat Khan, head of the Sufi Order International. Inspired by Vilayat's vision of a holistic learning center, the 195 acres that make up the Omega campus were purchased from a summer camp that was on the verge of bankruptcy. Then, as now, Omega was a nonprofit organization. The original blueprint was a communal-type situation wherein the resident staff would invite teachers to conduct in-house workshops. The public was invited to participate in these workshops at nominal fees designed only to keep Omega self-sufficient. Before long the popularity of the programs brought an increasing number of spiritual seekers to the campus, and the blueprint was compelled to expand.

Stephan was (and still is) a dedicated hooper, so one of the first renovations was to construct a full-length basketball court on a section of lawn just below the dining hall.

These days, more than twenty thousand people attend workshops, retreats, and conferences on the campus every year. Each season (April to October) features approximately 250 workshops in every esoteric area imaginable. From Qigong training to Raw Juice Purifications. From Transcendent Sex to Advanced Songwriting. From yoga to cooking, Buddhist meditations to the flying trapeze experience. Notable workshop leaders have included the likes of Ken Wilber, Pema Chödrön, Deepak Chopra, Alan Alda, Bruce Hornsby, Goldie Hawn, Donovan, Dr. Bernie Siegel, Jimmie Dale Gilmore, plus various swamis and rinpoches.

In 1985 Phil Jackson had completed his second full year at the helm of the Albany Patroons (we'd lost to Bill Musselman's Tampa Bay Thrillers in the Eastern Conference Finals). If Phil's achievements as a coach were known only to the most rabid of hoop-o-philes, he was still fondly remembered by many for his playing days with the Knicks (1967–78). Back then he was regarded with particular affection because of his long-armed defense, his uncanny lefty hook shots, and his hippie ways. Also, his honesty and intelligence were clearly manifested in his media appearances. It was also common knowledge that he walked from his "crib" on Twelfth Street to Madison Square Garden and was therefore accessible to friendly handshakes and advice from Knick-centric passersby (as opposed to Clyde Frazier, who always gadded about town sequestered inside his purple Rolls-Royce).

For sure, Dave DeBusschere was a lunch-pail player, and Captain Willis had the courage of a lion, but it was Phil "Action" Jackson who seemed to personify the way that New Yorkers liked to think of themselves. Smart. Hip. Honest. Compassionate. An overachiever. And, above all, a winner.

So it was through the initiative of Peter Reynolds, a part-time architect and neophyte hooper who was temporarily employed as assistant program director at Omega, that the first link was forged. For the occasion, I reprised my Patroons role as Phil's assistant.

There were close to fifty participants for that initial four-day workshop that convened over the July Fourth weekend. The only available basketball court was worrisome for several reasons:

- It was outdoors in full sunlight.
- The macadam surface held and radiated heat.

- The poles supporting the only two baskets were stationed just a few inches outside of the baselines. Each pole was padded with hard mats that could not be securely fastened and that constantly twisted and slid down so as to leave much of the poles unprotected.

Still, the court was situated just below the dining hall at a highly visible section of the campus. The workshop soon became a showpiece with administrators and other guests sitting on the sloping lawn areas.

But what to do with two hoops and fifty players?

Run drills.

Despite the fact that the Knicks' coach, Red Holzman, would not allow Phil to dribble the ball (except in preparing to launch his hook shot), PJ had a nifty handle. Indeed, his mastery and demonstration of the renowned Pete Maravich drills (dribbling between the legs, behind the back, etc.) became the basis for most of the drills we ran. Exercises in cutting, passing, and running lanes were also established. The highlights of these drills consisted of Phil and me playing tandem defense at one basket while the hoopers ran through a continuity 3-on-2-on-1 fast-breaking procedure.

Otherwise, Phil taught them the rudiments of the triangle offense, and we let them play 5-on-5 halfcourt. When the heat had drained some of their enthusiasm, I ran big-man drills at one basket while Phil ran little-man drills at the other. In the evenings, we conducted bull sessions.

In essence, the entire weekend resembled a fantasy camp, where middle-class fans typically paid inordinate sums of money to hang with a famous jock. Had Phil spent the weekend reading from the Manhattan telephone book, most of the participants would have been satisfied. Two years later, when Phil became an assistant coach with the Chicago Bulls, his NBA glow was even more of an attraction.

Then, in 1992, after Phil had been the Bulls' head honcho for two seasons, the traveling and the time required to continue leading the workshop became too onerous, so the whole shebang was turned over to me.

My first official act was to arrange for Omega to rent an indoor gym with two full courts during whichever weekend we'd be in session. After using several local junior and senior high schools, and even a health club, an annual agreement was made with Bard College, only ten miles away.

My second adjustment was to recruit my own assistant—Eddie Mast.

For a short while, Eddie and I led two workshops every summer. Sans Phil the enrollment dipped to twenty-five or thirty, but that permitted more hands-on teaching. With two available courts, twenty players could simultaneously indulge themselves. And the emphasis shifted to the participants themselves, how and why they played.

After Eddie's passing, Phil returned to headline a benefit workshop in which our honorariums and all the tuition monies were donated to his surviving family—who were all in attendance—Diane and the five kids, Derrick, Raina, Jonathan, Jared, and Kristina. Tears, laughter, and hoops—the workshop ran the full range of emotions. (I subsequently led two more benefit workshops on my own.)

By 1997 I was on my own again. In the winter of that year, I attempted to detoxify my body in hopes of conquering a chronic and painful case of gout that had been plaguing me for years (and had persisted partially because of some poor advice from several local MDs.) As a result, I became seriously (and painfully) ill, lost more than thirty pounds, and for several weeks was confined to bed.

I wasn't a very pleasant patient, to say the least. Writhing on my bed, the deep well of my anger surfaced, a reservoir left over from a childhood of physical abuse at the hands of my invalid father. Even more debilitating than the constant pain was the realization that I was replicating my father's status: I was a selfish, complaining, and self-pitying patient. At the same time, my wife, Daia, began a regular Buddhist meditation practice as a way of retaining a semblance of sanity in the face of my outrageous behavior.

After I'd recovered (and been properly medicated at last) I followed her lead and attended various Buddhist teachings and studied various Buddhist texts. Buddhism seemed to satisfy my need for a rational, nontheistic worldview. Before long I partook of certain preliminary ceremonies that declared my intention to become a practitioner of the Tibetan variety of Buddhism. These led up to my Taking Refuge with Trangu Rinpoche, a celebrated master and scholar who was visiting at a local center, Karma Tryana Dharmakaye (KTD) in nearby Woodstock. Later I also took Bodhisattva vows from Kartar Rinpoche, also at KTD.

At that point I began to look at my life from a different perspective. Naturally, my view of basketball changed as well and, along with that, my approach toward the workshop.

Beginning with the summer of 1997 and continuing into the present, I implemented a new game plan for Beyond Basketball.

After dinner in the massive dining hall on Friday night, I would meet with the participants in our assigned cabin and try to create an instant community. My starting point was always the same—how wonderful and miraculous it was that so many of us had spent so much time, effort, and money to come here and share a weekend in pursuit of the heart of The Game. Then the players would take turns identifying themselves in whatever terms they wished.

Over the years, the Omega hoopers have included a wide range of people:

- A high-ranking official of the American Civil Liberties Union
- A world-class jazz musician
- The surgeon-general of Massachusetts
- A young woman who had just been hired as the academic advisor to the Georgetown University men's basketball team; since she had never touched a basketball before, she simply wanted to get a taste of what her advisees routinely experienced
- The president of a prestigious New England college
- The younger brother of one of the minority owners of the New Jersey Nets
- A married couple: he was the superior shooter, while she was faster, more athletic, tougher, a better defender, and a much more earnest setter of screens
- A pharmaceutical salesman who has to this day never missed a workshop
- A fifty-something man who'd had triple bypass surgery just nine months before (and was participating with his doctor's permission)
- A seventy-two-year-old man who had recently recovered from quadruple bypass surgery

- A sixty-eight-year-old veterinarian who hadn't played basketball in nine years and said he was "well-rested"
- Various cardiologists, attorneys, therapists, teachers, fathers and sons, taxi drivers, students, plus an unhappily married man who snuck off to Omega after telling his wife that he was on a business trip

The average workshop was comprised of eighteen to twenty-three devoted hoopers, contained one to three women, ranged in age from fourteen to seventy-three, and featured about 85 percent returnees.

After Eddie's passing, I tried various assistants: several hoop buddies, a young woman who coached the girls' varsity at a local high school, and, for one fascinating session, Darryl Dawkins. With his amiable ways and charismatic presence, Chocolate Thunder provided an invigorating presence. Trouble was that he hated the vegetarian food served in the dining room and therefore stocked up on corn dogs and chips bought from a gas station/minimart that we passed on our way back to the campus from the Bard gym. In addition, Darryl was a mite too homophobic for the free-thinking clientele.

Eventually, I was fortunate to hook up with Scott Wedman, and we've been coleaders since 2006. Scott played in the NBA with Kansas City–Omaha, Cleveland, and Boston (1974–87), made the All-Rookie team, was an All-Star in 1980, was selected to the league's Second All-Defensive team (1980), and was an instrumental cog in two Celtics championships (1984, 1986). In addition, Scott used to meditate before every NBA game in which he played, was an accomplished teacher, and saw The Game the same way that I did.

For the 2007–08 season Scott was hired to coach the Billings (Montana) Sky Force in the CBA. Before the season was half-over, Scott had been fired, rehired, fired, rehired, and then fired for good.

In any event, our collaboration has been fun, instructive, and inspirational for all concerned.

Before reconvening in the café for more informal Friday night get-togethers, I would distribute diagrams of the camp offense (which I try to vary from year to year). This could be a UCLA set, a double-high-post alignment, a flex, a passing game, or an antizone wheel. The idea was to create as much confusion as possible.

Here's why: Since approximately only 10 percent of the attendees have played any form of organized ball—with 1 percent having experienced college competition, the rest being ex–high school hoopers—the very concept of a set offense is totally foreign to them. Whether they are YMCA lunchtimers, playground all-stars, or men's league veterans, all they have experienced is catch-as-catch-can basketball. Isolations leading to too many bad shots and bad feelings. Open teammates routinely ignored. Passes to nobody. Guys on the same team encroaching on each other's space and sometimes even bumping into each other. Some guys running on breaks while others spectate. All topped by casual defense.

The imposition of some kind of offensive structure forces the participants to forget virtually everything they know about playing the game and to relearn the basics in a hurry. In other words, they see the dynamics of basketball with fresh eyes and with no mind. And since they're paying for the privilege, their concentration and commitment are remarkable.

What's really intended is to fool them into undergoing an active meditation.

On Saturday, we adjourn to the Bard gym and walk through the specifics: how to get free to catch a pass, how to catch and throw a pass, how to cut, how to set and use a screen, how to prepare to shoot while curling around a screen, and so on.

Teams are formed by counting off by fives, equalizing trades are ordered, and each team goes to a basket to rehearse the patterns while Scott and I roam from team to team offering corrections and more specific instructions. We also stop action in the early scrimmages to continue the corrections-cum-instructions-cum-good natured cajoling.

The after-box-lunch scrimmages are interrupted only by our shouts. If we see that everybody is getting worn down, Scott will conduct an instructional on shooting and they'll partake of some low-energy shooting games.

On Saturday night, we convene for our traditional bull session. What do Scott and I think of Dirk Nowitzki? Talented but a choke artist. Mike D'Antoni? Thin-skinned and defensive about not coaching defense.

The coach of a league comprised of seven- to nine-year-olds asked if he should concentrate on skills or on playing with an unselfish attitude. "Skills are the way to go with such young players," I replied. "It's something like tennis where the game's no fun at all if you can't hit the ball over the net. Also, the basket should be lowered to about eight feet so that, instead of having to resort to sidearm push shots just to reach the basket, the kids can develop the proper head-high shot mechanics."

And Scott will always contribute some Larry Bird anecdotes.

"Kevin McHale was injured in the middle of the 1985–86 season, so I started in his place. During this time, I had a really good game, leading the team with 26 as we beat the Bulls in Chicago. Well, I was sitting in the hotel lobby the next morning, reading the newspaper and waiting to board the bus that would take us to the airport when, all of a sudden, somebody threw a folded newspaper in my face. I looked up to see Larry Bird, all angry and scowling.

"'You see this?' he said, pointing to the headline above the game story. WEDMAN SCORES 26 TO PACE THE CELTICS.

"Of course I'd seen it, but I wasn't in the habit of paying any attention to what anybody in the media had to say about our games. So I just nodded.

"'This'll never happen again!' Larry said. 'It's my fucking team! And don't you ever forget it!'

"And I never did."

After breakfast the next day, we generally meet in our assigned room for another traditional ceremony, one that dates back to the days when Phil ran the show. Over the years, it's come to be called "Charley's Sunday Morning Sermon."

It's different every summer, but I always start by reviewing the reasons why basketball is superior to other sports: The continuous action. The exquisite balance between offense and defense. Players having to make so many decisions on the run. The fact that all of the participants in every level of basketball competition need a certain, minimal mastery of all the basic skills—catchers don't pitch, defensive tackles don't throw forward passes.

With only five teammates on the court at the same time, it's also easier for each player to know the strengths, weaknesses, and personal habits of the other four guys in the same uniform. Along with this is a basic need to understand the extent and the limits to our own skills, which translates into understanding which kinds of shots we are most likely to make and which we will inevitably miss. The same self-knowledge must be applied to all the other aspects of the game, including passing, dribbling, setting and using screens. The point is to know the role we must play, especially within the context of the assorted skills and shortcomings of our team of the moment. While this role might change to a certain degree—for example, although our ball-handling skills might be erratic, we might be the best ballhandler in a particular combination of teammates—in general, we should try to avoid doing things we are not suited to doing. Practice is where we woodshed and work on the lesser parts of our games.

An essential part of knowing your teammates and knowing your own limitations is being able to trust your teammates. Take Michael Jordan, for example. Before Phil Jackson became the Bulls head coach and implemented the Triangle, MJ would most often try to win ball games by himself. In several playoff series against the Celtics in the mid-1980s, Jordan would fill up his stat sheet with 56 points, and then 61 points—and Boston still prevailed. Flash ahead to the finals between Chicago and Phoenix in 1993, where, with the sixth and deciding game on the line, Jordan passed up a contested jumper and delivered the ball to John Paxson, who connected on the game winner. Even Michael Jordan, arguably the greatest player who ever lived, had to learn that he was unable to impose his will on most games.

The unselfishness that's such a basic element of the game is specifically one of the lessons we can take with us when the buzzer sounds and we reenter the rest of our lives. Teamwork. Trust. Self-knowledge. Physical, emotional, and mental resourcefulness. Being so much in our bodies. Respect for all participants, except perhaps referees. And, most important, the awareness and enjoyment of the living moment. For those who love basketball it's so much easier on the court than most other places to just "be."

All of these things are easier to see and assimilate within the boundary lines of the game than they are in the so-called real world. We can know the rules of basketball. We can understand exactly what the various markings on the court signify—the time line at midcourt, the stripe at the foul line, the delineations of the three-second lane, and so on. And it's child's play to read and understand both the scoreboard and the game clock. Outside of the boundary lines, however, the rules are confused, the scoreboard is difficult to decipher, and the roles we have to play are infinitely variable. We might be sons and daughters, parents, grandparents, employers, employees, drivers, passengers, pedestrians, decision makers, decision implementers, laughers, criers, lovers, haters, players, or pretenders. Everything. Nothing.

So, like every undertaking that's possible to all of us— from chopping wood to fetching water—basketball can also be a way to peace, love, and happiness.

Indeed, I've often been asked if there's a secret to being a successful coach, and if there is, what might that secret be. I'm sure as hell way down on any list of successful coaches, but I do know the secret. Loving your players.

This was somewhat easier in the CBA than anywhere else, simply because it was easy to either trade guys I couldn't connect with or just cut them. In the NBA there are salary cap equations to be considered. In amateur competition, there are angry parents to be dealt with.

The key to what we can learn from the game, and what we can take with us into our civilian lives, is preparation. Just lacing up our sneakers and jumping onto the court doesn't give us the time to adjust our expectations.

After Eddie Mast passed away about fifteen years ago, I got into the practice of pausing before I was ready to play, just long enough to remember him and to remind myself too of how lucky I was to be alive and to still be playing.

Eddie's death was sudden. One day he was playing in a pickup game at Lafayette University, which is just down the hill from his home in Easton, Pennsylvania. He had just hit a lefty hook when he went down. Several guys who were there, including a doctor, said that he was dead before he hit the floor. Dead and gone.

Turned out that his eldest son, Derrick, was a football player at the school, and they were having a team meeting in the same building. Derrick was summoned, ran to his father's side, and, according to the same witnesses, Eddie literally came back to life for a brief second. Just long enough to smile at Derrick. Before he passed for good.

If Eddie could come back from the dead to smile at his son, then we can all smile to ourselves as part of our pregame preparation.

Whatever we do, when we cross over onto a basketball court, we have to leave almost everything else behind: our bosses, our jobs, the bills we haven't paid yet, politics, telephone calls. What we should keep is the consciousness of love.

By the time I finish my Sunday Morning Sermon, we have been at the camp for parts of three days, with one last section set aside for us to play. I remind the attendants that the camaraderie that has developed will go a long way in enabling all of us to transcend our egos. Regardless of our own individual skill levels, by playing the game correctly and with a correct attitude, we can raise our own consciousness and the consciousness of our teammates.

And it all comes down to realizing that we can take all of these understandings and all of these blessings with us when we leave the court.

At the end of my sermon I always conclude with the universal appropriateness of some fundamental basketball numbers.

Four quarters, which represent the four seasons.

Each quarter is twelve minutes, half of the diurnal cycle.

And of course, the 24-second clock represents the totality of that cycle.

Among many other things, the three-second lane stands for thesis, antithesis, and synthesis. The resolution of differences.

Here are some more numbers that should be considered. With two teams, two sets of uniforms, offense versus defense, and two opposing baskets, the game could be seen as a dualistic enterprise. Made shots are good if made by the good guys, and bad if made by the bad guys. However, given proper attitudes on both sides, the game can, and should be seen as ten players playing one game.

Bill Russell talks about this kind of thing periodically happening during his NBA career: both teams playing with all-out effort, with respect for each other, and with total concentration . . . when suddenly the final buzzer sounded and they all had to look up at the scoreboard to see who won the game.

That's what we should all be aiming for.

Overtime

I must confess that it took me at least five years to shake my Jones for the game. But now, with my fingers all crooked from the hard passes I failed to catch, with my arthritic left hip aching in rainy weather, and with my oft-broken nose making me a serial snorer, I hardly miss playing at all.

It has been a joy to reminisce about the people and places that filled my life for so many years. But I have to admit to a certain frustration because this account necessarily fails at fully capturing the totality of my experiences in the game. And although I have more or less put my basketball days behind me, I miss the delicious pressure of having to make righteous decisions on a play-by-play and game-by-game basis. Moreover, I miss so many of the players and coaches with whom I had the privilege to associate.

At the same time, I've come to appreciate all of the shots that I've bricked, the turnovers I've committed, and the challenges that I've sometimes met and sometimes failed. They've all led me to who and where I am here and now.

Ah, but at least once every week, I still dream that I'm wheeling and dealing in the low post.